# The Appian Way
## From Its Foundation to the Middle Ages

*Edited by*

Ivana Della Portella

*Text*

Ivana Della Portella

Giuseppina Pisani Sartorio

Francesca Ventre

*Photographs*

Franco Mammana

THE J. PAUL GETTY MUSEUM

LOS ANGELES

**The Appian Way**

*Edited by*
Ivana Della Portella

*Texts*
Ivana Della Portella
Giuseppina Pisani Sartorio
Francesca Ventre

*Photographs*
Franco Mammana

To my son

—*Ivana*

To Papa, who will read this with the eyes of his heart

—*Francesca*

To my husband

—*Giuseppina*

Printing
EBS Editoriale Bortolazzi-Stei
Verona

Italian edition © 2003  Arsenale-Editrice

English translation © 2004  J. Paul Getty Trust

First published in the United States of America
in 2004 by
Getty Publications
1200 Getty Center Drive, Suite 500
Los Angeles, California 90049-1682
www.getty.edu

Christopher Hudson, *Publisher*
Mark Greenberg, *Editor in Chief*

Robin H. Ray, *Copy Editor*
Stephen Sartarelli, *Translator*

Library of Congress Cataloging-in-Publication Data

Via Appia antica. English
  The Appian Way : from its foundation to the Middle Ages / edited by
Ivana Della Portella ; text, Ivana Della Portella, Giuseppina Sartorio,
Francesca Ventre ; photographs, Franco Mammana.
     p. cm.
Includes bibliographical references.
  ISBN 0-89236-752-0 (HARDCOVER)
1. Appian Way (Italy) 2. Roads, Roman—Italy—History.
3. Italy—Antiquities, Roman—History. I. Della Portella, Ivana, 1959–
II. Title.
  DG29.A6V613 2004
  388.1'0937—dc22
                        2003026175

The English text on pages 230 to 233 is taken from *Horace's Satires and Epistles* by Jacob Fuchs, translated by Jacob Fuchs. Copyright © 1977 by Jacob Fuchs. Used by permission of W. W. Norton & Company, Inc.

*All photographs are by Franco Mammana, except the images on p. 33 (upper and lower right), permission for which was generously granted by the publisher of the Pontifical Commission of Sacred Archaeology.*

*On page 6: the original entrance to the Castrum Caetani (Tomb of Cecilia Metella), closed off during the nineteenth century and decorated with archaeological specimens recovered during excavations along the Appian Way.*

# Contents

# Introduction

Every citizen of Rome has at least one personal memory of the Via Appia Antica (the Ancient Appian Way): an outing, a photograph, a family anecdote. For a journey through the history and images of the Appian Way is also a journey into the identity of Rome.

Like Rome itself, the Appian Way grew and extended over time, following the interests of the Roman people as they expanded. It was the work site for simple stonecutters as well as great artists, engineers, and merchants. It integrated cultures and religions, united territories, favored exchanges between the heart of Roman power and its provinces, and helped lay the groundwork for linking Rome to Constantinople and Jerusalem, West with East.

The "Queen of Roads" is Rome's mirror, reflecting its economic and artistic pride, its political life, its cultural openness, its ability to use the past to chart the course of its own development. The Appian Way is also a great environmental monument, a space where urbanization and landscape successfully meld in happy equilibrium, thanks to the technical skills of the Roman road engineers and the greatness of the artists who created the villas, sepulchers, stelai, mosaics, and paintings that we can still enjoy today.

The establishment of the Parco dell'Appia Antica (the Appian Way National Park), an idea first conceived by Guido Baccelli and Ruggero Borghi in 1887 and much cherished by Antonio Cederna, finally does justice to the historical, archaeological, environmental, and—I must add—emotional value of the place. My hope, and that of many fellow Romans and other Italians, is that people will become aware that a cultural treasure so complex and spread so far across the country's landscape requires exceptional tools for its oversight, use, and management, and that a national law will soon be established regarding the Appian Way.

*The Appian Way* tells the story of an artistic and cultural continuity that constitutes the most precious core of Rome's identity. This book, combining archaeological and historical rigor with the pleasures of erudite narration, allows us to retrace, mile by mile, through documentary description and literary suggestion, the identity of a city, a people, and a local culture that succeeded in becoming universal.

WALTER VELTRONI
Mayor of Rome

# Foreword: Wanderings along the Appian Way

IVANA DELLA PORTELLA

*Caminante, no hay camino,*
*se hace camino al andar.*

*Wayfarer, there is no way,*
*you make the way as you go.*
                    Antonio Machado, *"Proverbios y cantares"*

We make our way along its disconnected paving stones, measuring our steps along the dihedral sequence of that eastbound straightaway, experiencing once again the passionate desire to reconstruct, in a succession of memories and impressions, the traces of an ancient route.

Not just any road, the Appian Way—the *regina viarum* (the queen of roads)—was the noblest and most celebrated and the first of a noble network that made Rome great. We measure its distances, examine its way stations, retracing the steps of those who preceded us, and our advance becomes a catharsis. As one goes along, retracing the ancient route, the experience inevitably becomes charged with symbols and myths. It ripens into a lived experience of traditions and religions grafted onto a lively, fascinating substratum.

It is a long itinerary full of atmosphere and expectation, a journey that is not always easy, where diverse scenes and landscapes come together in a puzzle of colors and sensations that cannot always be resolved into words.

Nevertheless we set forth, not aspiring to travel literature, but with the rather more amateur spirit of one who keeps a travel journal dotted with literary quotations.

In any journey, the lived experience of moods, relationships, tastes, smells, and landscapes make the undertaking an indispensable stage in one's enrichment as a human being. Thus, in a partially didactic, partially introspective spirit, we made our way to the Via Appia.

We could have begun our journey along tortuous paths and over shabby sheep-trails; we would have grown weary, but in the end we would have seen the East. Trajan, however, wanted to smooth the way for us, providing Appius Claudius Caecus's road with new routes as well as renovating old roads. The second-century Greek physician Galen wrote:

*[Trajan renovated the] muddy roads covered with stones and brambles, overgrown, steep, marshy, dangerous to ford, overly long and difficult . . . by raising them up with viaducts and paving them, removing all encumbrances and endowing them with bridges, shortening the route where it had been excessively long, cutting into the land to lower the road where it had been too sharply inclined, avoiding mountainous, wooded, or desert areas, and favoring inhabited sites.*

The Appian Way made the Empire proud indeed with its long course of paving stones stretching all the way to Brindisi (see map on page 21), with the boldness of its bridges, the length of its canals, its perfect straightaways, its deep cuts straight into the mountainside. Almost all the emperors were proud of it: Septimius Severus wanted to mark its beginning and end points with monuments of great symbolic and dramatic effect, the Septizodium at the start of the road, and the two columns in Brindisi, standing like two giant monoliths, marking a terminus open to the horizons of the sea. For the eight centuries when Rome was at the center of the world, the Via Appia served as a link to a rich and civilized Levant, spanning all of ancient Latium, Campania, Samnium, and Apulia all the way to Brundisium, the gateway to the East.

But even when the dark centuries gained the upper hand, with their uncertainties and hardships, the road continued to be traveled by tireless Christian pilgrims who, with their gnarled walking sticks and baskets full of expiatory anxieties, would toil their way along that dangerous and impassable road.

Much of that road was lost, covered over by new state and provincial roads that unknowingly followed its route. Traces of the road can be found here and there in the Pontine countryside, and near the old farming estates along the upland plains of Le Murge. There, in splendid isolation, fragments of bridges and viaducts suddenly appear, their invasive presence exalting those splendid yet desolate rural districts. And yet to retrace its course, even where it has vanished, once more linking ancient way stations and *mansiones* (rest areas) into a single route, is a unique, extraordinary experience.

The original population centers, now transformed by centuries and events, still speak of their ancient bond with that thoroughfare and recall it to mind with epigraphs and their given names. Oftentimes the link to the Appian Way is expressed through milestones, arches, or even more imposing structures. And thus, one small step at a time, we take in the ancient marks of grandeur, and with them, the vicissitudes of a humanity that traveled this route for centuries upon centuries.

The bibliography on the Appian Way is large and ponderous. Nevertheless, the only text that travels the entire route from Rome to Brindisi, step by step, is a study by Francesco Maria Pratilli dating back to the first half of the eighteenth century. However, there are authoritative works that retrace it in part or summarize its history. And then there are numerous guides that describe the itinerary with varying degrees of detail: first and foremost, that by Lorenzo Quilici, which carefully retraces the route in full.

Finally, there is a rich and interesting crop of monographs and studies on specific parts and monuments of this road. There is not, however, a more recent comprehensive work that covers the entire route from Rome to Brindisi and backs up its documentary and descriptive qualities with cultural and literary annotations.

In conceiving the present book we intended to fill this gap and attempt to offer the reader a kind of sentimental journey. The idea was to create something reminiscent of the literary journeys of the Grand Tour, not so much as direct, personal testimony, but rather as an experience seen through the eyes of ancient and modern literati and poets. Every description is therefore accompanied and enriched by past commentary and experiences, which embellish the list of sites and complement direct analysis with introspective, lyrical viewpoints.

Three of us put together this long itinerary. To my archaeological colleagues I allotted the initial and central parts of the road, these being the most strictly "archaeological." For myself I left the final stretch from Benevento to Brindisi, or rather, the final two stretches (the one belonging to the original Via Appia, and the one that followed, the Via Appia Traiana), because these seemed more fitting, with their later monuments, for the spirit of an art historian.

To the richly experienced and distinguished Professor Giuseppina Pisani Sartorio fell the task of commenting on the history and construction of the road, as well as discussing the best-preserved stretch between Rome and the Alban Hills. To Dr. Francesca Ventre, in turn, went the task of describing the stretch from the Alban Hills to Beneventum, with all its noteworthy and original monuments. And to me, finally, fell the more circular route from Benevento to Brindisi, indeed the round trip. The itinerary includes the more ancient stretch of the Appian Way that turns toward Taranto and ends at Brindisi, and then the later route put in place by Trajan, from whom it takes its name. To me it seemed of interest to present this latter stretch, emphasizing above all the manner in which it became used, in the middle of its life, as a pilgrimage route to Brindisi, from whence one set sail for Jerusalem.

In this phase of its existence, the Via Appia Traiana may be rightly considered a southern branch of the Via Francigena and thus a vehicle for that cultural syncretism whose most outstanding specimens include the Apulian Romanesque cathedrals, the legends of the paladins, and the chivalric romances.

To the refined sensibilities of Vittorio Emiliani we owe the book's prologue, a kind of foretaste of the theoretical aspects of its journey. It is important to mention here the Parco dell'Appia Antica and its administrative authority (Ente di Gestione), on whose board of directors I was privileged to serve over the last few years. Initiatives concerning the safeguarding and conservation of the road are described by Gaetano Benedetto, president of the Parco dell'Appia Antica from 1998 to 2003, in the Italian edition of this volume.

Thus the book closes with the hope that, through legislative action, we might realize the expansion of the Parco from Rome to Brindisi, as has been urged by so many intellectuals and thinkers of the twentieth century, and consolidate this gain by having it declared the heritage of all humanity.

# The Appian Way as Literary Journey

VITTORIO EMILIANI

When I think of the journey, what immediately comes to mind are the milestones along the roads. We used to notice them once, when our manner of travel was slower than it is now. If we proceeded on foot or even by bicycle, we would sometimes stop to examine them, and we might even sit on top of them for a few minutes. And it was immediately like going back in time, to the journey the ancients—our very own forebears—used to make along these rocky roads, dusty in summer and muddy in winter, over which carts, carriages, and coaches passed for centuries, indeed millennia, with no real change in technology since the invention of the wheel. So it was, until the arrival of the first automobiles or even the first bicycles, which conformists considered to be instruments of a progress that had a whiff of sulfur about it.

When I think of the milestones, what comes immediately to mind are the consular roads that marked the lives of every Italian. In my own life, this meant, above all, the Via Emilia, dotted by all those cities and towns of importance to the existence of someone who, like me, bears a surname derived from the road itself. (In all likelihood, it means "those from the Emilia.") This consular road goes on for miles and miles, all flat plain, running along the edge of the hills, from the start of the Po Valley plain to its great river (see map on page 21); it was planned and courageously built in the middle of the few emerging, wooded lands in existence in the third century B.C., amidst all the valley waterways and torrents that were there at the time, all the way to Bononia-Felsina. At that time

there was still no mystery surrounding the true course of the Rubicon, over which Caesar decided to cast the die (the *alea*—though he said it, in more cultured fashion, in Greek) and determine what fate to give the history of Rome, which was already the history of the world itself. For centuries the Via Emilia passed through the heart of those population centers of brick and stone, becoming their central axis and bringing civilized commerce and military convoys. My father and grandfather's hometown was Forlimpopoli, Forum Popilii in Roman times, a town devoted to the livestock market, especially horses, whether for draft, carriages, saddle, or slaughter. The local horse-dealers always wore gaiters, even on holidays, and colorful shirts under short waistcoats, red handkerchiefs tied around their necks and held in place by metal rings, the inevitable wide-brimmed felt hat on their heads, often with a train ticket slipped under the band, perhaps to show proudly that they traveled from market to market, with their "travel certificate" in plain view.

The Via Emilia begins at Rimini, at the majestic arch of Augustus—the only intact structure, along with the bridge of Tiberius, that I could see when I went through the devastated city in 1945. And this same point serves as the terminus of another consular road that arrives from Rome, and to which, for many reasons, I also feel attached: the Via Flaminia, which starts at the Aurelian Wall at the Porta del Popolo, crosses Umbria and the Marches through the Apennines, a mountain chain at once sweet and harsh, land of raw winters, snow

11

and frost, windy springs, and gorges such as the Furlo. It is a landscape made for ambushing enemies such as the Carthaginian Hasdrubal, who was killed when he halted at the Metauro River. I spent many years in Urbino and have returned there many times since, in various capacities, and continue to return. It is difficult, I think, to imagine a landscape more Italian than this: hills lush with olive groves and vineyards, wood-darkened mountains, fortresses and abbeys, walled cities of gray stone, sanctuaries and soaring towers. Other convoys, other armies, other captains of fortune have passed between here and the Romagna: Alberico da Barbiano, Braccio Fortebracci da Montone, Federico da Montefeltro, Gattamelata da Narni, Giovanni dalle Bande Nere. Other processions have come through, religious ones this time, other travelers, pilgrims on their way to see holy visionaries named Francis, Claire, Benedict, Scolastica, Rita.

The opening scene of the film *Roma*, by Federico Fellini—who was Riminese, not coincidentally—is premonitory, if not downright prophetic: in a wintry, North Italian landscape, in a seasonally dim twilight, with snow beginning to swirl in the air, a handful of peasant women appear on bicycles, one of them carrying a scythe on her shoulder, and they ride past an old milestone bearing the inscription "Rome, 340 km." They are on the ancient Via Flaminia, which leads to the Porta del Popolo, near which Fellini lived for many years. That milestone contains the name and destiny of a man who would become, in the twentieth century, Rome's visionary poet.

In that film (do you remember?) it is a distant Rome that reemerges inexorably from the bowels of the subsoil, in the form of frescoes that decompose instantaneously, turning to dust during the work on the subway, as if fleeing that forced, mechanical modernization. Fellini loved to plan trips, he loved to fantasize on the subject of travel. In every one of his films, there is, one might say, a journey: the arrival of the young bride in *The White Sheik*; the departure of Moraldo (and an entire generation) in *I Vitelloni*; the protagonist's dream of returning to a mythic, primordial purity in *La Dolce Vita*; the arrival of the first-person narrator in Rome in the same film; the flight—even in dream—of the boy in *The Clowns*; the departure of Gradisca with her carabiniere after their wedding, at the end of *Amarcord*;

and if one cannot go en masse to the moon, one can, as in *The Voice of the Moon*, capture the orb live on TV. Until the end of his life Fellini spoke of making a cinematic tale about a violinist—*The Journey of G. Mastorna*—which he never realized. Some say it was because a psychic once told him he would die as soon as he had made it.

Thus Rome and our journeys. But how can one speak of Roman consular roads without speaking of their queen, the Via Appia Antica (the Old Appian Way)? I always say that if I were asked to name a place, a site, that more than any other embodies the fascination of ancient Rome, I would answer without hesitation: the Old Appian Way. It already announces itself at the Orti degli Scipioni, along the silent road that runs between the high walls, great espaliers of ivy and trees, a great many trees, cypress and laurel above all, turning toward the Porta San Sebastiano, and then descending toward the church of Domine Quo Vadis, still rustic and medieval. But when one reaches the Appian Way's shiny ancient paving stones, a sudden, necessary slowness, a mysterious silence surrounds us, taking us into a dimension far from the breathless, exaggerated speed at which we are forced to live. At the start of the *regina viarum*, there is everything: there is nature, featuring flora of exotic origin; there is fauna both migratory and nonmigratory, continually renewing itself; there is the extraordinary, unique engineering of the Roman road and aqueduct; there are villas and solemn sepulchers; there are the vast spaces, devoid of human presence, of the Circus of Maxentius; there are the rites and myths of a variety of religions, in nature or in catacombs; there are monuments large and small that accompany the modern wayfarers who are forced to walk slowly; there is the echo of nearby waters flowing and gurgling; there is the unique blend of cultivated lands and pastures with transhumant sheep that stay awhile, then move on, exactly as they did two thousand years ago and more.

As it runs southward, the Appian Way often intersects with the sheep trails along which so much of the history of our civilization has been written, on those journeys undertaken every October, when a certain lilac (the *cacciapastore*, or "shepherd-chaser") blooms, journeys that would take the flocks and herds from the crests of the Apennines toward the Adriatic Sea on one side of the peninsula, and toward the Tyrrhenian Sea on the other, or further south, toward the Ionian Sea, only to bring them back inland once the months of frost and snow had passed. Along the Appian Way, Magna Graecia, with its enormous, wind-shaken olive trees, rises up to meet us; we pass great farming estates of stone and lime with Arab names; we see very ancient cities. One evening I arrived in Taranto as a group of young archaeologists was ending a work campaign and, as is the custom, celebrating with a pleasant dinner. Inside their excavation site they showed me clear traces of Neolithic settlements, then Greek walls, then Byzantine structures with their trademark bricks. The only reason that there were no Roman remains was because those conquerors preferred to build in an area entirely apart from the Greek city. At what might be thought of as Taranto's gates—for example, at Massafra, called the Thebes of Italy—our itinerant eyes would soon feast on the deep green valleys of the gorges, sheer along the Ionian coast, rich in grasses and spring flowers, and featuring real cities among the rocks, safe refuges against marauding pirates come from the same seas that many centuries earlier had taken Diomedes and other *nostoi* from these shores to the war in Troy, including the carpenter Epeos, builder of the great wooden horse that spelled the end of Priam's city. One year, very long ago, I went to Brindisi, from which people set sail for Greece, and where now still-legendary convoys, this time from the railways, take the ferry before continuing eastward: the Orient Express. And I thought of my father, who told me that, as a boy, he used to go to the town train station with his friends at midnight to witness the screaming passage, like a deafening lightning in the night, of the Indian Mail, on its way south.

# Origins and Historic Events

GIUSEPPINA PISANI SARTORIO

path. It is also a road of written memories because of the epigraphs commemorating the great figures of Rome's history—the Cornelius Scipio family, the Metelli, Servilii, Messala, Claudii—as well as totally unknown people, such as the Publius Minaci, the Canulei, and Avili.

The Appian Way represents the production and exchange of the goods transported for centuries over its paving stones, which became deeply grooved from the passage of carts to and from Rome, the capital of the Empire. It represents a strategy of conquest, in ancient as in modern times: the conquest of new territories, but also of Rome itself.

It is a highway connecting different peoples, both Italic and Mediterranean. The Appian Way is, finally, an extraordinary example of ancient technology.

## The Appian Way: A Journey through Literature and Memory

This is a literary journey, not only because we shall repeatedly cite the observations of other writers, but because we shall try to provide a direct reading of the monuments and the events that produced them—events in which the Appian Way itself was a protagonist—through the voices and impressions of the poets, writers, and journeymen who traveled it over the centuries.

References to literary texts, travel memoirs, place descriptions, and works on architecture serve for the most part to re-create atmospheres and emotions. They might be references to music,

*Above: Funerary relief of Hilarius Fuscus. The relief is incorporated into an architectural structure that resulted from nineteenth-century renovations of archaeological finds discovered during excavations along the Via Appia.*

*Facing page: The Porta Appia in Rome, also called Porta San Sebastiano.*

*Via Appia: regina viarum*[1]
STATIUS *SILVAE* 2.2.12

O via Appia, consecrated by Caesar (Domitian)
venerated under Hercules' effigy,
you surpass all of Italy's roads in fame . . .
MARTIAL *SPECTACULA* 9.101

Thus did the poets Statius and Martial define the most celebrated, noble, and glorious of Roman roads, the Via Appia (the Appian Way). It is a road of memories, because of the tombs that line its

The Appian Way is not merely a road on which people of all races and all epochs traveled back and forth. It is a continuum of events and occurrences. The very monuments along its route never stay the same: They change, transform themselves, adapt, and accompany us on our journey. We see the Tomb of Cecilia Metella from afar, from as far away as Porta San Sebastiano, as a goal to be reached, towering above us like a castle on its foundation of lava; later, when we turn around, it is already different, no longer a castle, but almost a circular temple at the center of a courtyard.

Thus, in addition to providing information on individual monuments or topographical references that are essential for orienting ourselves, our journey will proceed by meaningful stages presuming that the reader-traveler is open to following an unusual itinerary. It will be part topographical, part historical, part time-travel; partly told through individuals, partly through events.

"Every grain of this soil, many times over," wrote modern Italian author Giorgio Vigolo, "was once the bodies of men and women, the columns of temples, the bricks of homes, trees, grass, tunics, bread."[2] Ours is not a journey through reality, but a trek through memory. And if life is a journey, along the Appian Way it is a journey—ad absurdum—through the life of death, and therefore through the immortality of nameless people of the past.

This does not mean that the Via Appia is funereal. The vast panorama that spreads out behind the tombs is like a painted backdrop tempering its funerary significance. The ruins that accompany us on the roadside tend more to remind us of time's passing, slipping by like the miles of road under our feet.

### The Road of Memory
*Hospes resiste. . . . Rogo te, viator. . . .Viator vale!*
Stop, stranger. . . . I beg you, traveler. . . . Adieu, traveler!

Tomb inscription, Mile 6[3]

The exhortations that we read on the tombstones of the Appian Way appear to want to strike up a conversation with the living who pass by. They invite us to stop, to remember, to say good-bye.

The tombs, even those without names, are a memory of the past accompanying the traveler on his

painting, history, or archaeology, but they all aim at putting individual elements into context, building correspondences between them to create a diachronic picture of the whole. In this picture, what was there yesterday and what we see today assume meaning and significance for a new vision of tomorrow.

journey, not only at the exits of Rome, but also at the gateways of the cities through which the road passes along its entire route. At Albano, Velletri, Terracina, Capua, Benevento, and Canosa, the first sign that one is approaching a population center along the Via Appia is the tombs themselves. Some of these are very famous, such as those at the entrance to Albano, or those on the way out of Capua.[4]

The Etruscans (like ourselves today) built cities for the dead not unlike the ones for the living, where the "houses" serve as tombs and look out onto streets traversed only during funerals. The Romans, by contrast, deposited their dead along the roads of the living, which were traveled not by funeral processions but by citizens going about their vital activities.

And the charm of the Appian Way, which seems a place suspended in time between life and death,

has endured over the centuries. For example, it was on the base of one of the green-and-white cipollino marble columns erected, perhaps by Septimius Severus, in the port of Brindisi that the Byzantine governor in the tenth century A.D. chose to commemorate himself and his times.

The cities along the Appian Way vigorously maintained their pride in the road. Holy Roman Emperor Frederick II of Swabia imitated the *fasti* (official registers of important persons or dates) of the ancient Roman triumphs by erecting, at Capua, a monumental arch at the head of the bridge where the Appia crossed the Volturnus (modern Voltorno) River.

But what leaves the deepest impression in one's memory are the images of the Appian Way propagated in later centuries by artists: the contrast between the "ruins of ancient magnificence"[5] and the desolation of the Roman Campagna, by then abandoned and prey to malaria, was repeatedly represented in paintings, etchings, and watercolors. These images were diffused all over Europe and aroused people's curiosity, eventually causing Italy to be invaded by a mob of intellectuals. Such works include the drawings of Giovannantonio Dosio and Etienne Du Pérac, the etchings of Giovanni and Francesco Piranesi, the aquatints of Carlo Labruzzi, and the paintings of Claude Lorraine, Hackert, Coleman, Caffi, and many others. The Appian Way's monuments, studied and drawn by such architects as Baldassare Peruzzi, Antonio da Sangallo, Andrea Palladio, and Raphael, also served to inspire the new forms and architectural works of the Italian Renaissance.

Poets and writers such as Byron, Goethe, Stendhal, and Chateaubriand found inspiration for some of their finest pages along the Appian Way. In the diary of his *Italian Journey*, on November 11, 1786, Goethe noted:

*Today I visited the Nymph Aegeria, the Circus of Caracalla, the ruined tombs along the Via Appia, and the tomb of [Cecilia] Metella, which made me realize for the first time what solid masonry means. These people [the Romans] built for eternity; they omitted nothing from their calculations except the insane fury of the destroyers to whom nothing was sacred.*[6]

In the early twentieth century, Thomas Ashby, the English archaeologist who immortalized the Appian Way in hundreds of photographs, wrote of the road's Roman environs that its "charm . . . is impossible to describe":

*[T]he wonderful lights that play upon its innumerable ridges and valleys, the beautiful outlines of the mountains by which it is bounded—many do not realize that from Rome one can easily see peaks in the Central Apennines which rise to over 8,000 feet above sea-level—the strange, desolate appearance of that part of it which runs towards the sea, hidden from us unless we ascend the dome of St. Peter's or the Alban or Sabine Hills, the loneliness of the flat Latin shore stretching away south-eastward towards that wonderful promontory of Monte Circeo, that dominates the whole coastline and the low-lying Pomptine Marshes . . . all these different scenes make up but a part of what few even of those who know and love it best have been able to convey to those who have but a slight acquaintance with it. It is very doubtful . . . whether the charm of the Campagna is meant to be described in prose: one might as well expect to understand a symphony of Beethoven from a printed description, if one had never heard it and could not read the score.*[7]

## The Road of Conquest

The course of the Appian Way advanced as Rome advanced on its path of conquest through southern Italy; and at Brindisi, it became a launching point for the conquest of the East. The legions set out from Rome along it; the orders given by the commanders were entrusted to swift messengers who then traveled in the opposite direction, bearing the tidings of victory and newly conquered lands back to Rome.

Strategic and tactical considerations lie at the very origin of the Appian Way. Once the war against the cities of Latium was over (348 B.C.), the Volsci subdued, a colony founded at Terracina in 329, and the Aurunci defeated, the Romans established the colony of Sessa Aurunca in 312 B.C. and those of Minturnus and Sinuessa in 296 B.C. This expansion made it necessary to move Rome's armies up and down the peninsula as quickly as possible and by the shortest possible route. Indeed the first stretch of the road—the 132 miles from Rome to Capua (see maps on pages 86 and 108)—was built as the war against the Samnites raged (326–304 B.C.).[8] The Romans had been defeated at Lautulae, near Terracina, in 315 B.C. and were forced to abandon Capua. The clash over the final conquest of the *Campania felix* and Capua—the area's number-three city in terms of size and importance—was blocking Rome's southward path.

The road was therefore first used for military operations during both the Second and Third Samnite Wars, and again in the war against Pyrrhus, which opened the doors for Rome's conquest of Magna Graecia. It took them across territories not yet annexed to Rome, though belonging to allied communities.

As the occupation of the new territories gradually got under way, the road was extended as well.[9] At first it went as far as Beneventum (an additional 33 miles), which was made a Latin colony in

**The Road of Commerce and Communication**

The Appian Way cut through the richest, most fertile regions of ancient Italy, and all traffic to and from southern Italy traveled along it. Once its military purpose faded away, the road naturally assumed the commercial role proper to a major artery of travel and communication.

The colonization of southern Latium in the late fourth century B.C. coincided with an impressive program of road building. Indeed the transport system was of great importance to the Romans in all their plans of conquest, first with Latium, then southern Italy, and finally, the entire Empire.[10]

The Appian Way crossed regions rich in agricultural products—wine, olive oil, wheat—and connected Rome with the regions of the East, whence came all the rarest and finest merchandise (perfumes, spices, silks, jewels, and rare and precious stones and marbles) destined for the inhabitants of the capital of the Empire.

Important branches of the Via Appia included the Via Flacca, from Terracina to Fondi (184 B.C.); the Via Domitiana, from Sinuessa to Cumae, Puteoli (Pozzuoli), and Neapolis (Naples) (95 A.D.); the Via Popilia, from Capua to Reggio and on toward Sicily (132 B.C.). By means of this road network, almost all the traffic of southern Italy, as well as that issuing from sea travel in the central and eastern Mediterranean, flowed into the Via Appia.

The public roads were the setting of the *cursus publicus* (*vehiculatio*): that is, the transport of goods, people, and messages serving exclusively public needs (a service reserved for officials—members of the imperial administration—the army, and the transport of victuals) and paid for by the state.[11] The *cursus publicus* was exercised sporadically in the Republican era, then reorganized by Augustus and endowed with an administration and personnel under the authority of municipal magistrates. Nerva later replaced these magistrates with the *mancipis*, who were under the authority of a *praefectus vehiculorum*. Under Trajan and Hadrian the Roman government covered all the expenses of organizing public transport over the entire territory of the Empire.

There were two kinds of *cursus*: the *celer* or *velox* (rapid), intended for bearing messages (the average daily distance traveled by a *cursor* was 70 km) and

262 B.C., then to Venusium (modern Venosa), which was already a Roman colony by 291 B.C. It was further extended to Tarentum (modern Taranto) after that city was taken in 272, and then, with the conquest of Messapia and the Salentum peninsula in 191 B.C., all the way to Brundisium (modern Brindisi), a strategic crossing point into Greece and a bridgehead for the conquest of the East. In all it covered 364 miles (538 kilometers) from Rome.

The eighteen-year-old Octavian was in Albania preparing an expedition against the Dacians and the Parthians for Julius Caesar when he learned that the emperor had been assassinated. He set off at once for Italy, and all along the Appian Way—at Capua, Casilinum, and Calatia—Caesar's veterans paid him homage, convincing him to enter Rome and claim the inheritance of his great-uncle and adoptive father.

But the Via Appia has also been traveled for the opposite reason: to lay siege to Rome and in some cases even to conquer the city. In 1536 Charles V, a new Scipio, made his triumphal entry into Rome on this road, and in 1571 Marcantonio Colonna celebrated his triumph over the Turks at Lepanto on the same road. The Appian Way was again to be the stage for triumphal entrances into Rome: in 1817, for Ferdinand, King of the Two Sicilies; and in 1819, for Francis I, Emperor of Austria.

Finally, even the Americans, in 1944, entered Rome by way of the Via Appia.

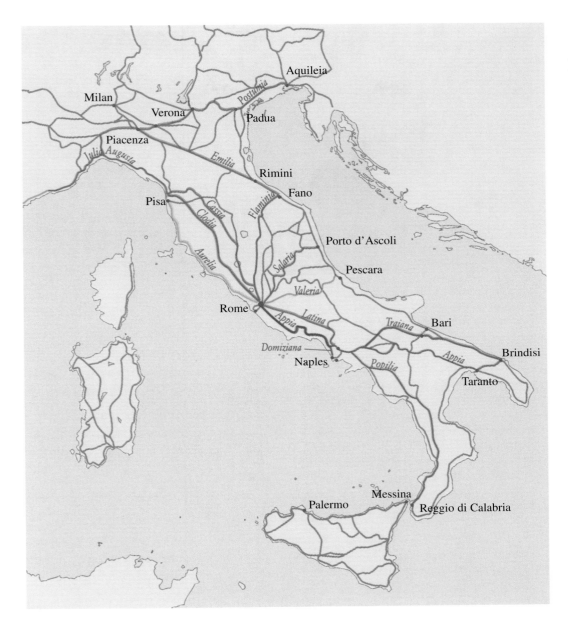

*Facing page: Relief showing scenes of building activity probably related to the Via Appia and the expansion of the port of Terracina (Rome, Museo Nazionale Romano at Palazzo Massimo).*

*Left: The network of Roman consular roads in Italy.*

travelers; and the *cursus tardus* or *clabularius* (slow) for merchandise.[12]

Essential to the *cursus*'s functioning was a network of service posts along the major roads of the Empire. There were the *mutationes*, rest stations or post houses for changing horses every ten miles; and at one day's journey from one another were the *mansiones* or *stationes*, establishments equipped for overnight stays that sometimes coincided with preexisting villages or population centers. Along the

Appian Way, these included Bovillae, Aricia, Forum Appii, and Tres Tabernas, while others were created specifically for the *cursus publicus* (Ad Nonum, Ad Sponsas, Ad Medias). Over time, these stations became the nuclei of new cities.

## A Model of Engineering Technology

One cannot follow the course of the Via Appia without thinking of the sophisticated engineering plans underlying the construction of its various

*Facing page: Detail of paving
stones on the Via Appia at
the archaeological site of
Minturno.*

stretches.[13] The road crossed the Italian peninsula from west to east, passing through impenetrable regions that at the time of its construction were nearly or entirely unknown—ancient Latium, Campania, Samnium, Apulia—and coming to an end at the port of Brindisi, the point of departure to Greece and the East. On the other side of the Strait of Otranto, the road system continued with the Balkan extension of the Appian Way, the Via Egnathia, the first road built by the Romans outside the confines of Italy, in 148 B.C. It ran from Durazzo (Dyrrachium), passed through Epirus and Macedonia, arrived at Thessaloniki, then passed through Thrace before terminating at Byzantium on the shores of the Bosporus.[14]

The Via Appia was supposed to meet the demand for a swifter, more direct route than that offered by the tortuous mountain road of the older Via Latina. Thus its designers chose a course along the shore and through the coastal swamps. Straight lines were preferred to shorter distances, often leaving important cities off the route.[15] To achieve this, engineers resorted to the boldest solutions available to Roman technology. At the same time, they experimented with new methods, perhaps for the first time. Eventually certain innovations were adopted more generally to create the complex, articulated system that became the Roman Empire's network of roads, which in turn is the foundation of all the transportation routes of modern Europe.[16] Such technologies included land reclamation, bridge-building, terracing, cutting into mountains (as, for example, the cut in the Pisco Montano, where the Appian Way passes through Terracina), viaducts, and tunnels.

Among the notable features of the Via Appia are the straightaways of the opening stretch (see maps on pages 86 and 108). The first of these is 24 kilometers long and passes through the Roman Campagna and the Alban Hills; the second is 59 kilometers and covers the Pontine region. But there are other stretches that are equally straight: the one before Terracina (3 km); those passing through the plain of Fondi (8 and 9 km); at the mouth of the Garigliano River (7 and 10 km); and through the plain of the Volturnus before Capua (more than 22 km).[17]

The road's dimensions eventually became the model for the other heavily traveled Roman con-sular roads. It was 14 Roman feet (4.15 m) wide, although the width might increase at particularly important places; running along both sides were walkways 11 Roman feet (3.25 m) wide, bringing the road's total width to over 10 meters. As Procopius of Caesarea relates: "it is wide enough to allow two carts to pass in opposite directions."[18]

It was paved with large stone blocks that appeared formless but in fact were well fitted to one another, making up a perfect network of leucitic rock quarried either from the heart of the Alban Hills outside of Rome or from the Roccamonfina mountains near Capua. Sometimes the builders used hard stone quarried from hillsides crossed along the route.

All this gives us an idea of why the promoters of public works such as roads, aqueducts, forums, temples, basilicas, and baths were so keen to associate their names with the works, whether they were magistrates or emperors. They were well aware of the lasting fame that would derive from it.

The triumphal arches along the Appian Way were the most tangible testimony of this sort of glorification: the arches of Drusus, Trajan, and Lucius Verus (these last two no longer standing) along the first part of the road inside Rome's walls; Hadrian's arch at Capua; Trajan's at Benevento (erected by Hadrian); and the triumphal arch at Canosa along the Via Appia Traiana.

In the construction of their great public works, the Romans drew inspiration from three very precise concepts: *firmitas*, the solidity of the plan; *utilitas*, the rationality of the route; and *vetustas*, the solidity and durability of the architectural forms. But another element was also borne in mind for the great public works: the entirely Roman concept of maintenance. Through constant vigilance, the works and services were kept functioning efficiently. Eventually a magistrature was created that was devoted solely to this end: the *cura viarum* (care of the roads), later restructured by Augustus. Its *curatores* were generally responsible, through special appointments, for a particular road and perhaps for the territory through which it passed.[19]

The roads were *viae publicae* in that they were for public use and built on public land.[20] In the Republican era, the initiative to build a road came from the Senate; the execution was assigned on a case-by-case basis to the censors, aediles, and consuls.

Only the latter, being invested with the *imperium*, had the power to exercise the *ius publicandi*, that is, the authority to expropriate lands. But execution was also sometimes entrusted to praetors and urban quaestors. During this period, there still was no magistrature for this purpose, and when the emperor eventually assumed all these offices unto himself, he became responsible for the maintenance of the roads. According to the dictates of the *lex Iulia municipales*, after its construction, the road fell under the administration of the aediles, who had jurisdiction within a ten-mile radius of Rome.

In 20 B.C., Augustus reorganized the service and took upon himself the expenses of the *cura viarum*, at which time he personally attended to the maintenance of the Italian roads.[21] On that occasion, or a bit later, in 16 B.C., a monument at once symbolic, useful, and commemorative was constructed in the Roman Forum (*in capite romani fori*): the *miliarium aureum* ("golden mile") or *Urbis*,[22] which marked, according to Plutarch, "the point at which all roads ended."[23]

Little is known about this monument. According to standard archaeological opinion, the milestone was a marble column covered in gilded bronze and inscribed with the names and distances from Rome of the most important cities or of the consular roads. In fact, the monument must have been built to commemorate the *cura viarum* exercised by Augustus.[24] Thereafter the magistrates were elected by Senate decree at the behest of the emperor, and thus began the real maintenance of the roads of the Roman Empire.

From the time of Augustus onward, every important road had its own *curator*, chosen from among the ex-praetors. The *curator* might be

responsible for more than one road. He would see to its maintenance and any repairs needed for its paving stones, sidewalks, road signs, and milestones. He was also responsible for the conservation of the road itself and for police regulations concerning the circulation of traffic.

Outside of Italy, responsibility for the roads fell to the governors of the individual provinces, as part of the broader jurisdictional and administrative powers they were invested with. After the period of the Tetrarchs (A.D. 293–305), however, the central power abandoned the maintenance of the roads and milestones. The milestones then erected along the roads served more as conduits of imperial propaganda than as actual indications of maintenance or restoration.

These same milestones bear witness to the public administration's constant concern for the efficiency of the Via Appia, along with all the other roads that led from Rome to the most distant provinces of the Empire. From the third century B.C. onward, these cylindrical pillars were placed one mile (1,478 m) apart from each other, to mark the distances.[25] Aside from indicating the progressive number of miles traveled from the Porta Capena within Rome's 4th-century-B.C. Republican walls, they also bore the name of the man who had them erected and who either built or restored the road or the milestone itself.[26]

In the sixth century, Procopius of Caesarea, in a tone of great admiration, described the perfect execution of the Appian Way's pavement, for which he gave credit to Appius Claudius:

*Once the stones were polished and flattened and cut at an angle, Appius Claudius put them together without lime or other binding material, and they now stand so united and so solidly together that anyone who sees them cannot believe that they are merely set one beside the other, but must think that they form a single whole. Yet despite all the time elapsed and the great multitude of carts that have passed over it each and every day, their unity has not been broken up in the least, nor have they lost any of their smoothness.*[27]

**Origins and Historic Events**

The Via Appia, like the older Via Latina, has its origins in and over the Tiber, near the river port of

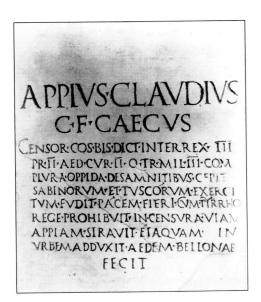

*Commemorative plaque of Appius Claudius, from Arezzo (copy, Rome, Museo della Civiltà Romana).*

*Facing page: The Appian Way at the Fosso di Sant'Andrea, near Itri.*

Rome. This was the focal point of the entire road system of what would later become the capital of an empire.[28]

On the river, and with the river as a catalytic presence, centrally located at the intersection of two ancient thoroughfares running along the north–south axis of ancient Italy[29]—the Latina-Appia to the south and the Via Salaria to the north, routes that already existed before acquiring their historic names[30]—lies Rome, the crossroads and point of equilibrium and fusion.

Thus, out of a combination of different ethnic, religious, commercial, and political interests, the city was born in an extremely favorable location, at the meeting point of two fundamental road axes and along a navigable river.

The Via Appia was laid down as far as Capua, 132 miles away, by Appius Claudius Caecus, as attested by Livy[31] and an inscription.[32] From him it would get its historic name.[33] The cost of the project must have been enormous and burdensome for the treasury. Indeed, as attested by Diodorus Siculus, it drained the coffers of the Roman state.[34]

For Appius Claudius, the building of the road was an instrument of power and a personal creation. He used all the authority granted the title of

*Portrait of Trajan, first half of second century A.D. (Ostia, Museo Ostiense).*

*Facing page: Detail of the Arch of Trajan at Benevento, the starting point of the Via Appia Traiana.*

censor over the eighteen-month period of his mandate to levy taxes on citizens and on their property, to determine the eligibility of candidates for admission to the elections for public office (whence derives the modern meaning given to the word *censor*), to exact customs duties, to administer state property, and to award public-works contracts.

In exercising this last function, Appius Claudius was incredibly efficient. As Livy remembered it: "That year the terms as censor of Appius Claudius and L. Plautius [actually C. Plautius] were illustrious, but the memory of Appius remains the more vivid for posterity, for he built the road and brought water to Rome, and he achieved these things alone."[35] Diodorus Siculus remembered him as follows: "Later he had paved with brilliant stone the greater part of the road that from him bears its name of Appia, from Rome to Capua, for a distance of one thousand stadia, leveling heights and filling holes and depressions in the land with appropriate works; and although he exhausted the public purse, he left behind an imperishable monument in memory of himself, having aspired to the common good."[36]

To allow him to realize both projects—the road and the aqueduct[37]—an unusual extension beyond the conventional limits was granted to his mandate as censor, but not to that of his colleague Plautius.

Appius Claudius left a lasting mark on the history of republican Rome. A member of one of the noblest Roman *gentes*, he was censor in 312 B.C., and consul twice—in 307 and again in 296—during the Samnite wars; he was dictator from 292 to 285; and he gave political room, voice, and weight, by means of the vote, to social strata previously excluded from the process. In 280 B.C., though old and blind, he delivered a famous speech before the Senate, fighting the proposal to make peace with Pyrrhus. An author in his own right, he penned many maxims, including his most famous one, which probably best represents him: *Fabrum esse suae quemque fortunae*, "Every man makes his own luck."[38]

The eulogy inscribed on the base of his statue in the Forum of Augustus remembers him as follows: "He took many Samnite cities, routed the army of the Sabines and Tusci, and forbade that peace be made with King Pyrrhus. During his term as censor he built the Via Appia and brought water into the city. He made the temple of Bellona."

For the purpose of counting the miles, the Appian Way officially began at the Porta Capena within the Servian wall. It was thus the first military road built *ex novo* by the Romans, as well as the first censorial road, inasmuch as Appius Claudius was censor when he had it built. In 296 B.C., the first mile (from the Porta Capena to the Temple of Mars) was paved under the supervision of the Ogulnius brothers, both curule aediles.[39] By 293, the paved surface reached as far as Bovillae.

Around 268 B.C.—after the conquest of Samnium in 272, the foundation of the colony of Beneventum, a strategic center in the heart of Irpinia, and the victory over Pyrrhus—the Appian Way was extended another 32 miles to Beneventum.

In the years that followed, the Pontine stretch of the road was improved. In 184 B.C., the censor L. Valerius Flaccus had work done around Formia, and in 179, the censor M. Emilius Lepidus did the same near Terracina.[40]

In 191 B.C., the Appian Way was paved all the way to Capua, and that same year the route was extended as far as Venusium, a Roman colony from 291 B.C. Around the same period, some time after 272, the link with Tarentum was completed. Finally, after the Messapii and Salentini were defeated in 266–267 B.C. and a Latin colony was founded in 244 at Brundisium,[41] around 200 B.C. the road was extended all the way to the Adriatic Sea, covering a total distance of 364 miles. The city of Brundisium, endowed with an excellent harbor, was an ideal base for operations in the East and natural distribution-point for products from the south of Italy. In 191 B.C., the road must have been completed as far as Brundisium, since Cato traveled it in five days.[42]

Julius Caesar, during his stewardship of the Appian Way between 69 and 65 B.C., lavished great care and expenditure on its renovation.[43] During the Augustan age, two restorations, in 17–16 and 2–1 B.C., were recorded, in the stretch between Venafrum and Beneventum.[44]

Many emperors set great store by the efficiency and proper maintenance of so important a road. Vespasian, in 76 A.D.,[45] and Nerva, in 97 A.D.,[46] renovated various stretches, especially the paving between Tripontium and Forum Appii.

Trajan promoted a great many paving projects between 98 and 112 A.D.[47] He was responsible for the Pisco Montano cut at Terracina, where part of

a mountain was cut away to allow the road to run along the seashore.[48] He also drained and paved the Decennovium, a nineteen-mile tract between Forum Appii and Terracina flanked by a navigable canal. One could thus choose to travel by boat rather than by cart.[49]

Emperor Trajan, however, is remembered most of all for having built the alternate route from Benevento to the Adriatic (see map on page 188), an event commemorated in that city by the construction of a magnificent arch.[50] The new road, called the Via Appia Traiana,[51] was probably built over a prior road, the Via Minucia, which Horace mentioned in passing in his *Epistles* (1.18.20): *"Brundisium Minuci melius via ducat an Appi"* ("Minucius's way leads to Brindisi better than Appius's"). The new stretch of road, which was completed in 112 A.D. and which shortened the route by twenty-eight miles (one day's travel), made the journey easier and facilitated troop movements. It became more widely used than the parallel, older road, which, *longa vetustate amissa* ("having fallen into ruin with the passage of too much time"),[52] was finally restored by Hadrian.

The Via Appia Traiana crossed the Apennine mountain chain at Paduli, continued on through Buonalbergo and, after passing the *mutatio* Aquiloni, went down to Troia, Ordona, Canosa, and Bitonto. From Egnathia (modern Egnazia), another port from which ships set sail across the Adriatic to Durazzo, the road continued on to Brindisi, its first stretch being rather tortuous, with bold bridges and viaducts—such as those over the Cervaro (340 m), the Carapelle (450 m), and the Ofanto (1000 m)[53]—the rest running generally flat over the vast upland plains of the Tavoliere and Le Murge. In all, it covered 296 kilometers. Two hundred milestones bore witness to Trajan's feat, which was completed in a single undertaking, with the inscription: *"Traianus Aug(ustus) . . . viam a Benevento Brundisium pecun(ia) sua fecit"* ("The emperor Trajan, with his own money, built the road from Beneventum to Brundisium").

The Appian Way continues via the route linking Brindisi to Otranto, which passes through Lecce (ancient Lupiae). In late antiquity, Otranto would eventually displace Brindisi in prominence on the Italian peninsula, becoming an increasingly important bridgehead of the Byzantine Empire.[54]

*Archaic-style altar, second half of first century A.D. (Rome, Museo Nazionale Romano at Palazzo Massimo).*

In A.D. 123, Hadrian renovated the stretch of the Appian Way between Beneventum and Aeclanum.[55] Antoninus Pius restored the bridge over the Volturnus at Casilinum, while Septimius Severus ordered numerous repairs done on the road, in addition to constructing the monumental facade marking and embellishing the Via Appia's entrance into Rome. This monument, the famous Septizodium, acts as a kind of stage set for anyone entering Rome from the East or from Africa along that route.

At the start of the third century A.D., Septimius Severus erected two monumental columns in Proconnesian marble, featuring capitals decorated with figures of Oceanus and the Tritons, at the terminus of the Appian Way in the port of Brindisi, between the eastern and western inlets. They were rather like terminal milestones, serving as the counterpoint to the stage set of the Septidozium built at the foot of the Palatine hill in Rome.

Around the end of the second century, between Miles 2 and 3 of the Via Appia, the preeminent cemetery of the Church of Rome came into being. Caracalla saw to the paving of the road for twenty-one miles past Fondi, in the area of Casilinum between Caudium and Beneventum.[56]

With the construction of a defensive wall around Rome by Emperor Aurelian and his immediate successors (271–77), the first stretch of the Appian Way was blocked by a grandiose double-arched gate, the most beautiful in the Aurelian wall: the Porta Appia, later renamed Porta San Sebastiano after the catacombs to which it led.[57]

At the beginning of the fourth century the road was renovated by Diocletian and the Tetrarchs, and again by Maxentius in 309. We know this from the milestones that bear their names, along with those of Constantine, Julian the Apostate, Jovian, Valentinian, Valens, Valentinian II, Theodosius, Arcadius, and Honorius,[58] whose interventions served to maintain the vitality of the principal link between Rome, southern Italy, and the East.

Leading to the south of the peninsula, the Appian Way was always a fundamentally important axis. Along its route we find not only tombs but also commemorative arches, gates, inns, houses, *mansiones*, *mutationes*, and villas—and in such abundance, and so rich and monumental, as to make it celebrated from ancient times for this fact alone. This is what caused the poet Statius, at the end of the first century A.D., to give it the name by which we know it today: *regina viarum*, "queen of roads," the most beautiful of the Roman roads for its engineering brilliance, and the most important for the regions it crossed through.

Its decline began in the fifth century, with the collapse of the organized Roman state: maintenance fell off, marshes crept in from the vast areas of plain, and the barbarian invasions drove much of the population out of the plains to seek safety on higher ground.[59] At the time of Theodoric (455–524), the so-called Decennovium—that is, the straightaway of the Via Appia flanked by the navigable canal for a nineteen-mile stretch between Tripontium and Terracina—became inundated and therefore unusable. Three inscriptions, and Cassiodorus, bear witness to Theodoric's wish to have the Decennovium restored.[60] The restoration must not have changed the appearance of the Appian Way in any substantial way, but it must indeed have been completed, since Procopius of Caesarea, working with Byzantine General Belisarius a few decades later, during the Greco-Gothic war, was able to celebrate the road, confirming its great efficiency after experiencing it firsthand in the course of an expedition.[61]

The proper functioning of the Appia would cease definitively when the Lombards occupied Capua in 593–594. However, despite the continuous plunder of its monuments, which began in late antiquity and continued throughout the Middle Ages (Saracen troops devastated the road in 946),[62] the ancient splendor could still be found here and there, preserved in part by Christian memorials that had filled in the gaps in the ancient pagan monuments and, in transforming them, had preserved their memory.[63] The faithful frequented such sites assiduously, especially the Memoria Apostolorum near the Catacombs of S. Sebastiano. The Appia became a road of processions and churches. Along its first stretch, we find the churches of SS. Nereus and Achilleus, S. Cesareo, Domine Quo Vadis, S. Sebastiano, and S. Urbano, often founded among the abandoned ruins, whose forms, structures, and columns they retain.

In the now-abandoned villas, farming colonies—the *domus cultae*—took up residence under the direction of the new ecclesiastical authority, which from the end of the age of Constantine owned the *patrimonium Appiae*, a vast property between the Via Ostiense, the Via Latina,[64] and the Alban Hills, consolidated by 604 A.D.[65] These lands later passed into the hands of the nobility and the powerful Roman families, who fortified them. The ancient monuments became towers and citadels, or *castra*: this was done, for example, by the Astalli at Torre Selce, by the Caetani at Capo di Bove, by the Savelli at Tor Carbone, by the Orsini at Fiorano, and by the Astalli at Roma Vecchia, in the ancient villa of the Quintili.

Up until the ninth century, the Appian Way remained in use along the stretch closest to Rome. But the transfer of the martyrs' relics from the suburban areas into the center of the city accelerated near-total abandonment of the road.[66]

In the eleventh century, the counts of Tuscolo fortified the sepulcher of Cecilia Metella and imposed a toll on travel over the Via Appia. This eventually favored the birth of alternate routes, such as the Via Appia Nuova, paved in 1574 by Pope Gregory XIII. But the old route between Cisterna and Rome remained active until the thirteenth century, though not continuously so.[67]

Then the Caetani family, to which Pope Boniface VIII belonged, fortified the area in order to control the road, incorporating the sepulcher of Cecilia Metella into its fortifications.[68] It became the Castrum Caetani at the center of a fortified village with some fifty houses and two churches.

In the Pontine stretch of the Appian Way, the absence of monasteries and castles, settlements typical of the medieval era, along the road and between it and the sea, indicates that it had by then been abandoned in favor of a more inland route along the foothills.[69]

By the fifteenth century, the monuments were being systematically stripped of their marble for reuse elsewhere, to the point where Pope Paul III, in 1534, established the Commissariat of Antiquities to safeguard the monuments and control excavations in search of antiquities. Appeals for the conservation of the Appian Way's historical memory had been made to Pope Leo X (1516–17) by Pirro Ligorio and Raphael himself.

Starting around 1500, thanks to the work of Cesare Baronio and Antonio Bosio, scholars of early Christianity, many of the churches that give the Appian Way near Rome its modern aspect

were restored: SS. Nereus and Achilleus, S. Sisto Vecchio, S. Cesareo, the Domine Quo Vadis, the nearby round *tempietto* built by the English cardinal Reginald Pole of the circle of reformers of the mid-sixteenth century, S. Sebastiano, and the sanctuary of the Madonna del Divino Amore.

Pilgrims to the six or seven churches of Rome would take the Via Appia on their way to the *basilica*

*Apostolorum* and then to the little Church of the Nunziatella and the Abbey of the Tre Fontane. Innocent XII (1691–1700) had a link road opened between the Via Appia Antica and the Via Appia Nuova, called the Via Appia Pignatelli. These were not the only improvements during this period. In 1568, the duke of Alcalà, Viceroy of Naples, promoted certain restoration projects along the Via

Appia in the Sant'Andrea Gorge near Itri, past Terracina between Fondi and Formia (see map on page 108).[70]

Abandonment, desolation, and the lack of maintenance allowed much of the Appian Way to be overwhelmed by swamps. In 1777, however, the Pontine stretch was newly renovated by Pope Pius VI Braschi: The pavement surface of the old road was brought back to light and a new road was built on top of it.[71] The ancient canal alongside, the Decennovium, was also restored. It was thereafter called Linea Pia in that pope's honor, as he had established an important direct postal route along the Via Appia, with stations posted every 81 miles.[72]

In Apulia the Taranto–Brindisi stretch of the Appian Way remained in use until the seventh century. During the Byzantine domination, Brindisi, terminus of the Via Appia Traiana, enjoyed a period of great splendor. A governor of that city even had an inscription cut into the base of one of the columns that had been placed there by Septimius Severus to mark the end of the road.[73]

Along the Appian Way near Rome, clandestine excavations grew in number when archaeological collecting became fashionable around 1600, and they continued through the eighteenth century. In 1780, the sepulcher of the Scipios was discovered, and excavations were carried out in the villa of the Quintili.

And thus it was without any great changes—aside from the gradual abandonment and submergence under swamp of the countryside populated by impoverished shepherds and farmers—that the road and its surroundings came into the nineteenth century. At that point, sculptor Antonio Canova, along with other illustrious men, was entrusted with safeguarding the road's monuments.

Not coincidentally, during the nineteenth century, the first works of conservation on the Appian Way immediately followed the great era of the Grand Tour, during which the intellectuals of Europe alerted public organizations of the need to safeguard historic patrimony. Archaeological research was fostered by the Pontifical Government of Pius VII and Pius IX, while scholars such as Carlo Fea, Antonio Nibby, and Ennio Quirino Visconti began to work on the Appia alongside artists such as Canova and a number of architects including Valadier.

Napoleonic policy for Rome—"second city of the Empire"—envisioned the creation of an archaeological park that was to include the Campidoglio, the Roman Forum, and the Palatine Hill, and was to be joined to the Via Appia.

But the first systematic excavation, documentation, and restoration of the Appian Way—proposed by Camillo Jacobini, minister of Commerce, Fine Arts, and Public Works of the Pontifical Government under Pius IX—was carried out between 1850 and 1853 by Luigi Canina between Miles 4 and 9.[74] Named Commissioner of the Antiquities of Rome in 1839, Canina embarked on a project of careful documentation and planning, which we can then compare with what was actually achieved on a budget of 16,000 *scudi*.

The research and excavations were carried out at the expense of the government. With great far-sightedness, the road was expropriated along with a respectful ten meters of land on either side. It was marked off with the low, stone dry-walls, a type of enclosure that, while separating the road from private properties, makes it still possible today to preserve a coherent relationship between the road and its "hinterland."

During Canina's excavations, more than four hundred monuments were discovered, including tombs, villas, and temples. These were dug up, raised, restored, and studied.

Canina's very modern idea was to create a kind of open-air museum. He gave the Appian Way between Miles 4 and 9 a personal image of its own, made up of reconstructed brick walls or restorations of ancient structures on which he "remounted" marble works recovered during excavations: epigraphs, sculptures, and architectural and decorative fragments. This created an archaeological landscape that has little to do with historical reality, but had the merit of preserving a context that would have otherwise been lost or scattered, leaving us, among other things, a testimony of the criteria of conservation as applied in the mid-nineteenth century.

It is to Canina, and to the foresight, scholarship, and moderation of his intervention that we owe today the preservation of the most beautiful section of the Appian Way just outside of Rome.

At around the same time, starting in 1849, Giovanni Battista de Rossi began systematically

*Facing page: Fresco in the central apse of the Benedictine basilica of Sant'Angelo in Formis, near Capua. It portrays the abbot Desiderius (later Pope Victor III) offering to Christ a model of the new basilica of Sant'Angelo, which he had rebuilt and expanded in the eleventh century. The more ancient part of the original church was built by the Lombards in the late sixth century, on the site where a temple to Diana Tifatina had been demolished.*

*Left: North portal of the Norman church of S. Giovanni al Sepolcro in Brindisi, the city that was the terminus of the Appian Way and a favored port of call for crusaders.*

*Right, top and bottom: Frescoes from the Catacombs of S. Senatore near the church of S. Maria della Stella in Albano.*

exploring the Catacombs of S. Callisto, giving new life to our knowledge of early Christian Rome. In 1859, in the Randanini vineyard in front of the Basilica of S. Sebastiano, an important nucleus of Jewish catacombs was discovered. Finally, in 1893 Guido Baccelli began work on organizing the Passeggiata Archeologica ("Archaeological Promenade") and the Park of Porta Capena, closely connected with the first stretch of the Appian Way.

In 1988, the Lazio Regional Government established the Parco Regionale dell'Appia Antica, guaranteeing the conservation of that stretch of road by the Commune of Roma (the municipal government) and the surrounding municipalities. In the stretch running between Miles 3 and 7, the Appian Way has been the beneficiary of careful recent restorations (the Villa of the Quintili, the Mausoleum of Cecilia Metella, other sepulchers at the sides of the road, and certain parts of the pavement itself) on the occasion of the Papal Jubilee of the year 2000,[75] which, with the removal of a major highway bypass, gave the site back some of its charm of yore.

## Maps for Ancient Travel

In Roman times one traveled by horse, in carriages (*rhedae* or *carrucae dormitoriae* for long stretches, or light gigs called *cisia* for short trips). But most travel was on foot. The broad sidewalks constructed at a slightly higher elevation to the sides of the main roadbed bear witness to the heavy pedestrian traffic along the road. This is also confirmed by Horace's memoirs of his journey to Brindisi, and the story of the apostles Peter and Paul's journey to Rome on foot.

Every itinerary and map published in antiquity records the different way stations (*mansiones* and *mutationes*) along the Appian Way.[76] However, as such itineraries were designed for different people at different times, the information given in one often fails to correspond to the information in another.

The *Itinerarium Antonini Augusti* was a road guide from the time of Caracalla that catalogues 256 itineraries along the principal roads of the Empire; the *Itinerarium Burdigalense* or *Hierosolymitanum*

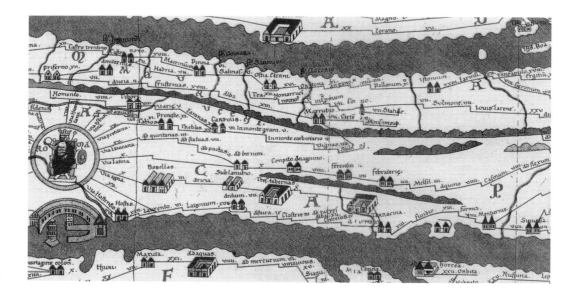

was a fourth-century A.D. guide for pilgrims traveling from Bordeaux to Jerusalem; the *Ravennatis Anonymi Cosmographia* was a highly detailed geographical survey published in the late seventh century that includes the Appian Way, along with a list of all the way stations. The *Tabula Peutingeriana*, a veritable road map of the Roman Empire probably compiled in the third century, with updates and corrections made in the fourth and fifth centuries, has come down to us in the form of a twelfth- or thirteenth-century copy. It is an extraordinary cartographic representation, on parchment scrolls oriented with east at the top, which because of the limited height of the scrolls greatly distorts the configurations of seas and landmasses. What is noteworthy is the fact that, as a road guide, it adopts conventional symbols to indicate cities, small population centers, and *mansiones*, just like modern maps.

### The Appian Way and the Grand Tour

The landscape that framed the Appian Way for the poets, writers, novelists, and scholars who traveled it from the seventeenth to the nineteenth centuries, in search of a variety of inspirations, was quite different from what we see today.

The Roman Campagna looked like a "timeless . . . land, perennial and unchanging under the weight of millennia, peopled by ruins and buffalo and sheep and foals and herdsmen still clothed in pelts like ancient fauns," according to Ugo Fleres, who published a widely read account of the Campagna in 1904.[77] It is a picturesque vision that attempts a reevaluation, a reconciliation between ancient and modern. Indeed, the Appian Way itself, along with its tombs, became a literary protagonist in the "Fifth Colloquy" of *Roman Nights*, by Pietro and Alessandro Verri.[78]

On the Grand Tour, an excursion along the Appian Way was customary, not only because of its beauty, the luminosity of its landscapes, and the richness of its ruins of monuments both pagan and Christian, but also because it was the obligatory route for the continuation of the Tour—whether overland by carriage or on horseback—in the direction of Naples and then Sicily, two other traditional destinations of the *Italienische Reise*.

Goethe was author of the most famous of these early travelogues. In addition to describing his journey, he made sketches in India ink and watercolor, as a sort of spontaneous commentary on sensations for which the written word was insufficient.

The pleasure of travel, of describing and drawing, also led Carlo Labruzzi, the Italian artist in the retinue of the famous traveler and antiquarian Sir Richard Coald Hoare, to favor the Appian Way between Rome and Capua.[79] Labruzzi "strips the palette of the superfluous, painting from life an entirely mental, abstract nature," with a descriptive stroke and a special sensitivity to the details of nature.[80]

## The Appian Way Today

But what do we ourselves expect from a visit to the Appian Way, or from a book about it? What does it mean, today, to tell the story of a road?

Its natural frame has changed, even compared to the early decades of the twentieth century. It is no longer a desolate countryside, but a landscape of intense construction that miraculously ends at an ill-defined limit, as if some great hand had stopped it, suddenly blocked its violent expansion.[81]

The houses that, despite restrictions and prohibitions, have been built along the "urban" route,[82] and not recently at that, in some way recreate the ancient relationship between burial sites and residential areas, but they no longer engage in the same dialogue as the Villa of the Quintili might have done with the adjacent tomb of a Sergius Demeter. On the contrary, it almost seems as if the new inhabitants, by defending their privacy with high walls and dense enclosures, reject all relationship with this road and its memories.

Today the Appian Way, in its most monumental, best-preserved part, is at last a protected site, far from the noise of the city, immersed in an almost motionless atmosphere, one that certainly invites the soul to reflect and investigate. It offers a kind of spiritual rest that can only do good to every one of us, a pause in the itinerary of our frantic pursuit of life, a chance to rediscover even the simple pleasure of going somewhere on foot.[83] This, and more, is what we can find as we walk along the Via Appia.

Much is being done, in spite of everything, to preserve this piece of history in as broad a context as possible, to allow people to feel the strong historic presence of the Appian Way, especially that part that begins at the Forum Boarium (near the Circus Maximus) up to the city limits of Rome.[84] But even more ambitious projects are in the works that envision the protected area of the ancient, noble road extending over the entire route between Rome and Brindisi, in a synergy between regional, provincial, and municipal administrations. And

they, we hope, will have far more power to realize their designs than Ruggero Bonghi and Guido Baccelli ever dreamed of.[85] This may prove to be the finest legacy our generation can leave to those that follow.

## Notes

1 *Horace's Satires and Epistles* (New York: W. W. Norton, 1977), pp. 12–14.

2 Giorgio Vigolo, quoted in F. Castagnoli, A. M. Colini, and G. Macchia, *La via Appia* (Rome: Banco di Roma, 1972), p. 30.

3 From the metered inscription of Caius Attilius Evodus, pearl merchant on the Via Sacra, at Mile 6 of the Via Appia.

4 The tombs called "The Distaff" ("La Conocchia") and "The Old Prisons" ("Le Carceri Vecchie").

5 *Via Appia: Sulle ruine della magnificenza antica*, eds. Italo Insolera and Domatilla Morandi, exh. cat., Fondazione Memmo, Rome (Milan: Leonardo Arte, 1997).

6 J. W. Goethe, "Italian Journey (1786–1787)," in *Selected Works of J. W. von Goethe*, trans. W. H. Auden and Elizabeth Mayer (New York: Knopf/Everyman, 2000), p. 512; Paolo Chiarini, "Goethe, Roma e il viaggio in Italia," in *Goethe a Roma, 1786–1788: Disegni e acquerelli da Weimar*, exh. cat. (Rome: Artemide, 1988), pp. 15–25.

7 Thomas Ashby, *The Roman Campagna in Classical Times* (New York: Macmillan, 1927), p. 21. See also S. Le Pera and R. Turchetti, "Thomas Ashby e la via Appia," in *Sulla via Appia da Roma a Brindisi: Le fotografie di Thomas Ashby 1891–1925*, exh. cat., British School in Rome (Rome, 2003), pp. 15–18.

8 The journey from Rome to Capua (132 miles, equal to 195 km) could, in fact, be made in four days by an army on the march.

9 As Rome expanded, the construction of roads and the founding of colonies kept pace. See F. Coarelli, "Colonizzazione romana e viabilità," in *Dialoghi di Archeologia*, ser. 3a, 6, 2 (1988), pp. 35–48; G. Uggeri, "La via Appia nella politica espansionistica di Roma," in *Via Appia, decimo incontro di studio del Comitato per l'archeologia laziale*, ed. Stefania Quilici Gigli, *QuadAEI* 10.1 (Rome: Consiglio nazionale delle richerche, 1990), pp. 21–28.

10 Pier Giorgio Monti, *Via Latina* (Rome: Libreria dello Stato, 1995), p. 13.

11 G. Pisani Sartorio, "Mezzi di trasporto e traffico," in *Vita e costumi dei Romani antichi* 6 (Rome, 1988), pp. 23–25; S. Bellino, *Dizionario Epigrafico De Ruggiero*, vol. 2 (2), pp. 1404–25, s.v. "*cursus publicus*"; H.-G. Pflaum, "Essai sur le *cursus publicus* sous le haut-empire romain," in *Mémoires de l'Académie des Inscriptions et Belles Lettres* 14 (1940); Lorenzo Quilici, *La via Appia: Regina Viarum* (Rome: Viviani, 1997), p. 93.

12 *Theodosian Codex* 8.5 ("*de cursu publico, angariis et parangariis*").

13 Lorenzo Quilici, *La via Appia da Roma a Boville* (Rome: Bulzoni, 1977); idem, "La via Appia Antica," in *Piano per il parco dell'Appia Antica*, Italia Nostra, Sezione di Roma, coord. V. Calzolari; ed. M. Olivieri (Rome: The Association, 1984), pp. 61–80; idem, *Via Appia*, vol. 1: *Da Porta Capena ai Colli Albani*, vol. 2: *Dalla Pianura Pontina a Brindisi* (Rome: Fratelli Palombi, 1989); idem, "Le strade. Viabilità tra Roma e il Lazio," in *Vita e costumi dei Romani antichi* 12 (Rome, 1991); idem, *La Via Appia: Regina Viarum*.

14 R. A. Staccioli, "La via Appia: Storia e monumenti della 'regina viarum,'" *Roma tascabile* 84 (Rome, 1998), p. 7.

15 These cities could be reached via the secondary road system.

16 The entire road system of the Roman Empire has been calculated at more than 100,000 kilometers (about 60,000 miles).

17 Lorenzo Quilici, "Il rettifilo della via Appia tra Roma e Terracina," in *Via Appia* (*QuadAEI* 10.1), pp. 41–60.

18 Procopius *De Bello Gothico* 5.14.7.

19 W. Eck, "Der Administration der italischen Strassen: Das Beispiel der Via Appia," in *Via Appia* (*QuadAEI* 10.1), p. 31 ff.

20 M. Bertinetti, "La Cura viarum," in *Viae Publicae Romanae*, ed. Rosanna Cappelli, exh. cat., Castel Sant'Angelo (Rome: Leonardo-De Luca, 1991), pp. 36–37.

21 Antonio Palma, *Le 'curae' pubbliche: Studi sulle strutture amministrative romane* (Naples: E. Jovene, 1980), pp. 186–95.

22 Tacitus *Historiae* 1.27; Cassius Dio 54.8.4; Pliny *Naturalis Historia* 3.36.

23 Plutarch *Galba* 24; see Gerhard Radke, *Viae Publicae Romanae* (Italian trans.), (Bologna, 1981), pp. 1453–54.

24 Z. Mari, s.v. "*Milarium aureum*," in *LTUR* 3, pp. 250–51 (with bibliography).

25 Radke, *Viae Publicae*, p. 64; R. Friggeri, "I miliari," in Cappelli, ed., *Viae Publicae Romanae*, pp. 39–40.

26 Elena Banzi, *I miliari come fonte topografica e storica* (Rome: École française de Rome, 1999), p. 2.

27 Procopius *De Bello Gothico* 5.14.8–11.

28 G. Lugli, "Il sistema stradale di Roma antica," in *Études Etrusco-Italiques* (Louvain: Bibliothèque de l'Université, 1963), pp. 112–18, republished in idem, *Studi minori di topografia antica* (Rome: De Luca, 1965), pp. 223–28.

29 F. Castagnoli, "Il tracciato della via Appia," *Capitolium* 44 (1969), pp. 77–100.

30 For the Via Appia, one thinks of the preexisting Via Albana, which connected Rome with the ancient cities of Latium and the provincial sanctuaries, such as that of Diana at Aricia, or that of Jupiter on the Monte Cavo. See G. Tomassetti, *La Campagna Romana antica, medievale e moderna*, eds. L. Chiumenti and F. Bilancia, vol. 2 (Rome: Banco di Roma, 1975), p. 11.

31  J. R. Patterson, in *LTUR* 5 (Rome, 1999), pp. 130–33; S. Bruni, in *LTUR Suburbium* 1 (Rome, 2001), s.v. "*Appia via,*" pp. 84–95. It is noteworthy that Diodorus Siculus, like Procopius of Caesarea after him, attributed the paving of the road to Appius Claudius, whereas in fact it was done at a later time.

32  *CIL* XI.1827=*ILS* 54= *Inscr.Ital.* XIII.3.79. Eulogy of Appius Claudius Caecus at the Forum of Augustus in Rome.

33  Before Appius Claudius, roads were named after their geographic destinations, such as the Via Nomentana, the Via Praenestina, the Via Laurentina, and the Via Ardeatina. In the case of the Appia, the road took its appellation not from its founder's surname, which would have made it the Via Claudia, but from his first name, Appius.

34  Diodorus Siculus 20.36.2.

35  Livy 9.29.5–7

36  Diodorus Siculus 20.36.1–2. Diodorus here erroneously credits Appius Claudius with paving the road, when in fact this happened later. If Appius Claudius had not acted this aggressively, today we probably would not have the Via Appia: see S. Mazzarino, "Aspetti di storia dell'Appia antica," *Helikon* 8 (1968), pp. 174–96.

37  In 312 B.C., the censors Appius Claudius Caecus and C. Plautius Venox gave Rome her first aqueduct, which also bore the name of Appius.

38  For a historical portrait of Appius Claudius, see Quilici, *La via Appia: Regina Viarum*, p. 11; and G. Staccioli in *Via Appia* (*QuadAEI* 10.1), p 8; *CIL* IX.1827= *ILS* 54.

39  Livy 10.23.11–12. In 189 B.C., the censors M. Claudius Marcellus and T. Quintius Flaminius repaved the same area in flintstone, according to Livy 38.28.3.

40  Livy 39.44.6; 40.51.2.

41  This last stretch must have already been functional by 200 B.C., possibly even by 212 B.C. Hannibal may have traveled along it from Tarentum. See Uggeri, "La via Appia nella politica espansionistica," p. 24.

42  Livy 36.21.5–6; Plutarch *Cato maior* 14.3–4.

43  Bruni, *LTUR Suburbium*, pp. 89, 91.

44  *CIL* IX.5977, 5978.

45  *CIL* X.6812 = *ILS* 5819; 6817.

46  These restorations are attested to by sixteen different milestones. Bruni, *LTUR Suburbium*, p. 92.

47  Ibid.

48  Previously the road, abandoning its rectilinear route, passed through the upper part of the city on the *decumanus maximus* and ascended up the Monte S. Angelo, where the celebrated sanctuary of Jupiter Anxur stood; thereafter it descended toward Fondi. The Pisco Montano cut allowed the Via Appia to pass through the lower part of the city along the sea and made it possible to build the port, works that are depicted in a relief from Terracina (Museo Nazionale Romano, inv. 231008).

According to Coarelli, this construction should be attributed to the period of the war against Sixtus Pompeius (41–36 B.C.). F. Coarelli "La costruzione del porto di Terracina in un rilievo storico tardo-repubblicano," in *Revixit Ars: Arte e ideologia a Roma* (Rome, 1996), pp. 434–54.

49  Strabo 5.3.6.

50  Erika Simon, *Die Götter am Trajansbogen zu Benevent* (Mainz am Rhein: von Zabern, 1981). Stefania Adamo Muscettola, ed., *Benevento, l'arco e la città* (Naples: Dipartimento di studi del mondo classico e del Mediterraneo antico dell'Istituto universitario orientale, 1985), with previous bibliography.

51  G. Uggeri, *La viabilità nel Salento* (Fasano: Grafischena, 1983). S. Bruni, *LTUR Suburbium*, pp. 91–92.

52  *CIL* IX.6072, 6074, 6075 =*ILS* 5875.

53  This bridge was still in use in the eighteenth century.

54  F. D'Andria, "La via Appia in Puglia," in *Via Appia: Sulle ruine*, pp. 95–104.

55  The 127 A.D. restorations, according to an inscription, cost more than 109,000 sesterces per mile, provided in part by the landowners affected by the road. See R. A. Staccioli, *Via Appia* (*QuadAEI* 10.1), p. 11.

56  *CIL* X.6854 =*ILS* 5822.

57  It was reduced to one arch in the early fifth century, making it easier to defend.

58  A. Mosca, "Restauri tardo-antichi sulla via Appia," in *Via Appia* (*QuadAEI* 10.1), pp. 182–85.

59  L. Cassanelli, "Schede di storia territoriale," in *Piano per il parco dell'Appia Antica*, pp. 81–108.

60  "*Decennovii viae Appiae, id (est) a Trip(ontio) usq(ue) Tarrac(inam): Iter et loca . . . restituit,*" *CIL* X.6850–52 = *ILS* 867: Cassiodorus *Variae* 2.32.33. Between 507 and 511, the patrician Cecina Mavortius Basilius Decius completed the draining of the swamps, and Theodoric agreed to let Decius take over the reclaimed land. This was a prelude to what much later would become the "feudal" system; see S. Mazzarino, "Aspetti e storia dell'Appia antica," *Helikon* 8 (1968), pp. 195–96; Mosca, "Restauri tardo-antichi," p. 183.

61  Procopius *De Bello Gothico* 1.14.6–10; 2.4.

62  L. Fiorani, "L'Appia Antica nel Medio Evo," *Capitolium* 44 (1969), pp. 121–26.

63  R. Paris, "L'Appia Antica oggi," in *Via Appia: Sulle ruine*, pp. 21–22.

64  Lucrezia Spera, in *LTUR Suburbium* 1 (2001), s.v. "*Appiae patrimonium*": this was made up of sixteen *massae* (parcels) and fifty-nine *fundi* (farmsteads). F. Marazzi, "Il *patrimonium Appiae*: Beni fondiari della Chiesa Romana nel territorio suburbano della via Appia fra il IV e il IX secolo," in *Via Appia* (*QuadAEI* 10.1), pp. 117–26.

65  Epistle of Gregory I the Great (January 25, 604); see Spera, ibid.

66 Lucrezia Spera, *Il paesaggio suburbano di Roma dall'antichità al Medioevo: Il comprensorio tra le vie Latina e Ardeatina dalle Mura di Aureliano al III miglio* (Rome: "L'Erma" di Bretschneider, 1999), p. 424; Bruni, *LTUR Suburbium*, p. 93.

67 J. Coste, "La via Appia nel Medioevo e l'incastellamento," in *Via Appia: Sulle ruine*, p. 128.

68 R. Paris, "Il mausoleo di Cecilia Metella e il Castrum Caetani sulla via Appia," in *Via Appia: Sulle ruine*, p. 54.

69 Coste, "La via Appia nel Medioevo e l'incastellamento."

70 Lorenzo Quilici, "La via Appia attraverso la gola di Itri," in *Lazio ieri e oggi* 38, no. 1 (2002). Restoration of this stretch of road is currently being undertaken by the Commune of Itri, with finances coming from the Regione Lazio in connection with the Parco Naturalistico dei Monti Aurunci.

71 Quilici, "Il rettifilo," pp. 41–60.

72 Andrea Carbonara and Gaetano Messineo, *Via Appia*, vol. 3: *Da Cisterna a Minturno* (Rome: Libreria dello Stato, 1998), p. 11. Rainwater was channeled off into ditches perpendicular to the road, called "mile ditches," because they were dug in correspondence with the milestones.

73 The other column, which fell during the earthquake of 1528, was moved to Lecce in 1666 and placed in the central town square as the base of the bronze statue of St. Oronzo.

74 L. Canina, "Esposizione topografica della prima parte dell'antica via Appia dalla Porta Capena alla stazione di Ariccia," *Annali dell'Instituto* (1851), pp. 303–24; (1852), pp. 254–300; (1853), pp. 132–87; idem, *La prima parte della via Appia, dalla porta Capena a Boville, descritta e dimostrata con i monumenti superstiti* (Rome, 1853). See also S. Bruni, "La via Appia Antica: gli scavi tra Settecento ed Ottocento," in *Via Appia: Sulle ruine*, pp. 23–24; R. Paris, "Luigi Canina e il museo all'aperto della via Appia," in *Tusculum: Luigi Canina e la riscoperta di un'antica città*, exh. cat. (Rome, 2002), pp. 221–24; M. G. Filetici, "Otto mausolei fra il terzo e quarto miglio della via Appia, dal restauro di Canina del 1851 a quello del Giubileo del 2000," in *Tusculum*, pp. 225–29.

75 Paris, "Luigi Canina," pp. 222–24; Filetici, "Otto mausolei."

76 Bruni, *LTUR Suburbium*, pp. 92–93 (with bibliography on subject).

77 U. Fleres, 1901, quoted in M. Fagiolo dell'Arco, "Esotico e pittoresco alle porte di casa," in *La Campagna Romana da Hackert a Balla*, exh. cat. (Rome: Museo del Corso, 2001), p. 13 ff.

78 Alessandro Verri, *Notti Romane* 2, notte V, colloquio V, and letter to his brother Pietro, April 20, 1782.

79 M. G. Massafra, *Bollettino dei Musei Comunali di Roma*, n.s. 7 (1993), pp. 46–56.

80 Fagiolo dell'Arco, "Esotico e pittoresco," p. 15. See also M. G. Massacra, "Via Appia illustrata ab Urbe ad Capuam. Un itinerario attraverso i disegni di Carlo Labruzzi e le memorie archeologiche di Thomas Ashby," in *Sulla via Appia da Roma a Brindisi*, pp. 33–38.

81 This is well-known to those who fought for over sixty years to safeguard the Via Appia Antica and to create a protected area broad enough to preserve not only the remains of the tombs at the side of the road, but also the road's "framework," that is, those elements that allow one to enjoy it and to fully understand its historical and environmental value. See *Piano per il parco dell'Appia Antica*.

82 This term refers to the Via Appia from the center of Rome to Casal Rotondo, and almost as far as the G.R.A. (Grande Raccordo Anulare [Great Ring Road]), the outer belt of highway considered the boundary of Rome in the year 2000 (see map on page 42).

83 On holidays, the Via Appia from Porta San Sebastiano to the Rome city limits is open only to pedestrians.

84 The 1880s project to salvage the monumental area of the Imperial Forums, together with the already realized Archaeological Promenade—an enlightened project of the recently established Unification government (law 4730 of 7/5/1887, proposed by Guido Baccelli and Ruggero Bonghi)—was not realized until 1907 (law no. 502, on the occasion of the fiftieth anniversary of the proclamation of Rome as capital of Italy). It was not inaugurated (and incompletely at that) until 1917. Still, today it allows us to enjoy an archaeological park in the heart of Imperial Rome that unfolds without interruption all the way to the Alban Hills and beyond.

85 Lorenzo Quilici, *Via Appia*, vol. 1: *Da porta Capena ai Colli Albani*, p 11.

# The Urban Segment from Porta Capena to Casal Rotondo

GIUSEPPINA PISANI SARTORIO

*Above: The first milestone column of the Appian Way, rediscovered in 1584 and placed on the balustrade of the monumental staircase of the Campidoglio in Rome.*

*Facing page: The seventh milestone column of the Appian Way, on the balustrade of the Campidoglio staircase since 1848.*

## The Natural Surroundings of the Appian Way from Porta Capena to Casal Rotondo, Yesterday and Today

The road at first wends its way through the tufaceous hills facing the Tiber River, then emerges into a small valley traversed by a stream, which is all that remains of the Almone River. It then ascends the slopes of the "lava flows of Capo di Bove"—a route chosen because it provided a more solid base for the roadbed than the lower-lying and potentially marshy areas—passing, as in ancient times, through alternating tracts of wild and arable land, orchards, gardens, and villas.

The particular geological strata underlying this stretch (impermeable clay soil with overlying tufaceous strata, pozzolana, and underlying impermeable tufa) makes the area rich in water sources (the Egeria springs, the channel known as the Marrana Mariana, the Almone River) and mineral and thermal springs (e.g., Acquasanta).

In ancient times, the landscape was rich in tree and plant species. This is attested by the presence, along the Appian Way, of sacred woods (such as the sacred wood of the Camenae, nymphs who together with Aegeria inspired King Numa Pompilius; and the sacred wood of the god Rediculus and the holm-oak grove of Pagus Triopius) and rose-and-violet gardens next to the tombs.

Among the ruins of the historic monuments, wild vegetation now thrives, while the rare but surviving thickets still have species native to the Rome area, including the holm oak, cork oak, common oak, maple, myrtle, pine, and laurel. There are also many species that have been introduced at different times, including willows and poplars in the wetter areas, walnuts and mulberries along the lanes, and English oak and hazelnut in the drier areas.[1]

Peculiar to the Appian environs, but also to the Roman Campagna in general, are the grassy plateaus cultivated as grazing land. In the plans for the archaeological park, these would be salvaged with natural grass areas featuring different species of perennial grasses.[2]

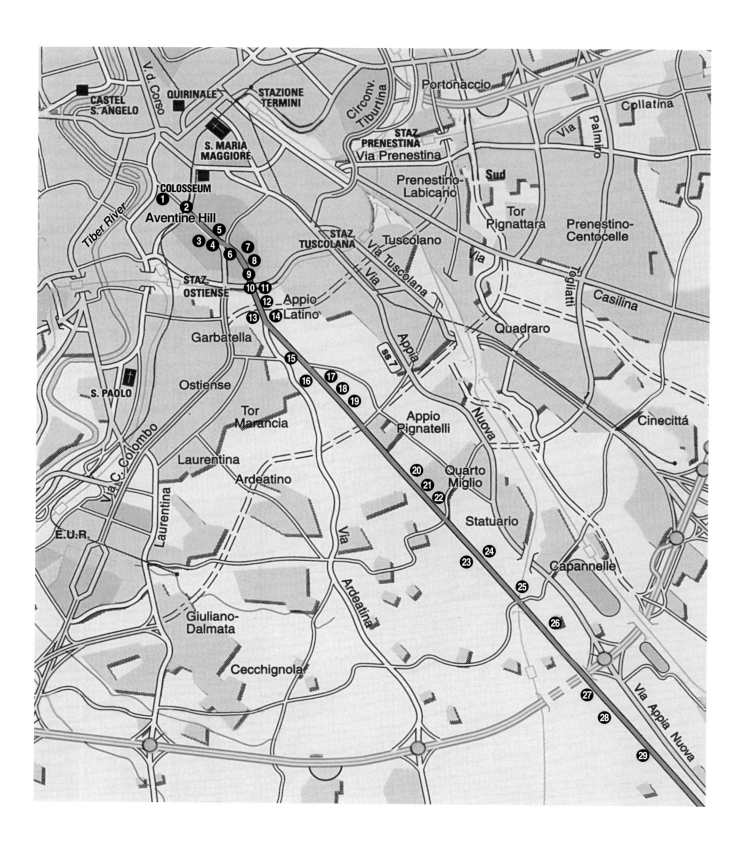

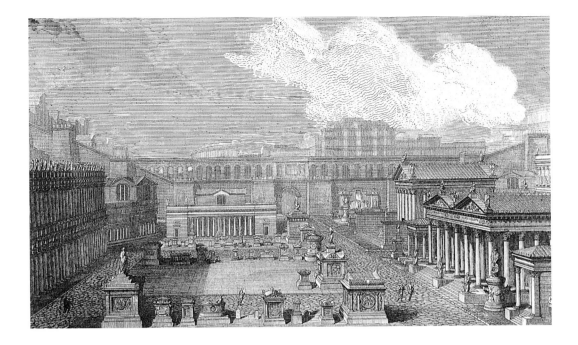

## Door to Door from Porta Capena to Porta Appia (Porta San Sebastiano)[3]

### The Appearance of the Road, Yesterday and Today

This stretch of the Appian Way is called the "urban segment" because it has been part of the city since antiquity. It runs from the Porta Capena within the fourth-century-B.C. Republican walls to the Porta Appia within the Aurelian wall, dated 270–277 A.D. It passes through the valley lying between the heights of the Celian and Aventine hills, and in ancient times it was flanked by mostly public buildings, often those connected to road-related services: the *area carruces*, a parking area for private carriages; the *mutatorium Caesaris*, where the emperor's carriages were changed; and the *area radicaria*, a kind of toll zone near the city gate. It was also flanked by baths, those of Caracalla and Commodus, and commemorative arches, such as the arch of Drusus (father of the emperor Claudius),[4] and perhaps also an arch erected in Trajan's honor and another commemorating Lucius Verus.[5] Then there were the dramatic facades, such as the Septizodium, which must have dazzled anyone entering Rome through the Porta Capena; the religious buildings, such as the Altar of *Fortuna Redux*; and the temples, such as that of *Honos* (Honor) and *Virtus* (Virtue). Here, outside the Republican walls—and outside the *pomoerium* (the ceremonial boundary of a Roman city)—was also the *Senaculum*, where the Senate convened for conference with consuls and magistrates returning from the provinces; there were other places designed for public ceremonies of departure and return (*profectio* and *reditus*) as well. All these monuments have disappeared.

The course of this stretch of the Via Appia must have followed that of the old Via Latina. Opposite where the current church of S. Cesareo stands, where one now finds a turreted medieval shrine—perhaps on the site of a more ancient *compitum*[6]—the two roads once forked: the Via Latina turned toward the foothills, while the Via Appia went toward the plain. They met up again at Capua.

At this fork began the area of the sepulchers. There aren't many remains of these left, but those that survived are significant, since they are mostly the tombs of important families, dating from the Republican era to the middle Empire. When the broader perimeter of the Aurelian Wall was built, the sepulchral area was moved outside the *pomoerium*, since by law one could not bury the dead inside city limits.

Today this segment of the road is clearly divided into two parts. The first runs from the Porta Capena to the church of S. Cesareo and constitutes the so-called "Archaeological Promenade." It comprises a vast area expropriated in accordance with course is perhaps the ancient Via Nova, built by Caracalla to serve his baths.

The second part of this segment, from the church of S. Cesareo to the Porta Appia, lies instead behind high walls that enclose private villas, public villas, and archaeological areas, which allow very little of the ancient tombs to be seen.

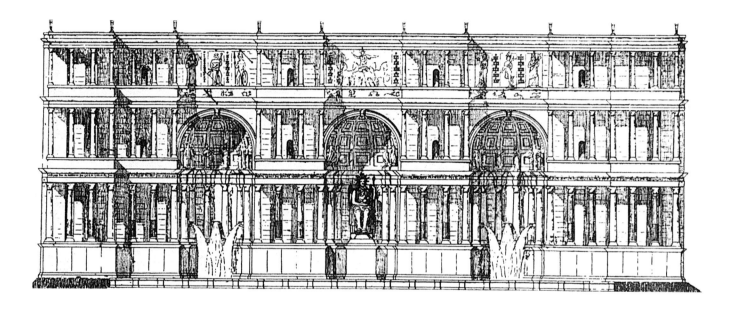

*Graphic rendering of the Septizodium. The monument, built by Septimius Severus, was a spectacular theatrical backdrop with astrological symbolism at the foot of the Palatine Hill. It was designed to welcome those who entered Rome along the Via Appia.*

an 1887 project—a project that echoed plans already formulated in the Napoleonic era—for a large archaeological park from the Campidoglio to the Via Appia Antica, including the Palatine Hill, the Roman Forum, the Colosseum, the Baths of Titus, part of the Celian Hill, the Baths of Caracalla, the Via Appia and Via Latina up to the walls, half of the Aventine Hill, and the Circus Maximus. Because of postponements, delays, and drastic reductions in the area to be expropriated, the Archaeological Promenade was not inaugurated until 1917. Tree plantings, excavations, and restorations of monuments were carried out along a route that some maintain is not that of the Appian Way (which probably ran closer to the Celian Hill), today the Via Valle delle Camene. The current

The typologies of the Roman-era tombs along the Appian Way, as along the other consular roads, vary immensely. In the tombs here, the typologies are even more diverse than usual. They are:

1. *Quadrangular tombs*, with pulvins on the sides, altar-style.
2. *Temple-style tombs*, with podium, staircase, rectangular chamber sometimes with niches in the walls, and pronaos (porch) with pediment.
3. *Circular-plan temple tombs*, with columned and pedimented pronaos, access staircase (Pantheon-style), and annular sepulchral chamber in the lower part.
4. *Tower tombs*, on high podium with volumes of decreasing size on top of one another

and sepulchral chamber in the lower part, sometimes with pyramidal roof.

5. *Aedicula tombs*, on high quadrangular base.

6. *Circular tumulus tombs*, on low podium with cone of earth on top.

7. *Tombs on quadrangular foundations*, with tall cylindrical base and conical covering.

8. *Quadrangular-plan tombs with chamber*, sometimes with hypogeum (cellar) and two stories on top; in the second century A.D., they were built with carefully made brick walls, decorative pilaster strips and trabeation in polychrome brickwork.

9. *Circular mausoleums*, from the third and fourth centuries, with domed vault.[7]

10. *Columbaria*, modern term for chamber tombs, for the most part entirely or partially underground, with numerous niches intended for cinerary urns or pots; the vaults are often supported by circular or square pilasters also covered with niches. The sepulcher assumes the general appearance of a dovecote or columbarium, whence the name.

### The Itinerary

The road led out from the heart of the city, the Forum Boarium, passing between the Circus Maximus and the slopes of the Palatine Hill, at whose foot, in the early third century, rose the Septizodium,[8] the unusual monument built by

*View of the Palatine Hill and the Circus Maximus. The most ancient stretch of the Appian Way passed through here.*

Septimius Severus (and demolished in the sixteenth century) for no precise purpose other than to serve as a kind of theatrical prop. Over thirty meters high, it greeted anyone arriving in Rome by the Via Appia from the ports of Campania, or therefore from Africa itself, birthplace of the emperor.

In Rome, the road exited through the Porta Capena, Martial's *arcus stillans* or "dripping arch,"[9] which he so dubbed because the two aqueducts, the *rivus Herculaneus* of the Aqua Marcia and Aqua Appia, passed overhead, and leaks from them made the city gate perpetually damp. To the right was the early-third-century monumental complex of the Baths of Caracalla, immediately followed by three church complexes: on the left, S. Maria in Tempulo and SS. Domenico and Sixtus, both founded in the sixth century, and on the right, the basilica of SS. Nereus and Achilleus, also sixth century, and S. Cesareo in Turri, twelfth century. Mosaics have been found beneath the latter's flooring, from a third-century bathing establishment possibly connected with the Baths of Commodus.

In the fifteenth century a country residence, attributed to Cardinal Bessarione, bishop of Tuscolo from 1449 to 1468, was built near the bifurcation of the Via Appia and the Via Latina. It is a rare specimen of a suburban Renaissance villa,

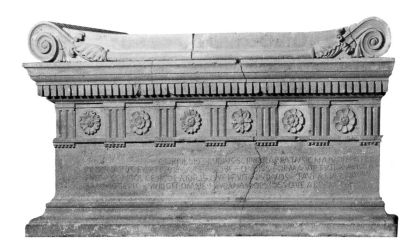

and today serves as a reception center for the mayor of Rome. Tombs from the late Republican era have been discovered in the building's foundations.

On the road's left, near the Pallavicini estate, is the Oratory of the Seven Sleepers. It lies within more ancient structures that bear paintings from the eleventh and twelfth centuries illustrating the legend of the saints of Ephesus, who were buried alive during Decius's persecutions and found alive two centuries later. Nearly the same age as the road is one of the most illustrious and well-known sepulchers of the Appian Way: the Tomb of the Scipios, the famous family that provided Rome with some of its most celebrated personages, including Scipio Emilianus and Scipio Africanus.[10]

Cicero recalled the family in a rhetorical question: "Do you, perchance, consider them modest, the tombs of Catalino, the Scipios, the Servilii, the Metelli, when you see them upon exiting the Porta Capena?"[11]

This tomb was already known by 1614. It was rediscovered in 1780, when the Sassi brothers decided to enlarge the cellar of their house, which was built on top of an older dwelling. Preserved under the Roman house, which dates to the third or fourth century, the Scipios' tomb was cut into the tufa and presented a painted facade with three arched doorways giving onto a side road of the Appian Way.[12] In a large quadrangular room supported by tufa pillars, it held some thirty-two sarcophagi,[13] either monolithic or made of slabs of peperino stone. Their inscriptions celebrated the glories of various members of the noble family, starting with L. Cornelius Scipio Barbatus, consul in 298 B.C., and continuing with Gnaeus Scipio Hispanus and many other men and women. It became the model for the tombs of the Roman *nobilitas* of the era. A portrait in tufa believed by some to be of the poet Ennius, friend of the Scipios, may instead be a likeness of Cornelius Scipio Nasica Corculum.

In the vineyard of the same Sassi family, a columbarium with over 470 cinerary urns was discovered. More were later found in the Codini vineyard: two (one with some 500 cinerary jars, the other with 600) were discovered between 1840 and 1847 by G. P. Campana, an antiquities scholar and collector, and a third by the proprietor himself, P. Codini, in 1852. The walls and pilasters supporting the vaults are entirely covered with burial niches, inside of which were placed the jars containing the ashes of the deceased. Many can be identified from their names as slaves or freedmen of the imperial family. Oftentimes their role or profession is actually indicated: a treasury cashier, a tax collector, members of a symphonic college, members of a guild of wreath-makers and florists, a midwife, an architect, and a jester of the court of Tiberius are among them. The columbaria were used from the late Augustan and the Tiberian age up until the second century A.D.

Before passing through the gate bearing its name, the Via Appia was spanned by a vaulted arch of the Antonine aqueduct, a branch of the Aqua Marcia, which provided water to the Baths of Caracalla. The arch is commonly and mistakenly attributed to Drusus, whose arch actually came first. Other arches of the aqueduct can in fact be recognized to the right and left, proving that the vaulting is only the monumentalization of an archway framed by two columns on high plinths and composite capitals surmounted by an architrave above. The architrave rises to the massive attic, adorned with a triangular tympanum, through which water flowed into the hollow.

In the fourth century, the arch was incorporated into the system of internal defense of the Porta Appia, the most imposing, best-preserved gate in the walls that the emperor Aurelian and his successors, Tacitus and Probus, had built to

*On pages 50–51: the Via Appia between the Piazzale Numa Pompilio (where the Via Appia and the Via Latina converge) and the Porta San Sebastiano.*

*Facing page: The so-called Arch of Drusus. Erroneously attributed to Nero Claudius Drusus (father of the emperor Claudius), the arch is a monumentalization of one of the spans of the Antonine aqueduct that brought water to the Baths of Caracalla. In the fourth century the arch was incorporated into the Porta Appia.*

*This page: The Porta Appia, the most imposing of the gates in the Aurelian walls built in the last quarter of the third century A.D. Its name was changed to Porta San Sebastiano in the Middle Ages, after the famous catacombs dedicated to the sainted martyr located a few kilometers away.*

*On page 54: A stretch of the Via Appia going toward Rome, as it looked in the nineteenth century (above) and as it was presumed by Luigi Canina to have looked in antiquity (below). In the background is the Porta San Sebastiano; in the foreground, on the left, is the Tomb of Priscilla; on the right, the Tomb of Getas.*

*On page 55: The so-called Tomb of Priscilla, wife of a powerful freedman of the emperor Domitian.*

Its architecture and its strategic position make it the finest example of a city gate inserted in an ancient fortification. Originally double-arched, the structure that we see today—with only one, more easily defensible arch—dates from the restorations of Arcadius and Honorius (401–2). It shows a two-story attic with arched windows and travertine facing, a crenellated catwalk, and semicircular brick towers on the sides, which were later surrounded by a quadrangular base faced with blocks of marble. The gate reaches a total height of twenty-eight meters and dominates the Almone River valley from above.

On the right side of the archway, crudely carved into the rock, is an image of the Archangel Michael bearing witness to the victory of the Roman Ghibellines over Robert of Anjou, King of Naples, who wanted to subjugate the city after the pope went into exile in Avignon. The inscription tells of the event in a simple, efficacious style: "Year 1327, proclamation XI, in the month of September, on the penultimate day, the feast of St. Michael, foreign people entered the city and were defeated by the Romans, with Jacopo de' Ponziani the district leader."

### From Porta San Sebastiano to the Domine Quo Vadis, between Miles 1 and 2

*The Appearance of the Road, Yesterday and Today*
Outside the gate, the road descended toward the Almone River, which flowed between open banks through a spacious valley. Here, in ancient times, there used to be a temple dedicated to Mars, and in the plain near the temple was the *transvectio equitum*, a sort of staging ground for military drills and parades.

The temple devoted to Mars Gradivus—that is, the "Mars who enters"—is generally believed to have been near the Clivus Martis, just before the Almone, "*inter miliarium primum et secundum.*"[15] An effigy of the god placed near the temple, which was probably built in 338 B.C., was possibly accompanied by images of wolves. On the fifteenth of July every year, the cavalcade commemorating the Romans' victorious battle against the Latins at the Lagus Regillus in 496 (or 494) B.C. would set out from the temple and head for the Campidoglio. Recent excavations, searching for the overpass of

protect the capital of the Empire from barbarian threats during the period from 270 to 277. Over time the gate became known as the Porta San Sebastiano, since it lay along the axis of the catacombs most visited by the faithful, the object of continual pilgrimage.[14]

Via Calicia on the left side of the road, have brought to light some tufa-block structures that have been interpreted as the remains of the Temple of Mars.[16]

Just after the bridge that spanned the small river, the road bent to the left and began a gentle ascent. Today the road along this stretch runs between two high walls that hide it completely, and it passes under two modern bridges, one for trains and the other for cars. In so doing, it passes over the ditch in which trickles what is left of the Almone River, now reduced to a polluted creek. Along this stretch, various business enterprises are inserted inside warehouse-like structures, former hamlets, and fenced areas.[17] These endeavors are not always compatible with the conservation or dignity of the road.

The *Almo flumen* crossed the Appian Way and flowed into the Tiber.[18] Its importance is linked with the mythology of Virgil's saga, since the name Almo is given to the young Latin who first comes into conflict with Aeneas's Trojans upon their arrival on Latin shores. The clash arises when Julius-Ascanius kills a deer belonging to Silvia, sister of Almo and daughter of Tyrrheus, guard to the Latin king.

The river was also linked to a religious ceremony inaugurated in 205 B.C.: the *lavatio Matris Deum*, the washing of the noniconic statue of Cybele. On March 27 of every year, the symbol of the goddess, a black stone, was carried in procession on a *carpentum* (a two-wheeled cart) and washed in the waters of the Almo along with her sacred accoutrements, in an orgiastic ceremony. The Almo also marked the boundary of the First Augustan Region.

In the Middle Ages the river was given the name of Acquaticcio and served as the main waterway of the Caffarella Valley, also called the *vallis marmorea*. In the sixteenth century, mills and industrial buildings were set up along the Almone, whose source lies at the foot of the Alban Hills. They exploited the force of the torrent for grinding grain and tanning sheepskins.

The presence of tombs along this stretch and the one that follows is attested to by numerous fragments of marble that were later reused. Such is the case of the drinking fountain located just after the start of the road on the left-hand side, which is made from the basin of a sarcophagus and a relief portraying the deceased.[19]

In 1850, in the Marini vineyard (along the same stretch of road, on the left), a columbarium was discovered with forty-eight *defixiones*, inscribed on little lead slabs and inserted inside the cinerary urns.[20] These are texts of "curses" written for the most part in Greek (only five are in Latin) and aimed against the *agitatores* of the circus, the factions they belonged to, and their horses. They can be dated between the fourth and fifth centuries and refer to the circus games that used to be held at the nearby Circus Maximus, or in the Circus of Maxentius at Mile 3 along the Appian Way.

These tablets contain other writings as well, and rather lively drawings that were part of the magic ritual. One of the figures represented has been identified as a demon expressing the power of horses; it may have been connected to deceased persons belonging to a Gnostic sect.

## The Itinerary

Just outside the Porta San Sebastiano, on the right, wedged into the defensive wall, is the first milestone column of the Appian Way, commemorating the restorations made by Vespasian in 76 A.D. and by Nerva in 97.[21]

Under the modern overpass, on both sides of the road, are a series of sepulchers dating from between the first century B.C. to the second century A.D.[22] One of them still features a polychrome mosaic representing the four seasons and the rape of Persephone, anticipating the elements that will characterize the later panorama of the road. There is a columbarium underneath the nearby restaurant Il Montarozzo, which the proprietors use as a wine cellar.

On the left, atop the defensive walls, are two cement nuclei of large sepulchers, commonly but mistakenly considered the tombs of Horace, the Augustan poet (the cube-shaped structure),[23] and Getas (the tower-shaped one).[24] Two little farmhouses were built on top of them in the eighteenth century. In point of fact, the two funeral monuments date from the early imperial period.

To this same period can be ascribed the tomb opposite these two. This is the so-called Tomb of Priscilla, wife of the powerful freedman of Domitian, T. Flavius Abascantus, whose unusual funeral is remembered in a poem by Statius.[25] The tomb has a cubical base and a cruciform sepulchral chamber that was used as a cheese room until the eighteenth century, and a cylindrical upper part with external niches, atop which a circular lookout tower was built in the thirteenth century.

The little church called the Domine Quo Vadis, or S. Maria in Palmis, sits at the intersection of the Via Appia with the Via Ardeatina. It is linked with the tradition according to which Jesus appeared to the apostle Peter, who was fleeing Rome to avoid persecution by Nero. Peter supposedly asked Jesus, *"Domine, quo vadis?"* ("Lord, where goest thou?"), and the Lord answered,

"*Venio iterum crucifige*" ("I've come to be crucified a second time"). He supposedly left his footprints in a slab of marble.[26] Peter then returned to Rome and was martyred.

### From the Domine Quo Vadis to the Via delle Sette Chiese and the Church of S. Sebastiano, between Miles 2 and 3

*The Appearance of the Road, Yesterday and Today*
At the church of Domine Quo Vadis, the Via Appia, after a slight bend to the left and uphill, began a long straightaway that crossed the Alban Hills and led to Terracina. At this point the Via Ardeatina branched off in the direction of the city of Ardea; the road's modern destination, the sanctuary of the Madonna del Divino Amore (Our Lady of Divine Love), is indicated by a marble plaque from 1768, pointing out the road to the faithful, who traditionally travel it on foot and at night.

Along this brief stretch, characterized by the entrances to the catacombs of St. Tarcisius and St. Callisto, the road is cadenced by ancient tombs that can be seen tucked into farmhouses that have been transformed into villas, or in gardens or the catacomb areas, some of them turned into restaurants. Their general state is often so deteriorated that it is impossible to determine their typologies.

At the start of this stretch, a small ancient road (the present-day Via della Caffarella) breaks off and follows the course of the Almone River, wending its way into the Caffarella Valley. Along this byway lie some famous monuments, among them the Vaccareccia house, built in 1547 in the middle of a rich farmland reclaimed from the valley of the same name and organized as a farming center; the so-called Nymphaeum of Egeria; and the so-called Temple of the Deus Rediculus, which is actually a small second-century temple erroneously said to be that of Annia Regilla. Ancient sources document the existence, near Mile 2 of the Appian Way, of a

sacred field and wood devoted to the god, who protected one on the way home (Rediculus deriving from *redeo*, to return). Anyone leaving Rome from this point would ask the god for protection on his journey, and upon returning, would thank him for a happy outcome. According to Roman tradition, the god himself appeared to Hannibal, who arrived at this spot in 211 B.C., ready to attack the city. The god so frightened him that the invader turned back.[27]

At the intersection of Via della Caffarella with the Via Appia is a small round aedicule, built in 1539, that blends into the landscape with the elegant yellow-and-red polychrome of its brickwork. It memorializes the spot at which Cardinal Reginald Pole escaped an assassination attempt by killers hired at the behest of King Henry VIII, whose reforms the cardinal opposed. The paving stones and plinths surfacing at the roadside remind us that we are walking along the exact path of the ancient road.

On the right, a *fundus rosarius* is remembered. This was a garden in which were cultivated roses and violets, flowers that the Romans used to place next to the tombs.[28]

Along this stretch, at the crossroads with the Via Ardeatina and the Via delle Sette Chiese, lies a ridge containing the largest and most interesting system of underground Roman catacombs. The complex extends for some sixteen kilometers of multistoried galleries, whence came the name "Via delle Catacombe" given to the Via Appia.

The complex of catacombs gets its name from the Catacombs of S. Callisto (St. Callixtus), the first such complex recognized and explored by the archaeologist Giovanni Battista de Rossi in 1849. Farther on, they are called the Catacombs of S. Sebastiano.

The Catacombs of S. Callisto are an ensemble of different galleries, starting with the Crypts of Lucina, the oldest nucleus, which dates from the late second century. These were joined, in the year 260, by the burial vault of Pope Cornelius in the Coemeterium Callisti, the "resting place of Callixtus." The word *coemeterium* meant "dormitory," and *Callisti* refers to the deacon Callixtus, whom Pope Zephirinus, in the year 215, had put in charge of Christian cemeteries.[29] The catacomb was later further enlarged with the addition of other "areas" until it reached its present size. Parts of the complex can be visited. It was the official burial ground of the bishops of Rome; apparently at least fourteen popes are entombed there.

Further ahead, along a side road off the Appian Way where a pagan necropolis had previously been built up, lies another important complex of catacombs, accessible from the Via Appia Pignatelli. These are the Catacombs of Praetextatus. They were created around a central gallery called the Spelunca Magna in the Middle Ages, and they feature an exceptional assortment of sarcophagi, including the famous monumental tomb of the emperor Balbinus, assassinated in 238.

The vast spread of the catacombs in this area occurred for the most part from the fourth century onward, when a triumphant Christianity—thanks above all to Constantine's Edict of Milan in 313, which granted freedom of religion—was able to satisfy the desire of the faithful to be buried near the tombs of the early martyrs. Once the available space on the property of private landowners and in the first Christian communities ran out, underground galleries were created in suitable areas, and thousands of faithful were buried there.

A poem composed by Pope Damasus (366–384), discovered in 1854, gives a sense of the multitude of "holy people" buried in such places, especially in the Catacombs of S. Callisto:

*Here, if you wish to know, rests a throng of righteous men, all together. Their venerable sepulchers hold their holy bodies, but their sublime souls were borne away by the heavens. Here the companions of Pope Sixtus brandish the enemy's trophies, here an array of martyrs guard the altars of Christ. Here lies buried the bishop who lived during a long time of peace; here the confessors who came from Greece, here the youths and the children, the aged and infants who wished to preserve their virginal purity. Here, I confess, I, Damasus, would have liked to be buried myself, but I feared disturbing the holy ashes of the righteous.*[30]

**The Itinerary** On the left side of the road, two large nuclei of columbaria, where many inscriptions were discovered, have been destroyed. They held the ashes of the freedmen of Livia. Discovered in 1725–26 in the Benci vineyard, they are well known from the descriptions of Ficorini, Gori,[31] and Bianchini,[32] and from engravings by P. L. Grezzi and by Piranesi.

The inside of the columbarium of the freedmen of Augustus,[33] also on the left side of the road, currently hosts a restaurant. It consists of three rooms adjoining one another, with vaulted communicating corridors and access stairs at the back. They used to contain an estimated three thousand burial niches.

On the right-hand side of the road, in front of the seventeenth-century Villa Casali, a columnar milestone of the second mile once stood; today it is replaced by a plaque. Further ahead, on the left, there used to be the hypogeum of Vibia and that of the Four Worshipers (Quattro Oranti).

Near the Villa Mereghiana is the Hypogeum of the Holy Cross (Ipogeo della S. Croce), named after a painted Greek cross at the entrance of one of its cubicles. The structure dates from the mid-fourth century.

At the corner of the Via Appia Antica and the Via Appia Pignatelli, one finds two mausoleums in a quadrilateral area. These are the mausoleums of the Cercenii and the Calventii: The first has a circular inner space with a dome vault on a tall drum, and six apses; the second has a cruciform plan, with columns supporting the groin vault. They are probably late-period mausoleums, fourth or fifth century, related to the sepulchral area of the Praetextatus catacombs, famous above all from the drawings made of them by Ligorio, Peruzzi, Palladio, and Giulano da Sangallo.

This same general area was probably also the site of the tomb of Claudia Semnes, which we know about only from drawings by Labruzzi, such as that of the columbaria of the Moroni vineyards.

The Via delle Sette Chiese (Seven Churches' Road) joins the Via Appia on the right. This was the preeminent road that pilgrims traveled on their way to visit the basilicas and martyrdom sites of the early Christians. An itinerary was mapped out in guides for visitors to Rome, especially in Jubilee years, featuring the seven (or nine) most important churches, including the Basilica of S. Sebastiano, which this road connected to the Basilica of S. Paolo.

### From Via delle Sette Chiese to the Tomb of Cecilia Metella, between Miles 3 and 4

*The Appearance of the Road, Yesterday and Today*
Here the panorama of the Roman Campagna opens up. Along this stretch of the road, some of the ancient suburban residences begin to appear, their remains scattered along the valley's slopes, bearing witness to the same commingling of life and death that we mentioned above. They were once villas that almost always combined a residential part with a series of buildings devoted to agricultural activities. They were villas, therefore, not only for *otium* (pleasure), but also for *negotium* (productive activity).

A dense web of minor roads intersected the Appian Way or branched off from it as service roads for the various villas, farms, and cemeteries, and then headed off into the countryside, connecting it with the networks of roads surrounding the city.

Between the intersection with the Via Appia Pignatelli—the road created by Pope Innocent XII (Antonio Pignatelli) along a more ancient route connecting the Via Appia and the Via Latina—and the Vicolo della Basilica, the landscape to the west of the road is dominated by the basilican complex of S. Sebastiano. A gully had once cut diagonally through the Via Appia and then descended alongside the basilica, opposite which there was once a sandstone quarry, later used for catacombs. The use of the term "catacomb" to designate Christian cemeteries was born in this very area. In fact the expression *ad catacumbas*, or *in catacumbas*, referred specifically to an area between the second and third miles of the Appian Way, before the road was extended to include the place where, according to tradition, the mortal remains of the apostles Peter and Paul were transferred in 258. Sometime after this, it went on to signify any underground cemetery. The etymology of the word remains obscure: It may derive from the Latin verb *cubare*, to "lie down in accordance with funeral arrangements" or from the Greek *kata kumbas* (κατὰ κύμβας), i.e., "near the pit" or pozzolana quarry, perhaps indicating the hollow or quarries that indeed existed near the Basilica of S. Sebastiano.

After the Maxentian complex—the villa, mausoleum, and circus on the left-hand side of the road—the final segment of Mile 3 is marked by a considerable incline that accentuates the monumentality of the Tomb of Cecilia Metella, which stands at the highest point of the upland plain called "Capo di Bove."

The buildings, villas, farmhouses, and rustic buildings along this stretch of the road, which is

two apostles are the hundreds of invocations to Peter and Paul scratched into the walls. In the fourth and fifth centuries, a number of central-plan and basilican-plan mausoleums were built around the church. One of these is called the Mausoleum of Platonia, the tomb of the martyr Quirinus.

Before the catacombs were built, the site was occupied by villas dating from the first to third centuries, and by a group of brickwork pagan tombs, still well preserved, with delicate stuccoes and paintings. Particularly noteworthy is the mausoleum of M. Clodius Hermes.

On the left-hand side of the Via Appia, between it and the Via Appia Pignatelli, two groups of Jewish catacombs have been brought to light: one in the Cimarra vineyard, damaged by a pozzolana quarry; the other in the Randanini vineyard. The latter is the more famous and can be visited. It features galleries on two different levels, and a synagogue in the area above ground. Both catacombs, as well as other rediscovered cemeteries around the city, bear witness to the fact that a Jewish community flourished in Rome, especially in the third and fourth centuries. One nucleus of this community was situated right around the Porta Capena.

Until a few decades ago, a modern cemetery adjoined some late-Roman sepulchers at the corner of the Via Appia and the Via delle Sette Chiese. The only tomb left after the modern cemetery was removed belongs to the painter Giulio Aristide Sartorio, who had expressly asked to be buried at this site. Near the entrance, one can see the remains of the Constantinian basilica.

Before the entrance to the basilica of S. Sebastiano, at a point where the Via Appia widens, stands a cross-bearing column; on its base, an inscription commemorates Pope Pius IX's 1851 project to salvage and draw attention to the monuments of the Appian Way.

Continuing on, we find on the left an imposing, square mausoleum at the center of a four-sided portico, connected with a villa standing on a low hill and with a circus, ensconced in a natural vale, lying at a diagonal to the road. A side road here once started out from the Via Appia Pignatelli and, after crossing the Via Appia, probably at a higher elevation, used to continue along the side of the basilica of S. Sebastiano. The villa was a suburban residence built by the emperor Maxentius (306–312) near his dynastic mausoleum.

*Eighteenth-century facade of the Church of S. Sebastiano.*

wider than the rest, are almost all constructed on top of ancient sepulchers.

***The Itinerary*** The S. Sebastiano complex consists of a church, catacombs, mausoleums, and tombs above and below the ground, and Roman villas. As a whole it is called *Memoria Apostolorum*.

The Church of S. Sebastiano's seventeenth-century facade, built at the behest of Cardinal Scipione Borghese, covers the structures of the grand cruciform-plan basilica built by Constantine. It was originally devoted to the apostles Peter and Paul, whose remains were already here, or were transferred here, in 258, at the time of Valerian's persecutions, to a site also famous for the relics of St. Sebastian. Bearing witness to the memory of the

The mausoleum is better known under the name of his son Romulus, the only one of the family buried there (in 309 A.D.). Maxentius was buried elsewhere, since he died in defeat at Saxa Rubra on the Via Flaminia, at the hands of Constantine, in 312.

The imperial residence was built on top of a villa from the Republican era. Herod Atticus had restructured it in the second century A.D., after the death of his wife, transforming it into a religious site called Pagus Triopius.

halls,[34] he was paid homage by his subjects in much the same way as he was applauded by the people and the court in the circus, where games were played in his honor. But it was also the seat of his posthumous cult, with a mausoleum that looks in every way like a little Pantheon, with a crypt for sarcophagi on the lower floor and the naos of a temple on the upper floor, for the worship of the emperor as *divus*.[35]

Of especial interest is the structure of the circus, the best preserved of the ancient circuses, though

*This page: Fresco showing villas along the seashore, in a Roman house under the basilica of S. Sebastiano.*

*On page 62: Funerary piazzetta within the Catacombs of S. Sebastiano, with the facades of mausoleums consisting of three sepulchral chambers of clearly pagan origin, built around the end of Hadrian's reign.*

*On page 63: Detail of fresco decorating the lunette over the arcosolium of the mausoleum of M. Clodius Hermes, in the S. Sebastiano catacombs.*

The fact that the tomb of Maxentius was built with an entrance onto the Appia, thereby inserting itself in monumental fashion alongside the more modest tombs already in existence along the road, seems logical enough. What is more difficult to explain is how the mausoleum is related to the circus and the residential building. If, however, one considers it within the typology of imperial palaces of the Tetrarchy, then both the mausoleum and the circus assume a specific meaning. It is one that we encounter as well in the imperial residences at Milan, Trier, Thessaloníki, Split, and finally in the palace built by Constantine in Constantinople, when he moved the capital of the Roman Empire there in 330.

The palace was the residence of the living emperor, where, in richly decorated basilican-type

small in size (seating 10,000). One can easily make out the twelve stalls from which the chariots used to emerge, the steps, and the *spina*, the barrier around which the chariots would drive seven times in their race. In the middle of the *spina* stood the obelisk, probably originally from a monument in the Campus Martius, that now adorns the Fountain of the Four Rivers by Gian Lorenzo Bernini at the center of Piazza Navona, where Pope Innocent X had it installed by the architect Carlo Fontana in 1651.

The road continues climbing until it reaches the finest sepulcher of the Via Appia, the Tomb of Cecilia Metella.[36] On a high, rectangular concrete base, formerly revetted in blocks of travertine that are now all gone, rises the drumlike cylindrical sepulcher in blocks of travertine, eleven meters

*Upper right: Plan of the imperial complex of Maxentius.*

*Lower right: Reconstruction of the carceres of the Circus of Maxentius (Alfred Recoura, 1899).*

*Facing page: The Circus of Maxentius. In the fore-ground, one of the towers that flanked the starting stalls of the racing chariots (carceres). In the back-ground, the Tomb of Cecilia Metella.*

*On pages 66–67: The Tomb of Cecilia Metella.*

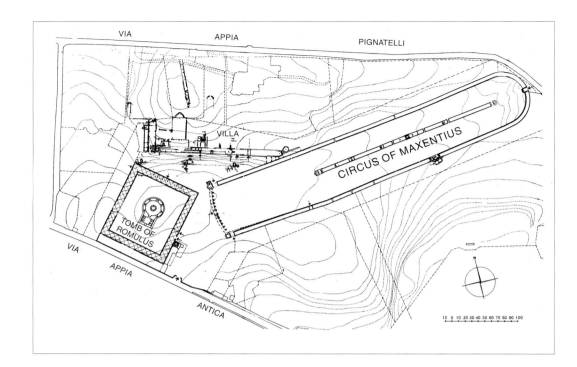

tall, with its Pentelic marble frieze of festoons and bucranes (ox-head motifs), which gave rise to the name by which the site has been called since the Middle Ages: Capo di Bove ("ox-head"). Added to the top of this structure, in the place of the orig-inal conical roof, are medieval crenellations. The entire mausoleum originally reached a height of twenty meters, with a diameter of one hundred Roman feet (29.6 m).

On the side facing the Via Appia, under a trophy of arms, is the inscription *Cecilia Metella, daughter of Quintus Metellus Creticus,*[37] *wife of Crassus.* The lat-ter was perhaps the eldest son of M. Licinius Crassus, the man famous for quelling the slave rebellion led by Spartacus in 72 B.C.; he was part of the Triumvirate with Pompeius and Caesar from 60 to 53 B.C. About Cecilia Metella little or nothing is known. The grandeur of her tomb must have been

fine, but now stripped, Gothic church devoted to S. Nicola of Bari, built in 1303; the roof is gone, but the side walls, propped up by eight buttresses and pierced with rosettes, still stand.

The *castrum* passed from the hands of the Caetani to the Savelli family, then to the Colonna, the Orsini,

*Above left: View of the Tomb of Cecilia Metella and the Castrum Caetani.*

*Above right: Detail of the structures linking the Tomb of Cecilia Metella and the castrum Caetani.*

*Opposite page: View of the Appian Way, toward the Villa of the Quintili.*

more an affirmation of her class, the *gens*, than of her individual person. The sepulcher is dated between 30 and 20 B.C. The sepulchral chamber was in the base of the structure; it was in brickwork, one of the oldest examples of this construction material so often used thereafter by the Romans.

Because of its elevated strategic position, it was turned into a fortress in the Byzantine era. In the eleventh century, it was incorporated into an actual fortified village with walls and nineteen turrets (240 m by 98 m) by the counts of Tuscolo, probably on the site of the ancient *statio* of Mile 3 of the Appian Way.[38] The citadel's central axis was the road itself, which thereby became blocked at the entrance and exit gates of the fortified area. In the fourteenth century, on the lava embankments, a baronial *palazzetto* (Castrum Caetani) was built by the Caetani family, who became owners of the land through the intercession of Pope Boniface VIII (Benedetto Caetani). A wall with arrow slits and battlements was added to the cylinder of the sepulcher. Also part of the medieval village was the

the Cenci, the Ospedale del Santissimo Salvatore, and finally to the Torlonia family in 1797, before it was ultimately expropriated by the government.

The mausoleum has always been seen as a symbol of the place, being so represented and described from the Middle Ages to this day. It was not immune to plunder, but when Pope Sixtus V agreed to its demolition in 1589, so that its materials could be reused in construction, it was saved by the intervention of Roman conservator Paolo Lancelotti and his colleagues Ottavio Gabrielli and Alessandro Gottifredi, who suspended the pope's approval. It is to them we are indebted for being able to admire today, on our journey along the Via Appia, the Tomb of Cecila Metella.

### From the Tomb of Cecilia Metella to Casal Rotondo, from Mile 4 to Mile 7 and beyond

***The Appearance of the Road, Yesterday and Today***
The stretch between the Tomb of Cecilia Metella and Mile 9 is characterized by tower tombs and

The temple-style tombs have outer facings in brickwork, sometimes two-tone, and a sepulchral chamber on the lower story. On the upper story, which one reached by means of a stairway on the front, the rites in honor of the deceased were performed.

Little by little, the ancient paving stones have been brought to light and restored, sometimes still with the deep grooves etched in them by the centuries of carriage wheels, and with the stone base of the sidewalks beside them.

Along the first stretch, many sepulchers have been privatized inside houses built during the 1950s and '60s and surrounded by luxuriant gardens. Though beautiful, these modern villas upset the rustic character of the road's setting and prevent it from being enjoyed by the general public.

Then, all of a sudden, the high walls and barriers come to an end, and the little walls restored by Canina return. Once again the eye can roam over a nearly uncontaminated landscape as far as the Alban Hills. In the background looms the Albanus Mons, known today as the Monte Cavo, where in ancient times stood the provincial sanctuary of Jupiter Latiaris and the seat of the Latin League.

It was from this point as far as the ninth mile that Luigi Canina executed his labor of excavation and restoration under the patronage of Pius IX in the mid-nineteenth century, inserting a frame of pine and cypress that to this today symbolizes the Appian Way. It is by far the most monumental part of the road. Here the ancient roadway and its framework constitute a single entity, showing the sequence of ruins—part excavated, part still buried—and the masonry facings and the marble revetments, many of them unfortunately looted and missing today.

Beyond the seventh mile, the funerary monuments become scarcer, and the continuity of the sepulchral wings at the side of the Via Appia ends. The few tombs one finds no longer belong to citizens of Rome, but to the people who owned the lands along the roadside.

***The Itinerary*** On the left is a tall cement nucleus of a towerlike sepulcher that over time has acquired the shape of a tree and is called the "Tower of Capo di Bove." A plaque here commemorates the astronomer Angelo Sacchi, who, in 1855, made trigonometric measurements of the Appian straightaway as

temple-style tombs. The tower structures have been reduced to strange geometric forms in timeworn concrete further eroded by humans, who long ago removed the more prized revetment materials, the marble and travertine. The remaining cement nucleus still occasionally bears the imprints of the removed blocks, and sometimes, though not always, these marks allow us to reconstruct the original forms.

far as Frattocchie. It was these measurements that verified the Italian geodetic survey of 1871.[39]

On the right, on the facade of Casale Torlonia,[40] a commemorative stone reminds us that certain experiments with the telegraph (called *elettrico relatore*) were conducted here, along the Appian straightaway all the way to Terracina, in the presence of Pius IX in 1853.

Further ahead, still on the right, we encounter the Forte Appia.[41] It was built, along with fourteen other forts and three batteries, along the main entrance roads to the city, after Unification forces captured Rome in 1870. It bears witness to a system of defenses already outdated at the time of its construction and never used. All the same, the area today serves as a military base.

The sepulcher of M. Servilius Quartus on the left, in front of the Forte Appia, was restored by Antonio Canova in 1808.[42] The so-called Tomb of Seneca, another brickwork coulisse reconstructed by Canova, was identified on the basis of a passage in Tacitus's *Annals*.[43] After returning from Campania to a suburban farm at the fourth mile of the Appian Way, Seneca was ordered by Nero to kill himself. He did so with serenity and courage.

A large metrical inscription from the first century,[44] carved into a slab of marble that Canova had placed on a brickwork shrine, identifies the sepulcher of the sons of Sextius Pompeius Justus: a poem in elegiac distichs recalls the premature deaths of the two sons, from the point of view of the desperate father.

On the right, the so-called Temple of Jupiter is in fact a third-century square hall-sepulcher in brick, with apses on three sides, probably originally crowned with a dome and preceded by a pronaos.

Also on the right is the so-called Tomb of St. Urban, who succeeded St. Callixtus as bishop of Rome at the start of the third century. It is recorded that Urban's body was moved by the noblewoman Marmenia to a sepulcher close to her villa on the Via Appia. Eighteenth-century excavators speculated that this site was the setting for these events. Recent excavations date the building around the early fourth century and relate the mausoleum to a variously attributed *pagus* (settlement) at Mile 4.[45]

A comic actor, C. Plinius Eutychus, is memorialized on a late-first- or early-second-century funerary altar. The inscription also mentions Pliny the Younger.[46]

A square-plan Doric sepulcher in *pietra albana* with a frieze of triglyphs and a metope with alternating helmets, bucranes, and flowers, is from the late Republican era.

The sepulcher of Hilarius Fuscus, to whom the five relief portraits of deceased individuals have been attributed, was also restored by Canina.[47]

The tomb with altar of the Rabirii is on the right.[48] The deceased who are portrayed in the relief and remembered in the inscription are: C. Rabirius Hermodorus and Rabiria Demaris, both perhaps freed slaves of Greek origin formerly belonging to an illustrious personage of the age of Caesar; C. Rabirius Postumus, merchant, banker, "minister of finance" to the Egyptian king Ptolomeus Auletes, whom Cicero defended in court;[49] Ursia Prima, called "priestess of Isis," third from the right, may have been a descendent of the couple. (She is represented a second time in the relief in the reworking of a male bust wearing a

*Above: The so-called sepulcher of Secundinus, near the Villa of the Quintili, an example of how archaeological specimens were transformed into monuments during the nineteenth-century renovations along the Appian Way.*

*Right: A stretch of the Appian Way near the Fossae Cluiliae. At this point the road curved to pass around the Fossae Cluiliae, site of the famous battle between the Horatii and the Curiatii.*

*On pages 76–77: A stretch of the Claudius and Anio Novus aqueducts, in the Roman Campagna.*

toga.) The relief is from the first century A.D.; the *sistrum* (rattle) and *patera* (bowl) one sees represented in it are symbols of the Egyptian cult of the goddess Isis.

Next, a tower sepulcher, called the "Tomb of the Frontispiece,"[50] features a family portrait in relief: A married couple makes the gesture of the *dextrarum iunctio* (joining of hands) with their children at their sides.

The archeological complex of Tor Carbone is centered around the fourteenth-century tower of the same name, which rises up from the remains of a villa from the Imperial era.

At Milestone 5, the road suddenly veers to the left and then to the right, circling round three tumuli before returning to its axis. It is believed the road was respecting the more ancient monuments in this area, which would confirm the antiquity of the route as preceding 312 B.C.

This may in fact be the early boundary between the Roman state (*ager romanus antiquus*) and the city of Alba Longa, near the Fossae Cluiliae, the place where the king of Alba Longa supposedly set up camp for his march on Rome during the time of King Tullus Hostilius.[51] Here, in the Campus Horatiorum of legend, the famous duel between the Horatii (the three Roman triplet brothers) and the Curiatii (the three Alban brothers, who were also triplets) is said

*Casal Rotondo, the impressive, cylindrical mausoleum attributed to Consul Messala Corvinus. Next to the mausoleum, an architectural coulisse was built under the direction of Luigi Canina, combining marble fragments from the mausoleum that were found during the nineteenth-century excavations.*

*Facing page: Detail of Luigi Canina's dramatic coulisse.*

to have taken place. An isolated tumulus, crowned by a cylindrical turret of tufa blocks, is supposedly the sepulcher of the three Curiatii and datable to the early Imperial period. The other two tumuli are supposed to be of the Horatii and can be dated around the end of the Republican era and the early Imperial era, respectively.

The tomb of Pomponius Atticus,[52] friend of Cicero, was also supposed to be in this vicinity. Cornelius Nepos writes: "He [Pomponius Atticus] was buried near the Via Appia, at the fifth mile, in the sepulcher of Quintus Cecilius, his grandfather."[53] Nearby, in fact, one finds the tomb of a Marcus Cecilius, with an inscription in clumsy saturnian verse: "This monument was made for Marcus Cecilius. I am pleased, O traveler, that you should stop at my home. May your business go well and yourself remain in good health. Sleep without worry."

The medieval Casale di S. Maria Nova, further on, is nothing more than a cistern from the Roman era with a tower added in the twelfth or thirteenth century.

Then, on the left-hand side of the Appian Way, comes the sprawling Villa of the Quintili with its grand nymphaeum, which served as its entrance. It is the largest villa of the ancient Roman suburbs. The story of this villa reads like a novel. It belonged

to the brothers Sextus Quintilian Condianus and Sextus Quintilian Valerian Maximus, both consuls in the year 161 A.D., and both writers of works on land-surveying and military matters. They were put to death by the emperor Commodus in 182 A.D. on the pretext of conspiracy, whereas the true motive was to appropriate their vast wealth.[54]

The villa consists of various parts, built at different times around the mid-second century and restored in the third and fourth centuries. The complex includes baths, which constitute the most imposing of the ruins; gardens; pavilions; cisterns; a hippodrome; a large, two-story nymphaeum, which serves as the entrance on the Via Appia; and an aqueduct possibly branching off from the Claudian aqueduct, or perhaps from the Anio Novus or the Iulia aquaducts. Its arches can be seen from a distance. In the Middle Ages, the counts of Tuscolo built a castle on top of the entrance nymphaeum. The structure was later passed on to the Astalli family around the twelfth–thirteenth centuries.

Rich in marble and gardens, the grounds once had many works of art that are now scattered throughout European museums and collections. The villa was expropriated by the Italian government in 1985; thereafter, restorations and excavations were carried out to enable the villa to be opened to the public.

In 1865, a second-century mosaic[55] was recovered from a tomb in the "Statuary Reserve" area near the Villa of the Quintili. Against a white background, it shows a skeleton, indicated in black tesserae, reclining on its left side on a triclinial cushion, looking as if it wishes to speak to the observer (see page 71). The right arm, bent at the elbow, seems to be pointing to the inscription below the cushion, the letters written in black tesserae. It bears the famous Delphic aphorism "Know thyself," here intended as a warning against the vanities of life from the unknown dead soul to the living who, passing along the road, might stop to visit his tomb.[56]

Casal Rotondo is one of the most important and imposing mausoleums on the Via Appia. It stands on the left, near the intersection with the Via di Torricola. The name, which means "round farmhouse," refers to its cylindrical form and to that of the medieval farmhouse that was built on top of it. It was once revetted with blocks of travertine, measures thirty-five meters in diameter, and dates from the Augustan age.[57] Nearby, there must have been a structure related to a *statio*, and the milestone of Mile 6.

Canina rebuilt Casal Rotondo with a conical, shingled cover and crowned it with a circular aediculum surmounted by a pinnacle. The fragments of the mausoleum are embedded in an architectural wing beside the sepulcher and include a decoration featuring theatrical masks. On the basis of a fragmentary inscription, the mausoleum is believed to be that of Messalla Corvinus, a friend of Tibullus and consul in 31 B.C. It is dated from the late Republican era, or perhaps from the Augustan. It is presumed to have been built by the deceased's son, Marcus Valerius Messalinus Cotta.

Torre Selce, another unusual monument along the Appian Way, is a thirteenth-century medieval tower that rises majestically in a bichromatic play of marble and flint, above a circular tomb on a square base. The tower rests on high buttress-walls. Flint quarries have been found nearby.

In front of the Torre Selce, there must have been tombs belonging to the winners of athletic, musical, and poetry competitions, all from the second century.[58] These competitions, or agons, included the Capitolia and Augusteia of Pergamum, the Koinon of Asia, the Olympia and Barbilleia of Ephesus, and the Aktia of Nikopolis. The sepulchers themselves have never been found, only the Greek inscriptions carved inside the agonistic crowns, sculpted in relief.

A bit further ahead, on the left, is the late-Republican-era tumulus sepulcher of C. Ateilius Euhodus, with a metrical epigraph that was brought to light in 1851:

*Wayfarer, stop and look at this burial mound on your left, where lie the bones of a good man who was merciful and a friend to the poor. I beg you, traveler, do no harm to this tomb. Caius Ateilius Euhodus, freedman of Serranus, pearl merchant of Via Sacra, lies inside this monument. Good-bye, wayfarer.*[59]

Just down the road lies the part of the Appian Way that used to be interrupted by the Grande Raccordo Anulare, the beltway created in 1960. It was recently restored in a major project on the occasion of Rome's 2000 Jubilee. The beltway now passes below the road by means of two tunnels.

Milestone 7, which commemorated the renovations made by Vespasian and Nerva, used to be situated here. Excavated in 1700, the milestone has stood on the balustrade of the Campidoglio since 1848.

Further ahead, on the right, are a group of column fragments. Based on references made in Martial's epigrams, they were formerly believed to have belonged to a temple of Hercules. Now, however, they are thought to have been part of a four-sided portico of the late Republican era, perhaps a *mutatio* with an aedicula devoted to Sylvanus.

Also on the right is a large rotunda topped with a hemispheric dome and a monumental entrance, surrounded by an ambulatory. Because of its unusual form, it is called the Beretta del Prete (Priest's Cap). It is a sepulcher of the late Imperial era, transformed in the early Middle Ages into a church to the Blessed Virgin, and later into a simple tower.[60]

The last sepulchral monument that appears along this stretch, half a kilometer after the intersection with Via di Fioranello, is the dome-roofed, cylindrical mausoleum of Gallienus, the emperor who died in 268 and was buried at Mile 9 of the Via Appia.

Also at Mile 9, according to the *Itinerarium Burdigalense* or *Hierosolymitanum*, is a *mutatio ad nonum*, used for changing horses after nine miles of travel.

Further on, the routes of the Via Appia Antica and the Via Appia Nuova will coincide at the place called Frattocchie.

## Notes

1   A. Battista and V. Giacobini, "Il paesaggio vegetale del comprensorio dell'Appia Antica," in *Piano per il parco dell'Appia Antica*, pp. 47–54.

2   The "artificial" gardens surrounding the homes built over the last fifty years are obviously not included in this survey because they often impose extraneous aesthetic and environmental models on the archaeological park and belong to a "different" history of the Appian Way.

3   For our discussion of the monuments along the Appian Way, we chose not to linger over every individual element, which might have had a diluting effect, but rather to focus on the features of those monuments—even those that are no longer extant—or those elements of the road or the surrounding landscape that we held to be most significant and important. In principle, a general description ("Yesterday and Today") should give the modern traveler a general, synoptic view and a key to understanding the specific stretch of road in question. To prevent the text from becoming too lengthy, and to keep to the subject stated, we will not describe buildings or monuments not strictly connected to the Old Appian Way or not visible to someone traveling it.

4   The arch probably gave its name to the nearby vicus Drusianus.

5   D. Palombi, in *LTUR* 1 (Rome, 1993), s.vv. "*Arcus Traiani*" and "*arcus divi Veri*," p. 112.

6   The *compita*, in ancient Rome, were shrines devoted to the *lares compitales*, guardians of crossroads. The *compita* were built at intersections of three or more roads, and the *lares* protected the site as well as the travelers passing through.

7   F. Castagnoli et al., *La via Appia* (Rome: Banco di Roma, 1972), pp. 163–67.

8   G. Pisani Sartorio, *LTUR* 4 (Rome, 1999), s.v. "*Septizodnium*," "*Septizodium*," "*Septisolium*," pp. 269–72 (with previous bibliography).

9   F. Coarelli, *LTUR* 1, s.v. "*arcus stillans*". Martial *Spectacula* 3.47.1: "*Capena grandi porta qua pluit gutta*" ("Where Porta Capena rains great drops . . .").

10  Africanus is not buried here, having died in exile in his villa near Literno.

11  Cicero *Tusculanae disputationes* 1.7.13.

12  F. Zevi, in *LTUR* 4, s.v. "*sepulcrum (Corneliorum) Scipionum*," pp. 281–85 (with previous bibliography).

13  The original sarcophagi and inscriptions have been in the Vatican Museums since 1792.

14  Inside the gate one can visit the "Museum of the Walls," which tells the history of the walls of Rome, and one can walk along the walls themselves for about one kilometer. A. Cambedda and A. Ceccherelli, "Le mura di Aureliano dalla Porta Appia al bastione Ardeatino," in *Itinerari d'arte e di Cultura: Via Appia* (Rome, 1990); G. Pisani Sartorio, in *LTUR* 3, s.v. "*Muri Aureliani: Portae, Porta Appia*" (Rome, 1996), pp. 299–300.

15  "Between the first and second miles." *CIL* VI.10234 from 153 A.D.

16  M. G. Cecchini, M. N. Gagliardi, and L. Petrassi, "Cavalcavia tra via Cilicia e via Marco Polo (Circ. I–IX)," *Bullettino della Commissione Archeologica Comunale* 91, no. 2 (1986), pp. 595–601.

17  Restaurants, construction warehouses, nurseries, and filling stations are among these businesses. A paper mill from the early 1900s, which was powered by the waters of the Almone, is the present-day office of the Ente Parco dell'Appia Antica (Park Administration of the Appia Antica).

18  G. Pisani Sartorio, *LTUR Suburbium* 1, s.v. "*Almo*," pp. 45–47.

19  V. Kockel, *Porträtreliefs stadrömischer Grabbauten* (Mainz am Rhein: P. von Zabern, 1993), p. 130, n. G5: late first century B.C.

20  G. Bevilacqua, *LTUR Suburbium* 1, s.v. "*Appia, via*," pp. 98–99.

21  *CIL* X.6812–6813= *ILS* 5819. This is actually a copy. The original milestone, discovered in 1584, is on the balustrade of the monumental staircase of the Campidoglio. According to certain writers, the first *miliarium* should be placed before the Porta Appia.

22  Cecchini, et al., "Cavalcavia."

23  This is because of Horace's famous journey along the Via Appia. In reality, the poet was buried on the Esquiline Hill, near the tomb of his great friend Maecenas.

24  Getas, youngest son of Septimius Severus, was killed in 212, in the arms of his mother Julia Domna, on the orders of his brother Caracalla.

25  Statius *Silvae* 5.1.

26  The marble slab with footprints (the one in the church is a copy; the original is in the Museum of the Catacombs of S. Sebastiano) is a pagan ex-voto for the good fortune of travelers. It shows two pairs of footprints pointed in opposite directions, to signify the *itus* and the *reditus*, that is, setting off and returning on a good foot.

27  Festus 355.

28  Tomassetti, *La campagna romana antica medievale e moderna*, vol. 2, p. 45.

29  Staccioli, *Via Appia* (*QuadAEI* 10.1), p. 25 ff.; F. Bisconti, "La via delle catacombe," in *Via Appia: Sulle ruine*, pp. 74–77.

30  A. Ferrua and C. Carletti, *Damaso e i martiri di Roma* (Vatican City: Pontificia commissione di archeologia sacra, 1985); F. Bisconti, "La via delle catacombe," p. 75.

31  E. Gori, *Monumentum sive columbarium libertorum et servorum Liviae Augustae et Caesarum* (Florence, 1727).

32  F. Bianchini, *Camera ed iscrizioni sepulcrali de' liberti, servi ed ufficiali della casa di Augusto scoperte nella via Appia* (Rome, 1727).

33 H. Kammerer Grothaus, "Camere sepolcrali de' liberti e liberte di Livia Augusta ed altri Cesari," in *MEFRA* 41 (1979), pp. 315–29; J. Kolendo, *Klio* 71 (1989), pp. 420–31.

34 The halls in Maxentius's palace were actually heated by means of air ducts beneath the floors and piping along the walls. The latter were decorated with colored marble inlays.

35 Giuseppina Pisani Sartorio and Raissa Calza, eds., *La villa di Massenzio sulla via Appia*, vol. 1: *Il palazzo* (Rome: Istituto di studi romani, 1976), pp. 131–41 (with bibliography); Giovane Ioppolo and Giuseppina Pisani Sartorio, eds., *La villa di Massenzio sulla via Appia*, vol. 2: *Il circo* (Rome: Colombo, 1999).

36 Quilici, *Via Appia*, vol. 1: *Da porta Capena ai Colli Albani*, pp. 40–43; R. Paris, "La storia del monumento," in *Via Appia. Il mausoleo di Cecilia Metella e il castrum Caetani* (Milan, 2000), pp. 5–25.

37 Conqueror of Crete, in 67 B.C.

38 *CIL* VI.3394.

39 Quilici, *Via Appia*, vol. 1: *Da porta Capena ai Colli Albani*, 61; S. Mineo, *LTUR Suburbium* 1, s.v. "*Via Appia, IV miglio*," 113.

40 Today it is the seat of the Moroccan Embassy.

41 S. Quilici Gigli, "Gli sterri per la costruzione dei forti militari," in *L'archeologia in Roma Capitale tra sterro e scavo*, eds. Giuseppina Pisani Sartorio and Lorenzo Quilici (Venice: Marsilio Editori, 1983), pp. 91–96.

42 P. Fancelli and P. Tamaro, "Antonio Canova tra archeologia e restauro: il monumento di M. Servilio Quarto sulla via Appia," in *Studi in onore di Renato Cavese*, ed. James Ackerman (Vicenza: Centro internazionale di studi di architettura Andrea Palladio, 2000), p. 230.

43 Tacitus *Annales* 15.60.

44 *CIL* VI.24520

45 Mineo, "*Via Appia, IV miglio*," 118: "*pagus Amentinus minor*"; see also L. Chioffi, "Epigrafia e insediamenti: il caso del suburbio di Roma," in *La forma della città e del territorio. Esperienze metodologiche e risultati a confronto*, ed. Stefania Quilici Gigli, exh. cat., S. Maria Capua Vetere (Rome: "L'Erma" di Bretschneider, 1999), pp. 56–60.

46 Pliny the Younger *Epistulae* 5.19.

47 This is a copy; the original was moved to the Museo Nazionale Romano in Palazzo Massimo.

48 This, too, is a copy, with the original in the Museo Nazionale Romano in Palazzo Massimo.

49 Staccioli, *Via Appia* (*QuadAEI* 10.1), p. 38.

50 Mineo, s.v. "*Via Appia, IV miglio*," p. 122. This, too, is a copy.

51 Livy 1.23.3.

52 Castagnoli, et al., *La via Appia*, p. 138.

53 Nepos *Atticus* 22.4.

54 Scriptores Historiae Augustae *Commodus* 4.9.

55 Now in the Museo Nazionale Romano at the Baths of Diocletian.

56 Mineo, s.v. "*Via Appia, IV miglio*," p. 128.

57 Ibid., pp. 129–30.

58 G. Bevilacqua, *LTUR Suburbium* 1, s.v. "*Via Appia*," p. 132.

59 *CIL* VI.9545; Mineo, "*Via Appia, IV miglio*," p. 132.

60 Mineo, s.v. "*Via Appia, IV miglio*," p. 135.

# From the Alban Hills to Cisterna Latina

FRANCESCA VENTRE

"I am convinced that the many treasures I shall bring home with me will serve both myself and others as a guide and an education for a lifetime."
J. Wolfgang von Goethe[1]

## Historical Events

From Boville to Cisterna, as soon as one has left Rome's immediate environs and the nearest countryside, the landscape changes in appearance. It becomes more opulent and prosperous.

This area used to be dominated, especially in ancient times, by the Latium volcano. It formed the lakes of Albano and Nemi, which still exist, as well as those of Turno and Vallericcia, which were drained by man, the former in the early eighteenth century, the latter in antiquity.

We are in Latium Vetus ("Old Latium"), the city of Rome's fatherland, a place still permeated with the evocative charm of its historical origins. It was here that Ascanius, son of Aeneas, after landing on nearby shores, founded Alba Longa,[2] progenetrix of Rome and a prominent population center more than a city in its own right. Indeed, Rome conquered it quickly, by the mid-seventh century B.C., triggering its rapid decline. The destruction of Alba Longa favored the formation and growth of other cities, including Aricia and Bovillae, which would prosper for four centuries.

During this time the ancient cult of Jupiter Latiaris thrived near Albanus Mons (present-day Monte Cavo), so much so that the site became a political and strategic reference point for all the cities of Latium Vetus.

The ultimate conquest of these centers, united in the Latin League in 338 B.C., gave Rome absolute supremacy over the territory. But the love and respect for religions linked to nature and primary deities would not diminish; on the contrary, it increased with the foundation of the Sanctuary of Diana near Lake Nemi and that of Juno at Lanuvium.

As Rome expanded, the surrounding territory, starting in the second century B.C., and especially by the mid-first century B.C., became an extension

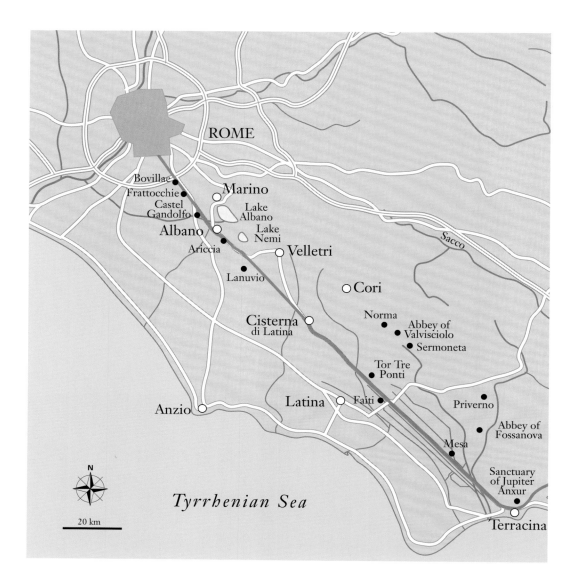

of the capital, as a holiday destination for aristocratic citizens and later for imperial families as well.

Over the centuries, in late antiquity and throughout the Middle Ages, with the growth or disappearance of these population centers, the spread of marshy and sometimes insalubrious areas, and rampant banditry, the original route of the Appian Way, though it survived, would suffer detours and be complemented by alternate routes.[3]

In the ninth century, the Church divided up the region and assigned areas to monasteries and emerging Roman families. New population centers sprang up, often on top of ancient ruins. This partitioning and parceling-out would lead, especially in the twelfth and thirteenth centuries, to the various struggles for power that resulted in the supremacy of this or that Roman family. Prominent among these were the Tuscolo, the Frangipane, the Colonna, and the Caetani families.

During this period, various types of fortifications were built for defensive purposes. From this point on, because of these edifices, the population centers of the Alban Hills would be called the Castelli Romani, the "Roman Castles."

In the sixteenth century, when the rivalries between the Church, the city government, and the local feudal lords had been fairly settled, a postal road was built linking Rome and Naples.[4] This road was not replaced until the end of the eighteenth century, when the Via Appia was reopened at the behest of Pius VI. He appointed the finest artists and architects of the age, such as Antonio Canova and Luigi Canina, to oversee the restoration and renovation of the historic road. They tried as much as possible to respect the ancient route, adding only a very few variants.

From the mid-nineteenth century onward, this postal road has been called the Via Appia Vecchia (Old Appian Way).[5] That was when Pius IX created the Via Appia Nuova (New Appian Way), which would remain the sole roadway to the south before the creation of the modern highways.[6]

**From Boville to Albano**

Let us resume the journey past Mile 12, from Boville, a village once called Frattocchie.[7] Here, as everywhere along the route of the Appian Way, the solid pavement, tenacious and eternal, echoed in Roman times with the rhythmic sound of the wheels of a *cisium*, *plastrum*, or *carrus*, accompanied by the dull clopping of horse and ox hooves. The road swarmed with vendors, soldiers, letter carriers,[8] and pilgrims.

Stops along the exhausting journey were made more comfortable by the presence of *mutationes*, where one could change horses, and *mansiones*, where, after a day of wearying travel, one could get a frugal meal and some sleep. These stopping points were usually created near population centers, as in the case of Bovillae, Aricia, Tres Tabernae, and Forum Appii. Or, conversely, population centers grew up around them, as in the case of Ad Nonum, Ad Sponsas, and Ad Medias.

One of these centers, Bovillae, echoes its bucolic vocation in its very name (*bovillus*, "cattle"). Throughout the region, which in the protohistorical period was already a station on the trans-

humance route,[9] Bovillae was known for cattle breeding.[10] This route, the Via Cavona, ran from Tivoli to Anzio (ancient Antium), thus linking inland Latium with the sea. Bovillae could not help but be a strategic meeting point of these roadways.

From its inception, the town was generous and grateful to Alba Longa, whom it served as a faithful colony, embracing its religions and population when Rome's expansionist ambitions were unleashed against it. Once its florid period of independence was over, and especially by the second century B.C., Bovillae became a preferred holiday spot for members of the Roman aristocracy, who built luxurious villas there.

Clodius, famous tribune of the plebs, owned a house outside the town. Some remains now inside the Villa Santa Caterina, at Herculanum, at Mile 14 of the Appian Way, can be attributed to Clodius's house.

The famous clash between Clodius and Annius Milo, two of the principal protagonists in the struggles that tore Rome apart in the first century A.D., took place not far from here, as demonstrated, among other things, by the presence of a tomb supposed to be Clodius's. The conflict is

*Left: The mausoleum attributed to the tribune Clodius near Bovillae.*

*Above: Lake Albano, which the nymphaea of the grandiose Villa of Domitian once looked out on.*

*Facing page, top: Plan of the Villa of Domitian.*

*Facing page, bottom: Statue of Polyphemus belonging to the group of the same name, from the Bergantino nymphaeum.*

recounted in great detail, and with great partisanship, by Cicero, in his oration entitled *Pro Milone*.

Publius Clodius, whose real name was Publius Claudius Pulcher, changed his name Claudius, which was of noble, aristocratic origin, to Clodius, which is in fact the same name pronounced in the popular manner. Aiming at the favor of the *populares*, and arranging to have himself adopted by a plebian, he was elected tribune of the plebs and thus began his political career. In 52 B.C., Clodius became a candidate for praetorship. At the same time, his longtime enemy and representative of the senatorial faction, Milo, was running for the sensitive position of consul. Indeed, two years earlier, in 54 B.C., the grave political situation made it impos-

sible to elect the consuls as was the rule, and in 53 B.C., the consulate entered a period of interregnum. In addition, both of these figures were duly favored and opposed by other figures on the political scene at that time. Clodius was protected by Caesar at one stage of his career, while Milo was supported by Pompeius and defended, even legally, by the skillful Cicero.

It was this complex situation, the salient features of which have been roughly sketched here, that led to the inevitable hand-to-hand clash between Clodius and Milo, when the two crossed paths on the Appian Way. On January 18, 52 B.C., Clodius was returning to Rome from Aricia, after stopping in at his villa. Milo was on his way to Lanuvium, where he served as dictator. When the two met up, their retinues provoked a brawl. Clodius, defending his men, was wounded and taken to an inn, before being dragged back outside and killed.

The road on which Clodius met his end had been built almost three centuries earlier by his ancestor, Appius Claudius Caecus, "as though the great Appius Claudius Caecus," observed Cicero, "had opened the road not to serve the (Roman) people, but so that his descendents could behave like brigands along it."[11]

Besides the abovementioned villa of Clodius, and that of Sextus Pompeius,[12] apparently many aristocratic homes were built along this stretch of the Appian Way, especially from the late Republican era onward.

The emperor Domitian was responsible for the construction of a grandiose villa between Castelgandolfo and Albano, which absorbed other structures from the preceding period. This Alban building complex was in use until the sixth century of the Christian era, when the destructive invasions of Goths, Lombards, and Saracens began. They were not to end until the ninth century.

The Albanum Domitiani sloped down toward the countryside on terraces supported by powerful substructures, overcoming the natural unevenness of the terrain. Its area included Lake Albano,[13] whose shores were ringed by nymphaea and porticoes, creating a theater-like atmosphere and a place where the emperor's guests went to be entertained. Every year, on the occasion of the Quinquatria Minervae, the celebration held in honor of the goddess Minerva, hunts of wild beasts, theater performances, circus games, and poetry and literary competitions were held for the amusement of a select public.

The historian Suetonius remembers the hunting parties that set out to capture the animals to be used in the festivities, which Domitian himself used to take part in: "Many people often saw him in his Alban retreat shooting arrows at hundreds of wild beasts of different species, and even intentionally hitting some with two shots in the head so that the shafts looked like horns."[14]

The emperor's villa also included the Nymphaeum Bergantino, a restoration of fragmentary marble statues representing the blinding of Polyphemus and a sculptural group of the monster Scylla. The artificial waters re-created the mythical context of these

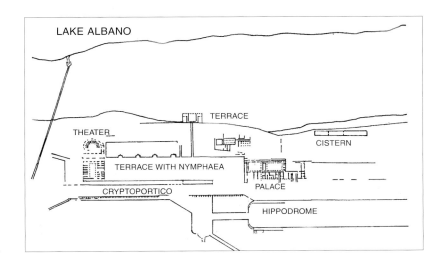

Homeric events. It was rather commonplace for imperial villas to have a monumental nymphaeum, a space often created in a natural cave, in which sculptures of characters from the *Odyssey* were artfully placed. Paradoxically, the natural setting was rendered artificial by human intervention, through the addition of such decorations as seashells or mosaics to create an aquatic or marine environment.

Tiberius (r. 14–37 A.D.) was the first to adorn his place of retreat—the Grotto at his Sperlonga

residence—with the two sculptural groups of the monster Scylla and the blinding of Polyphemus. This Homeric episode was also represented in the Nymphaeum at Punta dell'Epitaffio in Baia, the favorite Campanian retreat of the emperors Claudius (r. 41–54 A.D.) and Nero (r. 54–68 A.D.).

The Cyclops was also the subject of a mosaic representation in the Nymphaeum of Polyphemus in Nero's famous residence in Rome, the Domus Aurea.[15] Domitian (r. 81–96 A.D.), in particular, adorned his Albanum with a sculpture of the sea-monster Scylla killing Ulysses' companions, and another of a drunk, sleeping Polyphemus about to be blinded by Ulysses.

Finally, the emperor Hadrian (r. 117–138 A.D.) chose to embellish his villa near Tivoli with sculptural groups of these two famous episodes.[16]

The arrangement of the themes within both the Sperlonga Grotto and the Bergantino Nymphaeum is the same: The Scylla group occupies the center of the scene, in the water, and the Polyphemus group is in the background, to evoke the dark, disturbing lair described by Homer.

Near Lake Albano, one can still see the lake's artificial outlet. The Romans built it in order to irrigate the fields.[17] The historians Titus Livy, Valerius Maximus, and Plutarch have handed down to us the story behind this project. One summer, during the long, exhausting war against the Etruscan city of Veii, which the Romans had been besieging for ten years (406–396 B.C), the waters of the Lacus Albanus had suddenly swelled beyond all measure. The Oracle at Delphi was duly consulted regarding this anomalous phenomenon, and it was pronounced that the city of Veii would fall only after the waters of the lake had found an outlet to the sea, without invading the plain.

By now we are near the town of Albano, and before entering, we encounter a monumental mausoleum, identified as that of Pompeius Magnus, who had made his country residence here.

The first historical settlement of Albano occurred well after the construction of the Appian Way. It dated, in fact, from the reign of Emperor Septimius Severus, who, around the end of the second and the beginning of the third centuries A.D., created the Castra Albana, the camp of the Second Parthian Legion here.[18] As with the Albanum Domitiani, the unevenness of the terrain was overcome by the construction of four terraces. In the latter half of the third century, the legion was transferred, and the settlement acquired an increasingly civilian identity.

It was the presence of the soldiers, however, and therefore the inevitable influx of Eastern elements, that spread Christianity to this area at an early date. It was here that Constantine had the Church of St. John the Baptist built, for which a military camp was provided.

Of great visual and emotional impact are the great cisterns (*cisternoni*) that were built at the same time as the *castrum*, and which still survive underneath the town of Albano. A suggestive twilight atmosphere greets the visitor to their great hall,[19] divided into five naves by quadrangular pillars supporting the barrel vaulting. Light enters sporadically through great windows and skylights. One enters, even today, by descending thirty-one stairs. The space was once a reservoir capable of holding 10,000 cubic meters of water. It is partially carved out of peperino stone, and partially manmade. It was fed by two separate aqueducts and was situated at the highest point of the imperial encampment.

One more thing left to see is the Porta Praetoria, the monumental Praetorian Gate of Severus's *castrum*, which gives onto the Appian Way.

Before we depart the contemporary Italian city of Albano, we come upon a well-preserved mausoleum, consisting of a square-plan base in blocks of peperino, surmounted by four truncated conical elements on the sides, plus another in the center, constituting the burial chamber. A fascinating ancient tradition holds that the bodies of the Alban and Roman brothers, the Horatii and the Curiatii, are entombed here, after falling in combat along the Via Appia.[20] If one looks at the mausoleum in the light of Pliny the Elder's description of the Tomb of Porsenna at Chiusi, this monument, the only one of its kind, could actually be the tomb of Porsenna's son Aruns. He died in a battle fought in this very place between the Etruscans and the Aricians over the dominion of Rome itself, at the end of the reign of the Tarquinii, in 508 or 504 B.C.[21] After attacking Aricia on his way to Rome, Aruns, a member of the Etruscan Arruntia family,[22] had been defeated by the Cumaeans. At the time the latter were allied with the Latins and the

Left: The so-called mau-
soleum of Pompeius Magnus
at Albano.

Right: The Porta Praetoria
(Praetorian Gate), the monumental entrance to the
Castra Albana, on the side
facing the Via Appia.

Facing page: The famous sepulcher attributed by tradition
to the Horatii and Curatii,
near Albano. It is not to be
confused with the sepulchral
complex of the same name at
Mile 5 of the Via Appia.

Tarquinii, who did not want Porsenna and his descendants to take power in Rome.

In front of the sepulcher stands the Church of S. Maria della Stella, under which lies the small Christian catacomb of S. Senatore, created from a preexisting pozzolana quarry. The late-third/early-fourth-century dating confirms the early spread of Christianity in Albanum. The church's frescoes, which still survive, some of them representing Christ with Peter and Paul and beside the Virgin, date from a broad temporal spectrum ranging from the late fourth to the ninth century.

### From Aricia to Lanuvium

In order to allow the Appian Way to proceed in a straight line, even over terrain of varying altitudes, the Romans constructed, before Aricia, the famous, imposing viaduct that now unfortunately lies in a state of abandon, buried under dense vegetation.

Based on the work's structure, it is hypothesized that construction began in the period of the Gracchi.

The only surviving document relating to the via-duct's construction, however, is the inscription[23] attributing it to a well-known figure from the first century A.D.[24]

In the first half of the 1800s, a stretch of this viaduct, more than 230 meters long and over 13 meters high, with a width of almost 9 meters at the base, still existed. The facing was in *opus quadratum*—consisting of blocks of peperino arranged alter-nately lengthwise and breadthwise—and rested on a base of *opus caementicium* (a construction technique using cement, often mixed with fragments of brick and stone, *caementa*). Two arches along the viaduct also allowed for crossroads and waterways to pass underneath.

In the modern era, Pius IX emulated the grandeur of the ancient viaduct, commissioning Giuseppe Bertolini in the mid-1800s to build a bridge 312 meters long and with a maximum height of 200 meters, at a different spot from the ancient work.

*View of present-day Ariccia, with the viaduct built at the behest of Pope Pius IX.*

After walking along the viaduct, one enters Aricia, the first stop, in ancient times, for anyone coming from Rome. Horace, too, stopped here. The so-called "Osteriaccia" ("low inn"), in popular tradition, has been identified as the poet's "modest lodging,"[25] where he stayed after arriving in the company of Heliodorus the rhetorician, an erudite Greek.

This Latin city played a role of considerable political and religious importance for the whole territory.[26] In fact it was a provincial center for the local populations, as administrator of the goddess Diana Nemorensis, to whom the temple by Lake Nemi was devoted.

In archaic times the gods were worshiped in natural settings. The wood (*nemus*), once consecrated, took on the connotation of *lucus* (sacred wood), where the faithful would come to perform rites and bring offerings to the deity. The sacredness of the place was defined by its seclusion and the protective covering of its dense vegetation. Such was the case with the sacred wood of Diana Nemorensis (from *nemus*), as well as the wood of Feronia near the crag of Leano and the wood of the nymph Marica near Minturno. Usually, some time after the consecration of the site, a temple in simple forms, devoted to the deity, was built inside the sacred area. At times the sanctuaries were also situated on heights, as was the case with the Temple of Jupiter Latiaris on the Albanus Mons (Monte Cavo), where the people of Latium used to congregate.

The sacredness of the Sanctuary of Diana is perpetuated in the Park of Palazzo Chigi, which constitutes the last shred of the *nemus aricium*[27] devoted to Diana. Ovid described the wood as shady and possessed of a lake, "*lacus antiqua religione sacer*"[28] while Strabo pointed out that the *lucus* included all the woods on the left-hand side of the Appian Way and surrounded Lake Nemi.[29] The suggestiveness of the place fascinated poets like Martial, who called it "wood of the Muses," and Goethe, who passed through it on his "Italian Journey."[30]

The right to succession for the office of priest of the goddess (*rex Nemorensis*) was earned only by victory in a duel, by actually killing the reigning priest. A very ancient tradition explains this odd custom. Near the sanctuary, there was a tree whose

branches one was forbidden to remove. If, however, someone managed to tear one off, he could fight the priest of the goddess; if he should kill the priest, the victor would take his place as *rex Nemorensis*. The rite is explained in the Greek fashion by a myth: Orestes supposedly brought it to Nemi, having fled there after killing the king of Chersonesos (Thrace) and spiriting away an effigy of Diana.

Thus was born the famous Sanctuary of the Goddess Diana at Lake Nemi, initially frequented by Latin populations in league together against Rome's expansionist aims, and later, by Romans themselves and Latins, up until the Imperial era. Although its current vestiges date from the last building phase in the second century B.C., there is evidence of the cult in that area as early as the mid-sixth century B.C., when Etruscan dominion first went into decline. The three chambers of the temple must have held three effigies of the deity, each of which was supposed to represent Diana Nemorensis in her triple role of protectress of the hunt and the woods, goddess of the underworld, and goddess of fertility.

When Lake Nemi was drained in 1929, two boats that had been anchored there by the emperor Caligula (37–41 A.D.) were found on its bottom, almost two thousand years after they were launched.[31] They were in fact two elegant houseboats, designed for feasts, receptions, banquets, and holidays on the water.

Suetonius recounts that Caligula "had [several] Liburnian boats built, with ten rows of oars and gem-covered sterns, polychrome sails, with hot baths, arcades, vast tricliniums, and even a great variety of grapevines and fruit trees. He used to sail the shores of Campania on these vessels, lying down all the day long, amidst dancing and music."[32]

The boats' dimensions were out of the ordinary: One of them measured 73 meters long and 24 meters wide; the other, 71.30 by 20. The flat-bottomed hulls were so well preserved that as soon as they were brought to the surface, they were put to use for the study of shipbuilding techniques among the ancients.

Unfortunately, the boats burned during World War II,[33] and the local museum now has only faithful reproductions and a very few surviving remnants.[34]

*Left: Small bifrontal herm with maenads, a decoration from one of the ships recovered from Lake Nemi (Rome, Museo Nazionale Romano at Palazzo Massimo).*

*Below: Map of Lake Nemi showing the positions of Caligula's boats, recovered whole in 1932.*

*Opposite page: Head of Medusa, from the first of the boats recovered from Lake Nemi (Rome, Museo Nazionale Romano at Palazzo Massimo).*

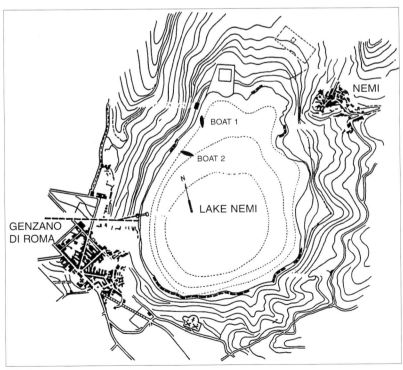

Getting back to our excursion along the Appian Way, at Mile 18 once stood the ancient city of Lanuvium. Evidence shows that the cult of Juno Sospita (Juno the Protectress) was already practiced here in the Archaic era—imported, like the cult of Diana, from Greece. It is further proof of the religious syncretism of the area of the Alban Hills. This goddess was in fact identified with Hera of Argo, imported to Italy by Diomedes.

The cult, centered around Juno, was agricultural and pastoral in character. Among the goddess's attributes were a headdress of goatskin and horns, oriental footwear with curling toes, a shield shaped like the number eight, and a lance. In a cave near the temple, a holy serpent was raised, and every year the virgin girls of Lanuvium would go to it in procession and offer donations of food in hopes of a favorable harvest. Archaeological vestiges of the sanctuary are contained today inside the seminary and the Villa Sforza of Lanuvio.

In 1934, a sepulcher was found in Lanuvio, the only one of its kind in Latium: the tomb of an aristocratic knight. Because of the richness and typology of its decoration—consisting of a full suit of armor—the sepulcher was named the "Tomb of the Warrior."[35] It has been dated around the fifth century B.C., and might therefore be an example of the armaments with which the Latin soldiers fought against Rome's expansion, around Lake Regillo, in 496 B.C.

At Lanuvium, according to the ancient sources, there was also a Villa of the Antonini, where the emperors Antoninus Pius (138–161 A.D.) and Commodus (180–193 A.D.) were born.[36]

Further on, at Mile 19, at Monte Cagnoletto, there still stands the milestone whose inscription commemorates the restoration of the Appian Way by the emperor Nerva. Just ahead on the right begins a strip of pavement about one hundred meters long that still has its stone base and the original retaining wall against the hillside. In the vicinity was also the way station of Sub Lanuvium, whose exact location has not yet been verified on the ground.

Leaving the area, one continues to find vestiges of road, *tabernae*, and ancient bridges along the route, as at S. Gennaro, Fosso di Mele, and Colle Ottone, before arriving in the district of Sole Luna. The place gets its name from the two deities (*Sole*, "Sun", and *Luna*, "Moon") to whom a temple was once dedicated here. It was a primitive cult based on the worship of the two orbs that were indispensable to the cycles of day and night, and to the seasons and life itself.

In this same area, at the crossroads with the Via Mactorina—which started at Velletri and headed to Satricum and Anzio—apparently stood the *mansio* Ad Sponsas, as the ancient remains attest.

## A Detour through Marino and Velletri, toward Cisterna

Let us now stray a bit from the Appian Way, toward settlements that existed before the road itself. These settlements clustered along far more ancient routes that were eventually replaced by the Via Appia, which ran further down in the plain, before they were revived in the Middle Ages.

Thus we arrive at Marino, originally the Sullan settlement of Castrimoenium.[37] Like other centers, it gravitated toward the Via Appia, although the road, proceeding directly along its straightaway toward Capua, never served it directly.

Of greatest interest in the modern town of Marino is perhaps the Mithraeum, which is hidden away and almost forgotten in a private cellar. The miraculously well-preserved fresco in it still conveys the inexorable power of the moment of taurochthony, the "slaying of the bull," from which the world is born and regenerated. It is easy to imagine the soldiers of the Castra Albana, or the miners from the nearby peperino quarries, gathering together in this darkened den to be initiated into the cult of Mithras.

Religions continued to overlap in this area. Not far away, near the ancient Albanus Mons, there used to be the provincial sanctuary of Jupiter Latiaris, the highest god first for the people of Latium, then for the Romans themselves. The latter, in fact, went so far as to diminish the importance of this sanctuary, transferring the cult of Jupiter to the Capidoglio, according to tradition, from the time of the Tarquin kings.

The Latin populations, who from time immemorial had gathered at this dominant point, sealed their alliances here during the *Feriae Latinae* (the annual festival of the Latin League). A white bull was sacrificed to the father of the gods and then dismembered, so that its flesh could be distributed among the forty-seven cities of the alliance.

*Facing page: The Via Appia at Monte Cagnoletto.*

*Below: Milestone 19 of the Via Appia, at Monte Cagnoletto, commemorating the restoration of the road by the emperor Nerva.*

*On pages 102–103: The Mithraeum of Marino. On the rear wall of the Mithraeum is a painting representing the taurochthony, or slaying of the bull.*

Let us now continue on to Velletri (the ancient Velitrae). The city is located at the geographic boundary between the Alban Hills, which lie behind us to the north, and the Pontine region, which we will head toward as we continue south, on the next itinerary.

Velitrae, at an altitude of 400 meters, controlled an important conjunction of roads predating the construction of the Appian Way which, when finally built, left the city off its route. One of these ancient roads linked Velitrae with the Pontine towns of Cora, Norba, and Privernum. Another, originating in Praeneste, went all the way to the sea, to Satricum and Antium. This was the Via Mactorina, which existed from Archaic times, though not beyond the sixth century B.C. A number of centuries later, Augustus sought to restore it.

The city was probably Etruscan in origin.[38] The culture, however, was shaped by the Volsci,[39] to such an extent that it remained perpetually in conflict with Rome as a matter of pride, until its final defeat in 338 B.C.[40] The punishment that Rome meted out to the city on this occasion was terrible. The city walls were torn down, and its senators were deported to the right bank of the Tiber and forbidden ever to return to Velitrae. A few centuries later, fate and luck, with their inscrutable designs, decided that the future first emperor of Rome, Octavian Augustus, should be born in this town.[41] The Octavii, in fact, owned a villa outside the town. The archaeological vestiges near the hill of San Cesareo are in all likelihood what is left of it.

As for the rest, there are no longer any visible remains of the ancient city, nor of such public buildings as the forum and amphitheater. We know, however, that there were three temples there. One was near where the Cathedral of S. Clemente now stands; the second near the Piazza del Comune; and the third underneath the Church of S. Maria della Neve. The local Museo Comunale, moreover, has a marble sarcophagus called the "Velletri Sarcophagus," which is adorned with two overlapping decorative bands of excellent Greco-Asiatic production, dated second century A.D.

It is also worth remembering that the origins of Christianity in the Velletri community are very ancient. Indeed, St. Peter, on the occasion of his journey to Rome, entrusted the followers of the new religion to St. Clement, who thus became the town's patron saint.[42]

Now let us leave Velletri and go to the last stop on this itinerary, Cisterna Latina. The name of the modern town derives from the presence of two reservoirs, which a twelfth-century medieval legend claims had served as a hiding place for Nero when he fled Rome.

Whatever the case, the birth of Castrum Cisternae, at Mile 35, is connected to the existence of the ancient Tres Tabernae, a center created, as the name ("Three Taverns") indicates, as a way station for travelers, equipped with places for food and refreshment (tabernae). It was here that, in 59 A.D., St. Paul, shackled in chains, met with the faithful of nascent Christianity.

And at this point we meet back up with the main axis of the Appian Way, leaving behind the Alban Hills, on our way to the Pontine Plain.

## Notes

1 Goethe, "Italian Journey" (November 1, 1786), p. 502.

2 The modern town most likely built on top of the site of the ancient Alba Longa is Castelgandolfo.

3 However, some maintenance work in the sixth century A.D. is indicated by the presence of Theodoric's milestones along the route.

4 This road passed through Marino and Velletri, but excluded Cisterna and the Pontine Marshes.

5 The name Via Appia Antica designates the Roman road built by Appius Claudius Caecus, which was extended and renovated throughout the Imperial period. The name Via Appia Vecchia was given to the postal road created by Pius VI when it was replaced by the Via Appia Nuova created by Pius IX in the nineteenth century.

6 Now State Route SS 107.

7 The name derives from *fratte* ("thickets"), the dense vegetation of shrubs and brush that came to invade the ancient ruins.

8 Antiquity's *tabellari*.

9 See Filippo Coarelli, *Dintorni di Roma* (Bari: G. Lazerta, 1981).

10 See Francesca Severini, *La Via Appia*, vol. 2 (Rome: Libreria dello Stato, 2001).

11 Cicero *Pro Milone*.

12 Some vestiges may still remain inside the Municipal Park of Albano, formerly Villa Doria.

13 Virgil *Aeneid* 9.525: "*atque lacus, qui post, Albae de nomine dicti, Albanus.*"

14 Suetonius *Domitianus* 19; Coarelli, *Dintorni di Roma*.

15 Elisabetta Segala and Ida Sciortino, *Domus Aurea* (Milan: Electa, 1999).

16 For all these places, see *Ulisse, il mito e la memoria*, exh. cat., Palazzo delle Esposizioni (Rome, 1996).

17 The conduit was 1.2 m wide and 1.6 m high, vaulted and made of blocks of peperino stone. The outlet was situated at the present-day village of Le Mole. The water reached this point after traveling about 1.5 km underground. Five kilometers later, it poured into the Tiber near Tor di Valle.

18 The Castra Albana covered an area of 240 m by 438 m and had four entrances. The main one gave onto the Via Appia, to the southwest.

19 Its long sides were 47.9 by 45.6 m, its short sides 29.62 by 31.90.

20 According to other sources, the Tomb of the Horatii and Curiatii is at Milestone 5 on the Via Appia.

21 508 B.C in the Roman chronology, 504 in the Greek. Filippo Cassola, *Storia di Roma dalle origini a Cesare* (Rome: Jouvence, 1985).

22 The presence of this family in this territory is well documented.

23 *CIL* XIV.2166.

24 This would be Tiberius Latinus Pandusa, who at the time was *quattuorvir viarum curandarum*, procurator of Mesia in 19 A.D. (Tacitus *Annals* 2.66).

25 Horace *Satires* 1.5.2

26 The Latin city dates from the sixth century B.C up to the Roman conquest in 338 B.C.

27 "Wood of Aricia." Also known as *Nemus Dianae* ("wood of Diana") or *Nemus Artemisium* ("wood of Artemis").

28 "Ancient sacred lake to holy religion," Ovid *Fasti* 3.264.

29 "*Dianae autem, quod vocant, Nemus ab sinistra viae parte est, qua ab Aricia Lanuvium versus ascenditur*" (5.3.12).

30 Goethe, "Italian Journey," 512.

31 Popular tradition held that there were probably boats at the bottom of the lake. In the fifteenth century, Leon Battista Alberti tried in vain to recover them. A century later, another attempt also failed. The third try, in 1895, was more fortunate. A diver managed to get a glimpse of the ships and give an account of their size and consistency. Unfortunately this episode indirectly led to the despoliation of the vessels, which were inconscionably stripped of many ornaments, including many of great value.

32 Suetonius *Caligula* 37; see also Coarelli, *Dintorni di Roma*.

33 May 31 and June 1, 1944.

34 Some bronze decorations, noteworthy for their size and great artistic value, are now in Rome, at the Museo Nazionale Romano (Palazzo Massimo).

35 Now in Rome at the Museo Nazionale Romano (Palazzo Massimo).

36 Remnants brought to light by recent excavations, at Genzano (Viale del Lavoro), belonged to a villa built on terraces (like so many others) that might be identifiable as the imperial villa.

37 Sulla founded this *municipium* in 80 B.C.

38 Its name apparently derives from *Velathri* – Volterra.

39 The most important inscription in the Volscian language was found at Velletri. It is a sacred document concerning the goddess Declona, and it is now in the Museo Nazionale of Naples.

40 The defeat of the Latin League, described above.

41 The ruins of a Roman villa found in the town of San Cesareo have for this reason been identified as being the Villa of the Octavii.

42 As mentioned, the cathedral of Velletri is named after St. Clement.

# From the Pontine Plain to Benevento

FRANCESCA VENTRE

*The majestic Roman aqueduct originating at the springs of Capodacqua and leading to the city of Minturnae (modern Minturno).*

*Facing page: The navigable canal that ran alongside the Appian Way for nineteen miles (the Decennovium) across the Pontine Plain, from Forum Appii to Terracina.*

## Historical Events

The region to the south of Latium Vetus (which we are now leaving behind), geographically situated between the Lepini and Ausoni Mountains and the sea, is known as the Pontine Plain.

This area would acquire a bad reputation in late antiquity and the Middle Ages, but in Archaic times, was neither poor nor unhealthy. Rather, it was a fertile flatland. In fact, the soil was very propitious to rich plantations of wheat, cereals, vegetables, olives, and vines.

The area became attractive to Rome quite early on. One tradition, often considered apocryphal, dates the foundation of Roman colonies such as Cora and Norba as early as the late sixth or early fifth centuries B.C., in the first years of the Roman Republic. The entire fifth century, in fact, was characterized by the ascendancy of the Volsci, who dominated the area, excepting only Cora and Norba, which were well defended and impregnable.

The Roman advance, turning south to the Pontine Plain, resumed after the fire set by the Gauls in 390 B.C. One year later, Camillus defeated the Volsci once and for all. Rome thus extended her supremacy, which was definitively sealed by the victory over the Latin League in 338 B.C.

Other colonies were then born—Fundi and Formiae in 334, Tarracina in 329—on the territory previously controlled by the Volsci. In 314 B.C., the Aurunci, who until that time had dominated the area south of Tarracina, rebelled against Rome and destroyed such centers as Ausona, Minturnae (which would reemerge as a colony in 295 B.C.), and Vescia.

The colonies of Tarracina and Minturnae, not coincidentally, were situated at two strategic points: the former controlled the barrier of the Monte S. Angelo (near modern Fornio), the latter the passage of the Garigliano river, the natural boundary between Latium and Campania.

Rome's expansion during this period was so great that the city found itself administering a vast territory. Only part of the territory was inhabited by citizens with full rights (*cives optimo iure*). The latter included the Roman colonists, in addition to the people belonging to the early core of settlers from the Roman expansion at the time of the kings.

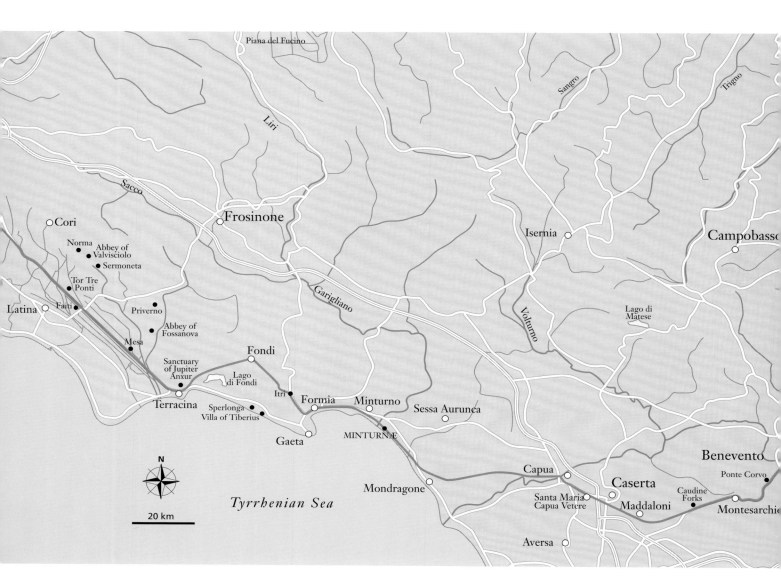

The colonists were granted the lands confiscated from the vanquished. Citizens of the Roman colonies held the right to vote in the Roman assemblies, but also enjoyed administrative autonomy. Tarracina (329 B.C.) and Minturnae (295 B.C.) were among the earliest Roman colonies to be founded.

Other types of colonies had less favorable conditions of existence. Their citizens, *cives sine suffragio* ("citizens without suffrage"), had the duties of Roman citizens (such as military service and tax-paying) but none of the rights. Such was the case for centers such as Fundi and Formiae, founded in 334 B.C., and Capua, founded in 341 B.C.

Over time, all the colonies were granted citizenship with full rights. For Fundi and Formiae, it came after more than a century of waiting, in 188 B.C. Capua, however, was treated more harshly. It was deprived of its autonomy, having taken the side of Hannibal in the Second Punic War.

In 312 B.C., the axis of the Appian Way was built through this region of Latium *adiectium*,[1] which ran securely from Tarracina to Minturnae, and the northern part of Campania, now totally under Roman dominion. It made possible the Roman expansion southward to Magna Graecia. Thirty miles of straight road established a link—still in existence today—from Cisterna to Punta di Leano, after which another straightaway led to Tarracina; in particular, the Decennovium,[2] flanked by a navigable canal, linked Forum Appii and Tarracina.

The special function and uniqueness of the Appian Way—shaped by the need, mostly military, that it be traveled in as little time as possible and with a minimum of obstacles and deviations—become particularly apparent along this stretch. The route along the foothills, and the population centers gravitating around it,[3] fell into decline as a result of the new, straight route. They would regain strategic importance and renewed splendor after the outcome of the Gothic War and the resulting, inevitable abandonment of the lowlands as the marshes began to encroach on them. Centers such as Cori, Norma, Ninfa, and Sermoneta were reborn, in some cases born outright, at the height of the Middle Ages, and the Cistercian monastic culture, radiating directly from France, spread through this area as well. Further south, cities such as Terracina, Fondi, Minturno, and finally Capua also experienced periods of strong growth.

In the flatlands, after many fruitless efforts conducted over the centuries, Pope Pius VI, in 1777, finally saw to the reclamation of the marshland and enabled the road to be rediscovered with repairs and serious restoration projects.

A valuable testimony to these projects and their value is provided by Ferdinand Gregorovius, a nineteenth-century German historian, who wrote:

*Whoever has never traveled through the Pontine Marsh, along the Appian Way to Terracina, has the most mistaken idea of its nature, because he thinks only of a putrid, swampy land. Obviously there are marshes and swamps there, but they lie between woods and thickets . . . and in May and June the Pontine Plain is a sea of flowers as far as the eye can see. Among the various popes, Sixtus V, a practical-minded Roman, was the first to undertake the draining of the swamp, and he was followed by Pius VI more than two centuries later. The latter pope reestablished the Appian Way, which he called the Linea Pia, renovated the large canal alongside it, had other canals dug, and transformed part of the marsh into arable land, to his everlasting credit.[4]*

Finally, in 1927, further intervention became necessary as the marshes had once again encroached on the land, due to neglect and abandonment.

Because of these complex phases in the Appian Way's existence, the first part of our itinerary, up to Terracina, will be divided into two sections. The first will be the route—archaic in origin and then revived in the Middle Ages—known as the "foothills" route;[5] the second will be the rectilinear route of the Via Appia Antica. The expansion of the road's limits through time bears witness to the fact that the *regina viarum* has always remained alive, and indeed has broadened its spiritual confines and influence over the centuries, beyond its merely physical route.

### From Cori to the Abbey of Fossanova: The Archaic and Medieval Route

One of the ancient Latin cities that fell into oblivion because of the uncompromising straightness of the Via Appia was the ancient Cora, founded according to legend by the Trojan Dardanus or the eponymous hero Coras, brother of Tiburnus.[6]

A very important route was the Via Setina, a road dating from no earlier than the sixth century B.C., which linked Rome to Terracina. It therefore existed before the Via Appia was built, its route lying further east.

Cora was a Latin colony of the fifth century B.C. and became a *municipium* in the third; after the civil strife between Marius and Sulla it fell into ruin, and much later it was sacked by the Ostragoth king Totila and by Frederick Barbarossa. Cori (as it came to be called) was well established on the foothills route by the time Innocent III ceded it to Pietro Annibaldi in 1212.

The few surviving Roman vestiges here are incorporated into later monuments and buildings, starting outside the circumference of the city walls and gates. The walls are notable for their imposing structure, in polygonal stonework (*opus polygonium*), dating perhaps from the fifth century B.C.[7] From the time of antiquity, terraces were created to overcome the natural unevenness of the terrain.[8] This led the roads to be arranged in concentric rings, interconnected by ramps and stairways.

*Detail of a segment of wall in* opus polygonium *from the Latin city of Cori, on the eastern side of the present-day Piazza del Municipio. Beside it is the church of Sant'Oliva, built atop an ancient edifice.*

*Facing page: The so-called temple of Hercules at Cori.*

Of the gates opened into the walls, the most important was the Porta Ninfina,[9] made up of a semicircular arch, dating around the third to second century B.C.

One of the city's main temples was devoted to Castor and Pollux. It was built as early as the fourth century B.C., and its still-visible structure should be dated around the late second or early first century B.C. In the front part of the temple are two rows of six columns, while the more internal area is divided into three spaces.

The most famous temple in Cori is the one built on two terraces and commonly said to be devoted to Hercules. The attribution to the mythical hero, however, appears unfounded; in fact it seems more likely to have been devoted to a goddess with curative powers.[10]

On the upper terrace stood the more ancient temple, of which no trace remains, dated between the mid-fourth and the second centuries B.C.[11] On the lower terrace, around 100 B.C.,[12] the second temple was built: Doric in style, it stood on a podium and was preceded by a portico with four columns in front and two on each side. Later, in

the Middle Ages, the Cathedral of S. Pietro was built atop this temple. The church was destroyed in World War II, and today only the campanile remains.[13]

Among the medieval vestiges to be admired inside the Church of S. Maria della Pietà is the paschal candelabrum, northern-barbarian in style and a rare specimen in this area. The stem rests on two lion supports (*protomi*) and is dated eleventh–twelfth century.

Past Cori, and continuing along the foothills route that used to lead to Norma, we arrive at the precious historic oasis of peace and tranquility that is the phantom garden of Ninfa. Imbued with the perfumes and smells of nature, in a serenity of near-total silence, cheered by the sight of so many colors, we are transported into a timeless feeling of delightful refreshment.

"Behold Ninfa," wrote Ferdinand Gregorovius, "behold the fabulous ruins of a city that lies with its walls: towers, churches, convents and buildings half-submerged in the marsh, buried under the dense ivy. . . . Over Ninfa there flutters a fragrant sea of flowers: every wall, every church, every house is enveloped in a veil of ivy. . . . Ninfa! It was the Pompeii of the Middle Ages, the city of dreams, immersed in the Pontine Marshes!"

Nearby were the sources from which the river Nymphaeus sprang, sacred to the noted deities of the waters, as recorded by Pliny.[14]

Documentation of the town of Ninfa, however, exists only as of the eight century A.D., when the emperor of Constantinople, Constantine V Copronymus, donated it, with its surrounding farming areas, to Pope Zacharias. The place gained increasing importance from its position as a way station. In the eleventh century, it belonged to the counts of Tuscolo, who in the following century ceded it to the Frangipane family. It was here that, on September 20, 1159, Rolando Bandinelli was elected pope under the name of Alexander III, in the church of S. Maria Maggiore, to avoid the riots in the city of Rome stirred up by the antipope Victor IV. The pontiff loved and rewarded Ninfa, building seven churches there named after the seven historic churches of Rome. But vengeance belonged to Fredrick Barbarossa, who was offended that the pontifical coronation was held outside of Rome. He wasted no time putting Ninfa to the torch and the sword.

It was the city's fate thereafter to pass from hand to hand among the local lords.[15] Its rulers included, in 1297, Benedetto Caetani, who in 1294 was made pope under the name of Boniface VIII.

The centuries ultimately forgot about Ninfa, and as a result, what became its ruins were enveloped by vegetation and relegated to neglect. But this ultimately also created its charm. The first to succumb to its seductions, after much time had passed, was Gelasio Caetani. Beginning in 1920, he lovingly devoted himself to restoring its historic buildings and creating a splendid garden, made from the inextricable symbiosis of plants, trees, and rare, varied, and brightly colored flowers, and the sober, pale shades of the surviving monuments.[16]

Continuing along the known archaic and medieval route past Norma, one reaches the town's Roman ancestor of Norba, clinging with its majestic polygonal walls to an impregnable hillside dominating the entire plain.

A Latin colony by 492 B.C., it was repeatedly but unsuccessfully attacked by the Volsci in the fifth and fourth centuries.[17] In 340 B.C. it took part in the Latin War, enjoying a period of splendor until it was totally and definitively destroyed by partisans of Sulla.[18]

*Left: View of the lake at Ninfa, with the fourteenth-century donjon of Caetani castle.*

*Below: Curtain wall of Caetani castle at Ninfa.*

More than seven centuries later, there was a brief attempt to re-inhabit the site, but the settlers finally decided to move to Norma. Indeed, the reason there are still vestiges of the ancient Roman city is because nothing was superimposed on it over time. The urban structure, arranged over terraces, had two high points called the Major Acropolis and Minor Acropolis. On the former, there were two temples; on the latter stood the Temple of Diana. In the southwestern part of the city was the Temple of Juno Lucina, protectress of women in labor.

Along the city's polygonal walls, which extended for roughly 2.5 kilometers, there were four gates, three of which are still extant: the Porta Signina, Porta Ninfina, and Porta Maggiore, all splendid examples of ancient fortification.

Leaving behind the ancient city of Norba, we next reach the Abbey of Valvisciolo. It is one of those presences that bear witness to the long life of the Appian Way, its persistence over time as it became the road carrying the message of the Christian

religion. This building, which was probably built atop a prior construction for Basilian monks, is a Cistercian work. The Abbey of Valvisciolo is named after Saints Peter and Paul, but also after the early martyr Stephen, patron of the more ancient Abbey of Marmosolio. The monks had left that abbey

after it was destroyed, moving to Valvisciolo. Some, apparently erroneously, have attributed the complex to the Templars, based on the recent discovery of a small Templar cross in the rose window of the facade.[19] All this really proves is the unusual, more meticulous craftsmanship of the rose window itself, which must therefore be dated before the suppression of the Order in 1312. The interior of the church, though restored in 1863–64 at the behest of Pius IX and again in the early 1900s, still manages to convey the sense of contemplation and sobriety characteristic of this ancient monastic order.[20] What distinguishes it from the other Lazio abbeys of Casamari and Fossanova, and thus from standard Cistercian schemas, is the lack of a transept. Moreover, the bell tower is positioned at the end of the right aisle and not over the center of the church, which is more in keeping with Cistercian dictates.

Just past the abbey lies the town of Sermoneta, an interesting center for its well-preserved quality and its location in the area of the Lepini Mountains. The town's name is supposed to derive from early, vanished settlements, such as Ulubrae and especially Sulmo, which then yields the toponym of *Sulmonetum.*

Sermoneta passed out of the Church's hands and into those of the counts of Tuscolo, and onto the Annibaldi, who then sold it to Pietro Caetani. Only Pope Alexander IV was able to wrest Sermoneta away from the Caetani, in order to give it as a gift to Cesare Borgia's son. He in turn used it as a headquarters in Latium. Julius II finally gave it back to the Caetani in 1504.

In the first half of the thirteenth century, the Annibaldi built the castle, symbol of the town. It was later modified and enlarged by the families that took it over. Its grandeur can still be admired almost whole: The different buildings are arrayed around the Piazza d'Armi, which is dominated by the thirteenth-century donjon.

Past the medieval towns of Sezze, Roccagorga, and Maenza, the foothill route leads us to the archaeological site of Privernum. The most ancient settlement here, controlled by the Volsci as a link between the hills and the coastal area, strategically dominated the lines of communication along the Amaseno River, between the Liri Valley and the Pontine Plain.

Virgil, in the *Aeneid,* held up Camilla, the daughter of Privernum's king, as an exemplar of the pride of the Volsci:

*Last, from the Volscians fair Camilla came,*
*And led her warlike troops—a warrior dame;*
*Unbred to spinning, in the loom unskilled,*
*She chose the nobler Pallas of the field.*
*Mixed with the first, the fierce virago fought,*
*Sustained the toils of arms, the danger sought,*
*Outstripped the winds in speed upon the plain.*[21]

Rome subdued Privernum after a conflict that lasted from 358 to 329 B.C. In 318 it was made a member of the Oufentine tribe, which took its name from the Ufens River.[22]

In the second century, the Roman settlement, with its regular layout, was founded on the plain. What remains visible of this urban structure are two temple buildings, the forum, the Capitolum, a few bathing establishments, and many houses, including one called the "Domus of the Emblem," which features mosaics in a Hellenistic style. Another rich, sumptuous *domus* of the Republican era, called the "Domus of the Nilotic Threshold," was decorated with a very fine mosaic in small tesserae, one section of which represented a landscape along the banks of the Nile.[23]

After the barbarian invasions of the region, the Roman district was abandoned by its inhabitants, who moved to what would thereafter be called Piperno, the corrupted medieval name of Privernum that was used until 1928. After that date, the town would be called Priverno. The medieval center of the town, like others we have mentioned, went through phases of shifting fortunes, owing to the fact that it repeatedly changed hands from one noble family to another.

The surrounding landscape, which enfolds these medieval centers and religious settlements, is enriched throughout by lookout towers, the survivors of a vastly more complex system of defenses against raids by barbarians or simple brigands.

At last we arrive at the Abbey of Fossanova, the model for the spread of Cistercian architecture in central Italy. The abbey complex, built at the behest of Innocent II in 1135, would remain forever linked to the mother house of Hautecombe in Savoy. Its first abbot, Gerardo, served from 1173 to

1187. By 1208, Pope Innocent was able to consecrate the altar of the completed church. In 1274, St. Thomas Aquinas died within its walls.[24]

In the second half of the fifteenth century, the abbey began its decline, which was to continue until Napoleon suppressed it altogether, consigning it to oblivion.[25] Since 1936, it has been in the hands of the Friars Minor Conventual.

The facade still has traces of a triple-arched ogival porch, with the imposing portal built around the central, broadest arch. Its architrave once bore the inscription testifying to the church's dedication by Frederick Barbarossa, but it was later covered by a mosaic in the Cosmati style.

Once inside the church, one is overwhelmed by the vastness suggested by the simple but imposing, gently soaring architecture of rib-vaults devoid of sculptural decoration and almost entirely without painting.[26] The plainness is a metaphor for the

sobriety to which the Cistercian order aspired. The nave, rightly taller and broader than the aisles, physically and spiritually leads the observer's gaze to the altar and the back of the church, illuminated by the light from the rose window.

Around the church are the spaces necessary to the ascetic lives of the monks: cloister, chapter house, dormitories, refectory, and infirmary.

### From Tor Tre Ponti to Terracina: The Route of the Appian Way

Returning to the original course of the Via Appia Antica, we find ourselves near the town of Tor Tre Ponti (ancient Tripontium). The simple place-name commemorates, according to two divergent hypotheses, the presence of either three bridges,[27] or of a bridge with three spans.[28]

The place corresponds to one of the ancient way stations along the Appian Way. Here, in 1780,

Pius VI erected a post office. Two milestone columns commemorate, respectively, the works of Emperor Nerva and the restorations made by Emperor Constantine.[29]

About half a kilometer later, a bridge constructed in *opus quadratum* with rusticated stones and a five-meter span crosses the Ninfa River. In the parapets, there are two surviving epigraphs that attribute the construction to Trajan,[30] who oversaw a vast restoration project for this stretch of road.[31]

At Mile 43 of the Appian Way, we come to Forum Appii, another place named after the censor who founded the road.[32] This was the starting point of the nineteen-mile stretch, the Decennovium, that led directly to Tarracina. It was flanked by a navigable canal, also restored by Pius VI, as far as the cliffs of Mount Leano.

The poet Horace tells us with irony and a little vexation of the ill luck he encountered in making this brief but tormented journey by water:

*Then, off to Forum Appi, full of boatmen and crooked innkeepers. We were lazy and spent two days getting there. Those with quicker legs do it in one. The Appian Way is easier if you go slower. Here, since the water was unspeakably bad, I declared war upon my stomach, waiting in sour spirits for the others in the party to finish eating. Now Night brought darkness forth upon the earth and prepared to flood heaven with stars. Now shout followed shout, slaves to boatmen and boatmen to slaves: "Land here!" "Don't overload us, dammit!" "Enough, we're packed!" Settling the money and hitting up the mule waste at least an hour. The horrible gnats and swamps frogs forbid all sleep. Drunk on cheap wine, the boatman sings about his girl back home. A passenger joins in to make a contest. Eventually he gets tired and goes to sleep, so the lazy boatman lets the mule feed itself its dinner, tying its rope around a stone, and then flops down and snores. Come daybreak and we see that our boat isn't moving at all; but finally someone with a temper pounces on the mule and on the boatman, whacking away at skulls and butts with a willow rod. By midmorning we've barely made port. We wash our hands and faces, Ferronia, in your waters.*[33]

Halfway along the Decennovium was the Ad Medias way station, whose named derived directly from its location. Included in the *Itinerarium*

*Above: Fossanova Abbey church, considered the model for Cistercian Gothic architecture in Italy.*

*Right: Plan of Fossanova Abbey.*

*Facing page: Interior of the chapter house of Fossanova Abbey.*

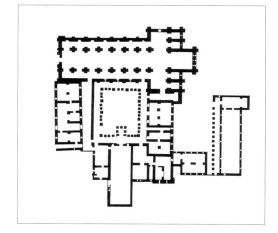

*Above and facing page: Views of the cloister of Fossanova Abbey. The cloister is square in plan, with three sides in the Romanesque style and one side in the Gothic. Inside is an aedicula built to shelter a wash basin, whose base incorporates a milestone from the Appian Way.*

*Burdigalense*, a map used by pilgrims on their way to the Holy Land by way of Brindisi, the site found new life when it was turned into the Casale di Mesa shelter, built by Pius VI as a postal station. It is still in good condition.

At its entrance, two milestone columns of Trajan's[34] note the distance from Rome (48 and 49 miles) and that from Tripontium and Forum Appii (6 miles),[35] according to the partial count of the Decennovium. The most ancient milestone of the Appian Way was also found here.[36] It names the two curule aediles P. Claudius (son of Appius Claudius Caecus)[37] and C. Furius.[38]

Inside the Casale, moreover, one finds an epigraph (commemorating the restoration, by Emperor Caracalla, of an altar devoted to Circe)

and two inscriptions bearing witness to the restoration work done at the behest of Theodoric[39] along the nineteen-mile tract, showing that the Appian Way was still in use in his time.

Finally, another item to be found in the Casale is the tombstone of Clesippus Geganius.[40] As Pliny tells us,[41] he was a slave of Eastern origin who lived in the Republican era, so misshapen that he was bought by a Roman matron, Gegania, to serve as a buffoon. He was ultimately set free, however, and became rich thanks to the same Gegania, who had fallen in love with him.

The mausoleum that precedes Casale di Mesa has for this reason been attributed to Clesippus, though without any certainty. It is a fine sepulcher, complex in structure: A circular element rests on a

Above: Terracina Cathedral, built in the early Middle Ages over the ruins of the Major Temple of the Emilian Forum. In the town's present-day Piazza del Municipio, a stretch of the Appian Way that once passed through the forum is still preserved.

Facing page: Detail of Terracina Cathedral.

quadrangular base, and inside it is a square, stepped tower. The area between the base and the inner circle forms a four-pointed star motif.[42]

Near Terracina, under the cliffs of Leano, at the end of the navigable canal, by clearwater springs, once stood the sanctuary devoted to the very ancient cult—widespread in central Italy—of the goddess Feronia, who guaranteed female fertility and natural bounty.[43] The poet Virgil calls her "*mater*,"[44] who here "rejoices in the green woods."[45]

At this point the Appian Way rounds the cliff and extends along a straightaway that was also the axis for the Roman division of these agrarian lands into plots, the traces of which can still be clearly discerned. The road here is once again lined by the ruins of tombs, some of them noteworthy. It continues on to Terracina, where the vista suddenly opens onto the Sinus Amyclanus, the modern Gulf of Gaeta.

## From Terracina to Benevento, By Way of Capua

*[T]he rocky perch of Terracina [looked] all the more desirable, and presently we saw the sea before us. . . . We had the sea on our right for a time, but the limestone hills close on our left remained unbroken. They are a continuation of the Apennines and run down from Tivoli till they reach the sea from which they have been separated, first by the Campagna di Roma, then by the extinct volcanoes of Frascati, Albano and Velletri, and finally by the Pontine Marshes.*

J. Wolfgang von Goethe, "Italian Journey"[46]

Terracina well deserves the name of "Thermopylae of Italy" for its strategic location. It stands at the point where the Ausoni Mountains, reaching the shore, divide the Pontine Plain, which we are now leaving behind, from the Fondi Plain.

Although Rome already controlled this area by the end of the sixth century B.C., the Volsci, in the fifth century, turned Terracina into their own stronghold, calling it Anxur. In 329 B.C., however, it became Roman once and for all, under the name of Colonia Anxuriana, and its citizens were enrolled in the Oufentine tribe.

After suffering a defeat at the hands of the Samnites in 315 B.C., at the battle of Lautulae, a mountain pass upriver from Terracina, the Romans regrouped the following year and thereafter asserted

their uncontested supremacy. From this time on, the city, like Minturnae, would enjoy a long period of social and economic splendor, most of it due to the export of its famous local wine, the Caecubum.

During this period the city was called Tarracina, a name that certain historians have seen as indicative of an Etruscan influence, though this is not supported by any solid archaeological evidence. In 217 B.C., Hannibal found his march toward Rome blocked at the abovementioned passage of Lautulae.

The Appian Way was of great importance in the geographical context of the area. Just outside of Terracina, the road forked: one branch went into the city, the other headed up toward the Monte S. Angelo before descending once again toward the sea at Fondi.

An important further modification of the road was the cut made in the Pisco Montano at the behest of Trajan. This resolved the problem of the coastal route, which had been blocked by the rocky spur. To get around the impassable height, a less invasive solution, reached in 184 B.C., had been to run another Roman road, the Via Flacca, along a dike in the sea.

Tarracina witnessed a period of intense building at the time of the war between Marius and Sulla. The latter, upon conquering the city, played an active role in its rebuilding.

The construction of the Emilian Forum, built for Aulus Aemilius,[47] dates from this period. A large part of its original flooring survives, cut in half by the passage of the Via Appia, which served as *decumanus*. A fine stretch of it is still preserved. The square known today as Piazza del Municipio once featured such monuments as the major temple, identifiable perhaps as the Capitolum or the Temple of Rome and Augustus. The splendid Romanesque cathedral, by being built on top of it, has helped to preserve it, protecting it from abandon and ruin.

Another important public edifice was the theater, which had a splendid natural backdrop, the sight of the Monte Circeo in the background.

Even in its medieval phase, Terracina—first the property of the Frangipane (great builders of fortifications), then of the Annibaldi—was prolific in its production of artistic monuments. The finest example of these is perhaps the abovementioned cathedral, consecrated in 1074 and devoted to

S. Cesareo. One cannot help but admire, inside the church, the paschal candelabrum, the ambo and the flooring, all excellent examples of Cosmati work.

Leaving the town behind, and traveling the stretch of road that ascends toward the Monte Sant'Angelo, we arrive at the famous sanctuary. From here one is dazzled by the extraordinary panorama, which to one side gives onto the Pontine Plain and the Monte Circeo, on the other, onto the Fondi Plain.

The sanctuary is surrounded by a defensive wall, characteristically white, built to keep Sulla from advancing onto Rome. The whole complex consisted of two buildings for worship, the more ancient of the two being dedicated to the goddess Feronia, who was also venerated at the sanctuary near the Leano cliffs. The Monastery of St. Michael the Archangel was built on top of this temple.

The sanctuary, like many others built in areas of uneven terrain, was constructed on a number of terraces incorporating powerful substructures. What

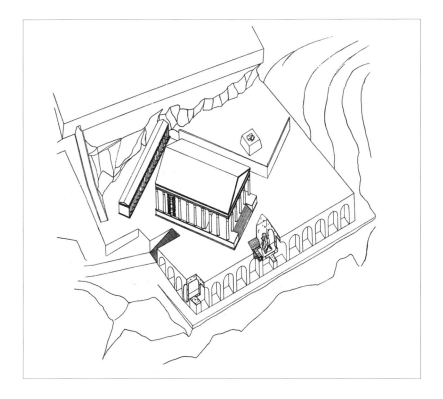

*Facing page: The so-called Sanctuary of Jupiter Anxur, at the top of Monte Sant'Angelo. The twelve powerful, pillared arches constituted the base of the former sanctuary.*

*Above: Reconstruction drawing of the Sanctuary of Jupiter Anxur.*

*Right: Cryptoportico of the Sanctuary of Jupiter Anxur.*

*On page 128, top: View of the Fondi Plain from the Sanctuary of Jupiter Anxur.*

*On page 128, bottom, and page 129: The massive artificial cut in the Pisco Montano allowed the Appian Way to run along the shoreline. Figures carved into the rock-face indicate the height of the stone removed.*

remains of these are the arcades and porticoes, which make for a very charming visit. Above these terraces usually stood the place of worship, one or two temples devoted to the deity worshiped in the sanctuary. In the case of Terracina, the major temple—the more important one—has been erroneously attributed to Jupiter Anxur, known as the principle god and the city's protector. We do know there must have been a temple dedicated to him near the Acropolis. This god was worshiped in his beardless, adolescent aspect, as would seem clear from the attribute of *Anxurus*, which in Greek means "not needing to shave."[48]

Recent studies and discoveries of votive objects, however, make it possible, with near certainty, to attribute the temple to the cult of Venus,[49] which grew up alongside the original, more ancient cult of Feronia and eventually replaced it. The cult of Venus was Sullan and was linked to commerce, the production of the famous local wine, and the activity of the port below.

We shall now go back to the other stretch of the Appian Way that includes the cut of the Pisco Montano. It is an impressive feat of engineering, at least 120 feet high (about 36 meters), according to the figures carved directly into the rock face.

The project is normally attributed to the emperor Trajan, who we know devoted a great deal of attention to work on the Appian Way. But in recent times his paternity has been cast into doubt, in favor of two alternative hypotheses. The first theorizes that it was part of Nero's attempt to build the famous canal that was supposed to link Rome and Puteoli (modern Pozzuoli), a town that served Rome as a port.[50] The second hypothesis dates the cut to around the period of the war against Sextus Pompeius (41–36 B.C.).[51]

After leaving Terracina we come to the Tower of the Epitaph, which marks the historic boundary between the Papal States and the Kingdom of Naples. The tower gets its name from a nearby monument bearing an epigraph. Put there at the behest of the viceroy of Naples in 1568, the epigraph welcomes the foreigner and invites him to enter the kingdom with peaceful intentions.[52] A short distance away is La Portella, the roadblock at the border, consisting of two cylindrical towers joined by a portico, which the Appian Way passed under until 1933.

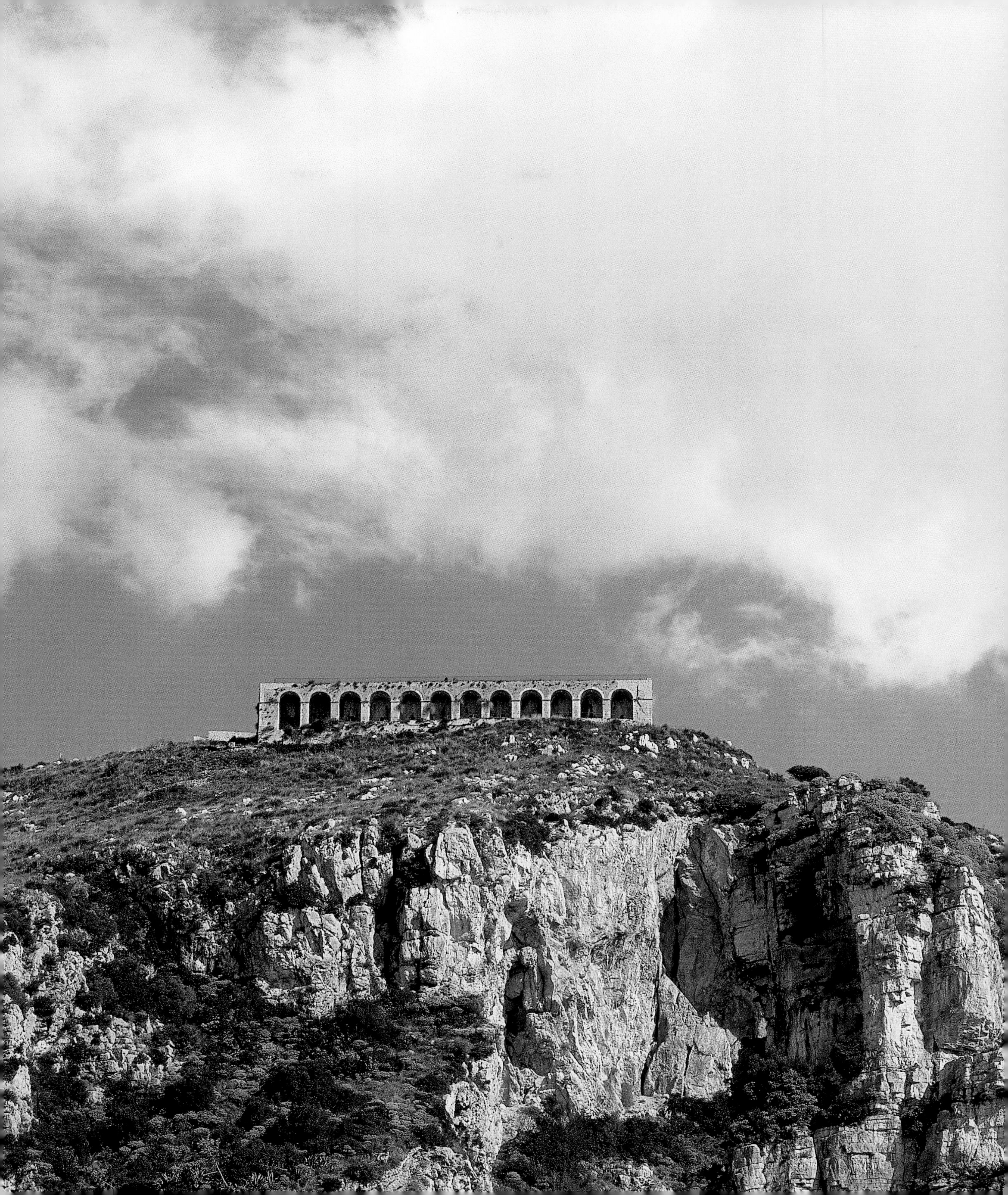

Hemmed in by the Ausoni and Aurunci mountains, the ancient city of Fundi (modern Fondi) stands just inside the marshy, unwholesome coastal area. Perhaps originally an Aurunci population center, then later definitely Volscian, it was recognized as *civitas sine suffragio* in 334 B.C., so that, as Livy tells us, "the road passing through its territories would be always safe and peaceful." In all probability, he was referring to the nearby passage of the Appian Way.

In 188 B.C., Roman citizenship was definitively granted to the residents of Fundi, which subsequently also became a *municipium*. Its territory soon became dotted with aristocratic villas, where Caecubum and Fundian wine was made.

Centuries later, in 846 A.D., the city was devastated by Saracens. Like all the other cities in the area, it then passed from one noble family to another, including the Caetani. They were responsible for the construction of the castle, which remains one of the city's most imposing buildings.

The arrangement of the urban fabric still preserves the Roman layout: the quadrangular perimeter of walls embraces the entire city, which was divided and serviced by a street system based on two major axes, the *cardo maximus* and the *decumanus maximus*, the latter consisting of the Appian Way itself.

And thus we resume our journey along the Appian Way, heading inland into charming, secluded areas, to admire the archaeological vestiges near the Fosso di S. Andrea.[53]

Here, thanks to recent research and study conducted by Professor Lorenzo Quilici,[54] grand polygonal structures and stretches of road have reemerged from the past, along with small rest areas and clearing stations, some of which may date all the way back to the time of Appius Claudius Caecus, and others at least to the time of Nerva and Caracalla.

A spectacular work of terracing on five levels, in *opus incertum* and *opus polygonium*,[55] represents the most sensational discovery. This was once a sanctu-

ary of Apollo, one that must be numbered among the most important in Latium, together with the Sanctuary of Jupiter Anxur in Terracina, that of Hercules at Tivoli, and that of Fortuna Primigenia at Palestrina. Joined to each terrace are reception rooms and, underground, no less than twenty-one cisterns.

Over the centuries, on top of the temple—of which, unfortunately, very little remains—there rose an early Christian church and the Fortino di S. Andrea. The road underwent restorations in the 1500s[56] and, more importantly, in 1767–68, under Ferdinand IV, when ancient paving stones were reused to build rest areas, and new milestones were erected on elegant little columns.

Let us hope that this spot in the National Park of the Monti Aurunci, so rich in historical, archaeological, and natural importance, and yet unknown to most, can be used to its best advantage and protected for the future.[57] It is a splendid illustration of how a monument gains value by being set in as broad a cultural and natural context as possible, as an example and part of the area's civic and social

*Left: Stretch of the Appian Way, near the Fosso di S. Andrea.*

*Below: Sixteenth-century milestone created on the occasion of the restoration of the Appian Way near the Fosso di S. Andrea.*

development.[58] Another hope is that this area might become just one of several links in a far more extensive chain of parks, desired by many, that would stretch from Rome to Brindisi and include the entire Appian Way.

As we return to the population centers, we immediately pass through Itri, recognizable from afar by its medieval castle and its Gothic churches. Its name in all likelihood recalls its function (*iter*, "journey" or "trip")[59] as a junction of some very ancient routes, when the Aurunci controlled the area.

At this point in our wandering, we find ourselves at Mile 85 of the Appian Way. Along the road nearby is a sepulcher, consisting of a cylindrical element resting on a paralellepidal base, as is often the case.

It is unlikely—since there is no archaeological proof—that this is the tomb of Marcus Tullius Cicero, the famous orator and politician, who was beheaded by the assassins of Antonius on December 7, 43 B.C. But the tradition is now so deeply rooted that one takes a certain pleasure in

believing that the body of that rhetorician, one of the major figures of the last phase of republican Rome's troubled history, lies here.

Here are the last moments of his life, and a portrait of his character, as recounted by Livy:

*[H]e was disgusted with fleeing and with life itself. As he leaned out of the litter and craned his neck without a shudder, his head was severed. . . . They also cut off his hands, blaming them for having written against Antonius. The head was then brought to Antonius, and on his orders was displayed, together with the hands, on the rostra, the very place where he had inspired more admiration in his listeners than any other human voice had ever done before. He could not bear any adversity like a man, except death; . . . at the hands of the victorious enemy he did not have to suffer anything more cruel than he himself would have been capable of doing, had he been able to attain the same success. But if we wish to counterbalance flaws with virtues, then we must acknowledge that he was a magnanimous man, quick, and worthy of eternal remembrance, so much*

so that to celebrate his merits would require the elo-
quence of another Cicero.[60]

A short distance away there is another tomb that
the same tradition, with equal plausibility, claims is
that of Tulliola, Cicero's daughter.

Let us now resume our journey and continue on
toward Formia (ancient Formiae). Before reaching
the town, we notice a fine public drinking-fountain
from the late Republican era, in excellent condition, whose waters have refreshed wayfarers along
the Appian Way for many centuries.

Formia also boasts ancient and mythic origins,
owing on the one hand to a legend maintaining
that the Laestrygonians, of Homeric memory, had
their base here, and on the other hand, to a tradition claiming that it was founded by the Spartans.

It came into being as a center of the Aurunci,
another of the Italic populations living in Latium
in the early days. By the fifth century B.C., it had
become a Volscian center.

In 338 B.C., as is well known, Formiae fell under
Rome's control, and its inhabitants acquired full citizenship in 188 B.C. Its port, long an important
place of commercial activity,[61] suffered severe dam-
age, like the port of Minturnae, at the hands of
Cilician pirates. The city also suffered incursions
from forces led by Pompey (Pompeius Magnus) in
67 B.C., and, following the internecine struggles
that erupted in Rome after the assassination of
Caesar in 44 B.C., was sacked from 41 to 38 B.C. by
Sextus Pompeius, Pompey's son.

Nevertheless, Formiae was chosen, like nearby
Gaeta, as the privileged site of many villas of the
late-Republican and Imperial eras. Roman notables
would spend their summers there, as the heat
became intolerable in the city.[62]

The most notable example of this genre of villa
is the building preserved within the Villa Rubino,
identified by some as the residence that Cicero
kept in these parts. Built on three terraces, it looked
out over the gulf and had many different environ-
ments, including a vivarium, two nymphaea, a private dock, and perhaps a warehouse.

A foretaste of ancient Minturnae is announced
by the 150 majestic arches of the aqueduct built

*The so-called tomb of Marcus
Tullius Cicero near Formia.*

*On pages 134–35: The town
of Minturno, preceded by the
150 arches of the Roman
aqueduct.*

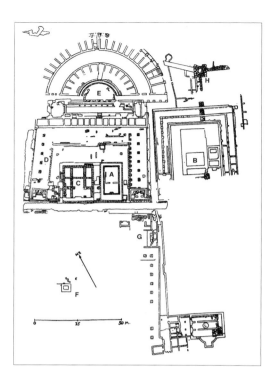

*Plan of the area of the forum and theater in ancient Minturnae: a) Temple A; b) Temple B; c) Temple of Jupiter; d) double portico; e) theater; f) central area of the forum; g) schola of the forum; h) castrum tower; i) building near forum.*

*Below: A stretch of the Appian Way in the archaeological area of Minturno. The road used to pass through the ancient city and served as its decumanus.*

between the end of the Republic and the beginning of the Empire. About eleven miles long, it is a fine example of *opus reticulatum*, a construction technique using small pyramid-shaped blocks of tufa set in a core of *opus caementicum*, which creates a play of chromatic alternation between the calcareous whiteness and the darkness of the tufa, framed by pilasters in *opus quadratum*.

The most ancient population of Minturnae is said to have been now Ausonian, now Auruncian. The Aurunci, after allying themselves with the Samnites and being defeated by Rome in 314 B.C., suffered very severe repression at the hands of the Romans for having taken the wrong side. Minturnae, thus subdued by Rome, became a colony in 296 B.C.

Certainly its position, from the late pre-Roman era onward,[63] was strategically important: It stood at the mouth of the ancient Liris, a good landing spot and also an outlet for the inland roads hooking up with the coastal route that was later retraced by the Appian Way.

The Roman *castrum*, in any event, was not built on the site of the preceding Auruncian center. The latter must have coincided rather with the medieval and modern city of Minturno, located further inland in a more defensible position.

The Via Appia Antica, after it entered the town through the Porta Gemina,[64] constituted the *decumanus* of the urban street system. On one side of the street one still finds the Republican forum, the Capitolium (dedicated to the triad of Jupiter, Juno, and Minerva), and the principal temples (the Republican Temple A as well as Temples B and C).

Gravitating to the other side were the *macellum* (market), behind which there is a large bathing complex, and the *tabernae*, meeting places where day-to-day commercial and social activities took place.[65]

The shiny, curved pavement and the perfectly preserved roadbed accompany us on our visit. This is one of the most stirring points along the route that runs all the way to Brindisi. It leaves an indelible memory in the eyes of the soul.

The theater, built at the end of the Republican era or the beginning of the Empire, looms a bit further on. It held up to 4,500 spectators, arrayed on the steps according to their social and civil status, protected from rain and sun by the *velarium* (awning) that extended over the entire auditorium.

Minturnae then began to die a slow death until it was definitively abandoned in 580 A.D., probably when the Lombards cut off the aqueduct. The inhabitants then moved to safer places in the hills nearby, and the new center took on the name of Traetto, named after the *traghetto*, or ferry, allowing passage to the opposite bank of the Liri River.[66] In the Roman era, the river was spanned by the Pons Tirenus, as Cicero tells us.[67]

In 915 A.D., the Battle of Garigliano was fought near the ancient city. It led to the victory of the Christian League, under Pope John X, over the Saracens, who until then had been terrorizing and devastating the surrounding area with their raids.

Let us now go into the medieval center of Minturno, which didn't get back its ancient name until 1879. Let us enter, if only briefly, the Cathedral of S. Pietro. We cannot help but stop for a moment, enraptured by two masterpieces created by the hands of Cosmati artists: the paschal candelabrum,[68] and the ambo,[69] both geometrically embroidered with thousands of little tesserae.

Then, leaving behind the sites of ancient as well as medieval Minturno, and wandering off the main road, we find ourselves in a place called Le Grotte ("The Caves"), at the Sanctuary of the Goddess Marica.[70] The site was dedicated to a very ancient cult, documented as early as the seventh and sixth centuries B.C., continued by the Romans until the second century A.D., and perhaps converted by them into the Egyptian cult of Isis and Serapis.

This marshy spot was deep in a sacred wood where the goddess, a nymph, was honored. Marica was an Oscan-Sabellian deity, but known to the Aurunci as well. Her simple, ancient Italic temple of tufa was frequented by shepherds and peasants, whereas her Roman temple attracted sailors and navigators when they returned safely to the river-port after a dangerous sea voyage. The wood served as a hiding place for Marius in his flight from Sulla, enabling him to arrive safely in Africa.[71] For centuries the river's silt was full of coins, tossed there to propitiate the goddess and ensure safety.

*The Roman theater of Minturnae, built in the late Republican era or at the beginning of the Empire.*

The deity's name derives from *mare*, the Latin word for sea, and her identity includes elements of both light and water, as well as fertility and life.[72] Because of these attributes, the cult of the goddess Marica has been likened to that of Diana-Artemis, Marine Venus, and Ino-Leucothea. She was included in an unusual triad with Leucothea (the "white goddess) and the Mater Matuta ("mother of the morning") whom Lucretius defined as "Matuta, goddess of fertility, the dawn, life and nature."[73]

Mater Matuta is an Italic deity, well deserving of this expressive, tender name because of her bond with the fertility of the earth, animals, and the human race, through birth and procreation. All ancient cultures, in fact, turned their devotions to a female deity as protectress of nature and therefore, most importantly, of mothers.

She is Potnia Theròn, mistress of Mycenean wild beasts; she is the Greek Hera; she is the Latin goddess Feronia, whom we've already met on our itinerary. But she is also the Eastern Cybele, and the Roman Magna Mater (Great Mother).

From the sixth to the first centuries B.C., the Italic women of the Campania region used to dedicate effigies of mothers with many newborns. These were tokens of thanks for divine benevolence, offered to the Mater Matuta of Capua, the fundamental goddess of the early cults. The precious, unique, and at the same time modest Museo Campano[74] of Capua has a collection of tufa sculptures representing mothers devoted to the goddess Matuta, hugging babes in swaddling clothes to their fertile breasts. They are ex-votos thanking their protectress in an often-spare figurative language.

All these statues were found in 1845, near ancient Capua, at a place called Petrara. They bear witness to how deeply rooted this cult was in the region. Women about to give birth would bring the sculptures to this holy place, to thank the goddess for a fertile pregnancy. Also found was a lone statue of a woman holding a pomegranate in one hand and a dove in the other, symbols of life, fecundity, and peace. It most likely represents the goddess herself.

Leaving the museum, we may now wander about the present-day town of Capua, the ancient Casilinum,[75] terminus of the homonymous medieval road, the Via Casilina, which retraced the more ancient route of the Latin and Roman Via Latina.

*Left: The Roman amphitheater at S. Maria Capua Vetere, second only to the Colosseum in size.*

*Below: Underground passages of the amphitheater at S. Maria Capua Vetere.*

Here, at the bridge over the Volturno River, the Via Casilina intersected with the Via Appia.

We enter the town through the once-monumental Porta Capua, protected by two powerful cylindrical towers in rusticated marble, erected by Frederick II in 1239. Ancient vestiges bearing witness to medieval Capua's inheritance of its Roman past are displayed along the roads, on the facades of the old palazzi, and in the squares.

Now we come at last to S. Maria Capua Vetere, the town corresponding to ancient Capua, after 132 miles (196 km) of intense travel. It marks the end of the Appian Way built by Appius Claudius Caecus, the terminus of the route designed in 312 B.C.

At this point the road met back up with the Via Latina, while the Via Popilia set out southward, all the way to Reggio by way of Nola, Nuceria, and Salernum in Campanian territory.

At the entrance to S. Maria Capua Vetere, whose name recalls its ancient origins, we are greeted by the Arch of Hadrian (117–138), which unfortunately has lost much of its majesty over the centuries.

During its long history, ancient Capua took on several different identities. Geographically, it is situated in what was considered a very fertile area. The ancient authors, Virgil among them, considered Campania's agricultural production nothing short of miraculous.

Capua, the principal population center of ancient Campania, appears to have been founded in the ninth century B.C., according to an assertion made by Velleius Paterculus. Born, in fact, as an Oscan center (its name was Latinized to Volturnum), it was considered an Etruscan city in the sixth century B.C.[76] It fell to the Samnites in 438, and finally, in 343 B.C., it appealed to Rome for help.

After the famous battle of Cannae in 216 B.C., during the Second Punic War, the city was taken by Pacuvius and Vibius Virius, who had rebelled against Rome, and turned over to Hannibal. The latter was happy to remain in the city, which famously offered him the possibility of a life of leisure. Indeed, Capua was celebrated, sometimes excessively so, for being a rich, opulent city.

The city paid a high price for its support of the Carthaginian leader. In 211, it fell definitively into Rome's hands. The Romans decided to deprive the city of all education and all political authority, with the exception of religion and the priesthood, and it was reduced to a way station and a farmer's market. These measures, however, did not succeed in negating Capua's identity and did not cause any decline in its economic development. Indeed the center enjoyed a long period of splendor. Its commercial production distinguished itself above all for its wine, Falernus, the most renowned in Roman circles.

The city was recognized as one of the most important in ancient Italy. Historian Titus Livy called it "the greatest, most opulent city in Italy," while Cicero dubbed it "the other Rome." While monuments from other time periods are few, Capua's ancient stature is attested by the presence of important monuments from antiquity, such as the two forums, two theaters, a Mithraeum,[77] and an amphitheater.

The fame of the latter is perpetuated by its perfect state of preservation, which is rivaled only by the Flavian Amphitheater in Rome. Built between the end of the first and the beginning of the second centuries A.D., it is a four-storied building measuring 46 meters tall, 165 meters long along its major axis, 135 meters along the minor, with 80 arches and a *velarium*. The latter was maneuvered by sailors from the Cape Misenus fleet, who performed the same function at the Colosseum in Rome.

Spectacular competitions between men and beasts, and between gladiators trained at the amphitheater's school, were held in this grandiose arena, before tens of thousands of spectators thirsty for bloody sports. The sand spread over the ground absorbed both the blood of the injured and the sounds of the struggle.

It was in this amphitheater's famous school that Spartacus, the Thracian gladiator-slave, received his instruction, before heading out from Capua in 73 B.C. to mount one of the most famous rebellions in human history.[78] He was followed, in what is proving increasingly to have been an organized undertaking, by a throng of tens of thousands (some say 30,000,[79] others as many as 70,000[80]) that included gladiators, slaves, but also freedmen, of the most diverse origins. They came from many cities to protest social conditions that had become unbearable.

In its early phases, the importance of the phenomenon was underestimated. The Roman army, under the leadership of Marcus Licinius Crassus, met the rebellion head on, as some of Spartacus's

followers were beginning to defect from its initial purpose and unity was breaking down.

Spartacus got as far as Reggio Calabria with most of his army, who defended themselves fiercely. He then went on to Lucania (today southern Calabria and Basilicata), where he died a hero's death on the field of battle in 71 B.C. Ancient sources number the dead at 60,000, but those who managed to flee suffered an even crueler, more ignoble fate. Six thousand of them were crucified and exposed in their torment along the entire stretch of the Appian Way from Rome to Capua, as a warning of the just punishment meted out to the fomenters of this *bellum servile*.

It is one of the few historic moments in which the Via Appia has been the dark witness of massacre and bloody deeds. This eternal road, scene of trade and commerce, the flow of ideas, expansionist ambitions, and pilgrimages, became the sad, unwilling stage of cruel death.

Just outside the walls of ancient Capua there is another monument, the Carceri Vecchie (Old Prisons), whose name accords with the tradition that the gladiators were locked up here. In fact it is a sepulcher, the largest in Campania, dated first century A.D.[81] It is circular in form, adorned with half-columns, blind arches, and a chromatic alternation of light and dark bands.

A bit further on is another funerary monument of the same period, symbol of ancient Capua: the Conocchia, or "distaff," tapered in shape, with alternating protuberances and recesses, concavities and convexities, which create a pleasant play of architectural forms. On the facade, commemorating the restoration work commissioned by the king of Naples (1751–1825), is the inscription "King

*Right: The Arch of Hadrian, which marked the entrance of the Via Appia into ancient Capua, the modern-day town of S. Maria Capua Vetere.*

*Below: The so-called Old Prisons (Carceres), where, according to tradition, the gladiators were housed.*

*Facing page: The tomb called the "Conocchia" ("distaff") at the side of the Appian Way on the way out of S. Maria Capua Vetere.*

Ferdinand IV, father of his country, restored me, a surviving structure of antiquity, when I was crumbling from old age and on the point of ruin, reinforcing me from the foundations on up."

At this point we leave S. Maria Capua Vetere behind us, continuing on our way along the Via Appia to Benevento, which now lies near.

Heading further inland, we reach the narrow valley of Caudium, in the vicinity of modern Arpaia. It was the unhappy scene of one of the most embarrassing episodes in Roman military history. It was here that the soldiers of consuls Sp. Postumius Albinus and T. Veturius Caudinus, after being defeated by the Samnites, were forced to file through the Caudine Forks (Furculae Caudine) of eternal and iniquitous memory. This was in 321 B.C., in the thick of the Second Samnite War (326–304 B.C.). Montesarchio and its castle now dominate the scene in the background. In far more ancient times, it was the Samnites, a proud and often unconquerable people, who dominated.

Along the route, there used to be three bridges to cross—the Tufara, the Apollosa, and the Corvo. These are now destroyed.[82]

The city of Benevento is just down the road.

## Notes

1. This term refers to the part of Latium that Rome, in this period, added (*adiectum* means "added") to the more ancient Latium Vetus. The exact boundaries are hard to determine, since they varied over time and even in the indications given by the ancient authors.
2. A nineteen-mile stretch, also documented by the most ancient milestone, which was found near the Casale di Mesa.
3. Cora, Norba, and Setia.
4. Quoted in S. Bruni, *Via Appia: Sulle ruine della magnificenza antica*, exh. cat. (Rome: Fondazione Memmo, 1997).
5. As J. Coste pointed out, "La Via Appia nel Medio Evo e l'incastellamento," *Archeologia Laziale* 10, no. 1 (1990), pp. 127–37, the "foothills" route was not the only medieval route, as is commonly asserted. There was another that passed halfway up the slopes of the Monti Lepini. And it is more precise to say that in the Middle Ages, the Appian Way was more a "direction" than a specific, well-defined route.
6. Founder of Tivoli. Cori was also held to be the foundation of Alba Longa.
7. The period when the colony was founded.
8. Based on the building techniques used, these should be dated sometime after the walls of the city.
9. So called because the road headed toward Ninfa.
10. Based on the typologies of materials found in a deposit of votive objects.
11. This dating, too, was based on a deposit of votive objects connected to the temple.
12. The date is almost certainly confirmed by the inscription over the door of the temple chamber, which names the *duoviri* who oversaw the construction, Marus Matlius and Lucius Turpilius.
13. The present bell tower, which replaced the medieval one, is from 1842, and is the only surviving element of the cathedral.
14. Pliny *Naturalis Historia* 3.57.
15. It was passed from the Frangipane to the Ceccano, then, in 1230, to the Annibaldi and after that, to the Caetani.
16. Gelasio's work was carried on by Roffredo and by his wife Marguerite Chapin. When Lelia, the last of the Caetani family, died in 1977, Ninfa was donated to the Fondazione Roffredo Caetani at the behest of Lelia and her husband Hubert Howard. The foundation still oversees the site, with the collaboration of the WWF [World Wildlife Fund].
17. Especially the Volsci of Privernum.
18. Pliny *Naturalis historia* 3.68
19. The cross was discovered during early twentieth-century restorations.
20. The cloister itself has undergone restoration, but more recently, in 1959–62.
21. *The Aeneid of Virgil* (7.1094–1100), trans. John Dryden (New York: Macmillan, 1965), p. 245.
22. Today called the Uffente.
23. Another mosaic with scenes of the Nile is in the Museo di Palestrina, from the Roman town of Praeneste.
24. His relics remained a long time at Fossanova. Later they were taken to Fondi, and finally to Toulouse, on the orders of Pope Urban V.
25. In 1812 it was used as a stable; in 1825, Leo XII gave it to the Carthusians of Trisulti.
26. There are a few traces of frescoes.
27. According to Lorenzo Quilici, *La Via Appia dalla Pianura Pontina a Brindisi* (Rome: Fratelli Palombi, 1989).
28. The bridge is that of the River Ninfa, mentioned below. See *Sulla Via Appia da Roma a Brindisi: Le fotografie di Thomas Ashby, 1891–1925*, exh. cat.
29. *CIL* X.6820, 6837. They stand in front of the church of S. Paolo, also built by Pius VI.
30. *CIL* X.6819.
31. From Tripontium to Forum Appii.
32. The modern-day Borgo Faiti.
33. 1.5.3–24. Trans. Jacob Fuchs, in *Horace's Satires and Epistles* (New York: W. W. Norton, 1977), pp. 12–13.
34. *CIL* X.6833, 6835.
35. Nerva paved this stretch, which was initially covered with gravel, for four miles; Trajan then paved the Decennovium. Caracalla paved it past Fondi for 21 miles, in 216 A.D. (G. Uggeri, "La Via Appia nella politica espansionistica di Roma," pp. 21–28).
36. *CIL* I2, 21 and p. 718; X.6838 and p. 1019; *ILS* 5801; *ILLRP* 448.
37. The P stands perhaps for Pulcher, consul in 249 B.C.
38. Perhaps Pacilus, consul in 251 B.C.; the milestone can perhaps be dated 255 or 253 B.C. (see Uggeri, "La Via Appia nella politica espansionistica di Roma," pp. 21–28). *CIL* I2, 21 and p. 718; X.6838 and p. 1019; *ILS* 5801; *ILLRP* 448.
39. *CIL* X.6850 and 6851.
40. *CIL* X.6488.
41. Pliny *Naturalis historia* 34.11–12.
42. Because of this typology, which may have been cone-shaped on top, the sepulcher was called the Trullo ad Medias in medieval documents.
43. The Lucus Feroniae, a sacred wood near Fiano Romano in Latium, were also devoted to this goddess.
44. *Aeneid* 7.564.
45. *Aeneid* 8.800.
46. Goethe, "Italian Journey" (February 23, 1787), pp. 559–60.
47. See Maria Rosaria Coppola, *Terracina: Il foro emiliano*, exh. cat., Comune di Terracina (Rome: Quasar, 1986).

48  Absorbed into the Greek language with this meaning, the term is originally Volscian.

49  The Temple of Jupiter Anxur was therefore located elsewhere, probably inside the city.

50  This view is shared by Federico Zevi.

51  F. Coarelli, "La costruzione del Porto di Terracina in un rilievo storico tardo-repubblicano," in *Revixit ars* (Rome, 1996), pp. 434–54.

52  The text of the epigraph reads as follows: "Hospes hic sunt fines regni Nea(polis)/si amicus advenis/pacata omnia invenies/et malis moribus pulsis bonas leges/MDLXVIII."

53  It gets its name from the small fort built in the late eighteenth century by the brigand Fra' Diavolo.

54  See Lorenzo Quilici, "La Via Appia attraverso la Gola di Itri," in *Le vie romane nel Lazio e nel mediterraneo*, Atti della Giornata di Studio (Rome, 28 May 2001).

55  Ranging 5 to 12 m in height, with a length of 125 m and a breadth of 60.

56  At the behest of the duke of Alcalà, Viceroy of Naples.

57  The archaeological area was expected to open in spring 2003.

58  The contributions and sensitivity of the municipal administration of Itri and the Lazio Region are noteworthy in this regard.

59  Others believe the etymology is to be found in the former presence of a Mithraeum on the site.

60  Handed down to us by Seneca the Elder; see Ettore Paratore, *Storia delle letteratura latina* (Florence: Sansoni, 1986), pp. 229–30.

61  The Gulf of Gaeta, dominated by Formia in antiquity, was in fact called Formianus Sinus.

62  Noteworthy are the villa and mausoleum of Munantius Plancus at Gaeta, and the vestiges of a villa near Gianola.

63  Unfortunately there is no known testimony from this period.

64  Also called Porta Roma and Porta Appia. It was called Porta Gemina because it had two openings.

65  As Cato recalls in his treatise on agriculture, Minturnae was an important market center for clothing and metal farm implements.

66  In 1828–32 the famous "Bourbon bridge" (Ponte Borbonico) was built, a work of avant-garde engineering that shows some of the Egyptianizing taste of the time. It was destroyed by the Germans in World War II.

67  Pons Tirenus or Tiretius. Cicero *Epistulae ad Atticum* 16.13.1.

68  Made in 1264 by Peregrino da Sessa.

69  Made in 1260, and remodeled in 1618.

70  M. T. D'Urso, *Il tempio della Dea Marica alla foce del Garigliano*, vol. 1 (Scauri, 1985).

71  Plutarch *Marius* 37–40.

72  Another theory as to the etymology of the name of Marica suggests a derivation from *Maro, Marus,*

*Marius, Maros,* etymon of the Italo-Etruscan magistrature of *Marones* and *Maronatus.*

73  Lucretius *De rerum naturae* 5.656–57.

74  Located in the historic Palazzo Antignano.

75  A garrison from Praeneste and Perusia heroically defended itself here against Hannibal in 216–215 B.C.

76  One of the most important of the very rare epigraphic texts in the Etruscan language, the famous tile of Capua, confirms this.

77  It is one of the best preserved of all Mithraea. In the back is a fresco of the taurochthony.

78  For Spartacus's origins, and for more general information on the historic event, see *Sangue e arena*, ed. Adriano La Regina, exh. cat., Roman Colosseum, 2001–2 (Milan: Electa, 2001).

79  Orosius 5.24.2.

80  Appian *Bella civilia* 1.116.

81  Probably the second half of the century.

82  They were destroyed by German troops during World War II, in 1943.

# From Benevento to Brindisi

IVANA DELLA PORTELLA

*Above and facing page: Ponte Leproso, the bridge by which the Appian Way entered Beneventum.*

**Benevento**

On his interminable journey to Brindisi in the company of Heliodorus the philosopher and Virgil, Quintus Horatius Flaccus—better known to us as Horace—after passing through Caudium, headed on toward Beneventum. On this passage through the arid, treacherous land of the Samnites, what worried him wasn't so much his diplomatic mission as the various events that befell him. It was as if he could grasp, in the multiplicity of developments, the substance of human sentiment, distilling it in paraphrase.

On board the *rheda*,[1] a four-wheeled carriage of Gallic origin, he sees the harsh, wild Samnite countryside rolling past him, the olive trees, in their robust contortions, themselves lamenting the crude dryness of the land. It's a long, tiring road, exacerbated by the clouds of dust and the infernal racket kicked up by the wheels over the paving stones. In the hard, dizzying monotony of it all, the journey seems endless.

Horace, however, lingers over that desolate, sirocco-burnt landscape, to reflect—with his unquestionable sagacity, or better yet, his *curiosa felicitas*—on the meaning of things and the route he has been traveling. Every episode, even the most apparently irrelevant, is sublimated in the clarity of the poetic experience, including his subtly captivating erotic anxiety.

*From here on, Apulia starts to display some mountains familiar to me, those with the sirocco parches, and which we would never have crawled over if near Trevicum a farm hadn't given us a reception, including teary smoke from wet branches and leaves smoldering in the fire. Here, utter moron that I am, I lie awake til midnight waiting for a liar of a girl who never came. Sleep takes me in the middle of a fantasy and my dreams are so real that I make a mess on my clothes and on my belly.*[2]

Far less comfortable in those days than now, such journeys proceeded along the consular roads at a fast pace from one *mansio* to another. The

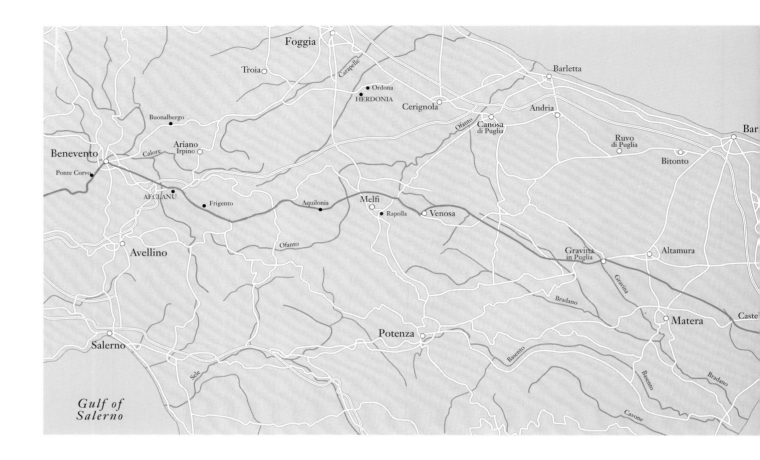

Map showing the route of the
Appian Way from Benevento
to Brindisi.

*mansiones* were stopping places, well equipped and
well managed, located for the most part a distance
of ten to forty kilometers from one another. They
afforded weary travelers rest and refreshment and
were furnished with inns (*cauponae*) and baths,
changes of horses, and anything else that might give
physical and mental comfort to travelers.

Innkeepers, ruffians, and prostitutes were the
human backdrop of such places. Although in certain cases they attained the dignity of small and fully
equipped citadels of comfort, they were most often
ill-famed and dirty, frequented only by boorish,
drunk, and brawling types.

*Then we go straight to Beneventum, where a dili-*
*gent host nearly burns his place down while cooking*
*bony thrushes. For through his old kitchen a*
*vagrant flame veered, from a fallen volcano of logs,*

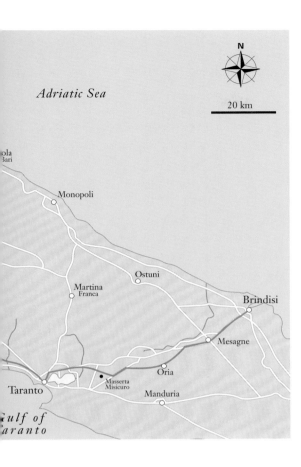

Adriatic Sea

20 km

*mounting high to lick the roof. Hungry guests, terrified slaves, snatch the food to safety, everyone tries to put the fire out—quite a scene.*[3]

Once he reached Naples, the Roman traveler, whether Italian or foreign, and later those from beyond the Alps, would go visit the Mefitis, and then proceed on muleback through the narrow passage of Arpaia, and shortly thereafter he could coast downhill to Benevento.[4]

The settlement had been called Maluentum, but the famously superstitious Romans, after defeating Pyrrhus in 275 B.C., immediately changed its name to Beneventum. It was a small Samnite center, peopled by sunburnt peasants, shepherds, simple folk who grazed their flocks on the snowy mountain slopes and cultivated grapevines with the knowledge they had gained from their fathers.

However, with the extension of the Appian Way through Beneventum, this city became a crucial transport hub of southern Italy and continued to expand until it became one of the main centers of the Empire, blossoming with trade and commerce. George Berkeley, Bishop of Cloyne and an early traveler to the region, described it cryptically in his journal:

*Beneventum situate on a rising ground. . . .
The country round it hill and dale various open. . . .
Streets paved with marble / many fragments of
antiquity in the walls of houses, friezes, architraves
&c broken / Amphitheatre the ruins of it consisting
of prodigious stones & brick work like those of Rome
and Capua tho not near so much remaining /
Cathedral clean & in good repair / Granite pillars
ten built supposedly on the foundation of an old temple; several fragments of the like pillars lying in the
streets.*[5]

One reached the city from the Leproso bridge,[6] which with its six majestic arches spanned the waters of the Sàbato River and led to the center of town.

Here one entered through the Port'Arsa, and along the way one saw the theater, the forum, the Iseum (temple of Isis), and other precious monuments.[7] Today it is hard to imagine the center of town as it was in antiquity, but it must certainly have been a beautiful city, noteworthy for its structure and fine architecture, as we can tell from the vestiges that have come down to us. Another early traveler, Luigi Vanvitelli, wrote:

*I saw this renowned city, and it is rather humble,
nor does it show any of the sovereignty in which it
lived for many centuries. It is situated on a small
hill in the middle of a valley entirely cultivated with
wheat, like the Roman Campagna, and therefore
entirely stripped of trees. Two rivers encircle it, the
Sabato and the Calore, but they are not navigable.
The nearby hills are somewhat covered in vegetation, but are hardly delightful. To get there the road
is unimaginably bad and one risks being overturned,
so uneven are the stones, with ascents and descents.
To give you an idea, it is twice as bad as the postal
road was from Otricoli to Narni before it was
repaired. Poor Via Appia! This is what passed*

*Right: Fresco depicting the Annunciation to St. Zacharias in the left side-apse of the Church of S. Sofia. The fragment, which dates from the ninth century, is one of the surviving elements of a fresco cycle devoted to the life of Christ.*

*Far right: Interior of the Church of S. Sofia in Benevento, where one may still admire the highly original architecture, one of the boldest and most imaginative structures of the early Middle Ages.*

*through Benevento toward Puglia. One sees three or four ancient Roman bridges over which one passes, and inside Benevento one sees an arch made for Trajan, which is exceedingly beautiful, full of very finely carved, indeed excellent bas-reliefs.*
*The barbarity of our age has had a city gate built within this splendid arch, and its walls have cut in half the bas-reliefs on the inside of the arch. It is a pity to see them so maltreated.[8]*

When the Lombards came out of the northern mists to this territory to found the greatest duchy in southern Italy, Paul the Deacon celebrated their achievement.

In all likelihood, when the first travelers of the Dark Ages journeyed along the already ancient paving stones of the Appian Way, they found not a tumbledown, decrepit road, but a comfortable, fascinating, if dangerous, thoroughfare. It was along this same road that Benedictine culture entered the Benevento area. And once there, it wanted to be known as "Beneventine" culture.

*Above: Romanesque lunette over the main portal of the Church of S. Sofia. The bas-relief shows Christ enthroned between the Virgin and St. Mercurius the Martyr, with a kneeling monk to the side, perhaps Abbot Giovanni IV, who restored the church in the twelfth century.*

*Facing page, and pages 154–55: The enchanting Romanesque cloister of the Church of S. Sofia. The capitals and pulvini of the columns are magnificently carved with plants and mythical animals.*

Bearing witness to the solidity and strength of this monastic culture is the splendid Church of S. Sofia and especially its adjoining monastery, center of one of the most famous *scriptoria* of the early Middle Ages.[9]

A central-plan structure of Lombard stamp, its sober, austere interior is cadenced by the stately, symbolic sequence of columns and pillars. It is a highly original weave, the fruit of an intriguing symbiosis between hexagonal and stellar structures which, in the nervous repetition of the centripetal and centrifugal forces produced, creates a sense of lucid disorientation.[10] "Out of the eighteenth-century shell emerges a Lombard church of odd shape," wrote Guido Piovene in his *Italian Journey* of 1956, "a star inside a circle, a decagon inside the star, a hexagon inside the decagon, with an altar at the center."[11]

Next to it, in the monastery proper, we find a dense alternation of four-light and three-light arches: the splendid Romanesque cloister (twelfth century), whose geometrical perfection echoes the medieval *hortus conclusus*. It is a cultural cross-roads that displays Lombard, Sicilian, and local influences, coming together in the rhythmical sequence of the sculptures and reliefs that adorn the pulvin capitals of the columns. They comprise a three-dimensional allegorical poem of great impact and beauty that depicts—in a disturbing medley of beasts, plants, and fantastical creatures—a wondrous universe expressing the eternal struggle between good and evil.

From here we move on to the Museo Provinciale del Sannio, whose collections are of great interest. The archaeological section contains a few finds from the era of Trajan, belonging to

Trajan's Arch. Two milestones from the Via Appia Traiana merit particular attention.

**From Benevento to Aeclanum**

Outside the city, the Appian Way ran through the Beneventine countryside all the way to the Mirabello Eclano pass. It's not well known, but its route is pretty much retraced by the current route, the State Route SS 7.[12]

The course is hemmed in by a landscape of hills, between tobacco plantations in flower and row upon row of vines and olive trees. The first known route of the Appia is along the Calore River, where between the cornstalks rise the scattered remains of the so-called Ponte Rotto ("Broken Bridge"),[13] a viaduct from the time of Hadrian[14] whose seven arches spanned the Calore and carried the Appian Way on toward Apulia.

At Mile 15, there was once the city of Aeclanum. In the ancient Antonine Itinerary, it is indeed located fifteen Roman miles from Beneventum, which explains its medieval name of Quintodecimo, a site confirmed in the *Tabula Peutingeriana*.

"We know nothing of the origins of Aeclanum," wrote F. M. Pratilli, another early wayfarer, in 1745. "But we do know that it was an ancient city, since we find mention of her in the historians I cited, and also in Cicero's letters to Atticus. It is to be surmised that [Aeclanum] suffered devastation and misfortune during the long and obstinate war of the Samnites against the Romans, and that afterward it kept itself in a state of middling good fortune with the passage of the Appian Way."[15]

An ancient Hirpinian center, crossroads of the transhumant routes, Aeclanum owed its fortune to its strategic position, fanned out over the natural

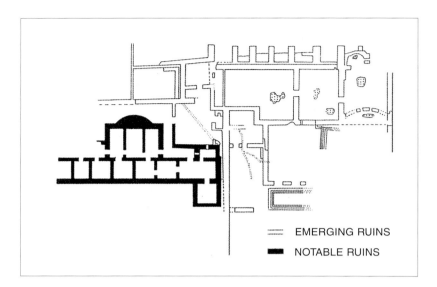

```
·····  EMERGING RUINS
■■■■  NOTABLE RUINS
```

*Above: Plan of the bath complex at Aeclanum.*

*Right: General view of the archaeological zone of Aeclanum. The population center rose up on a plateau through which the Via Appia passed; from here a byway set out, leading to the Via Appia Traiana at Herdonia.*

terracing that dominates the valley below as far as the Picentini Mountains. Excavations have demonstrated its prosperity, due mostly to commerce and trade that ranged across the entire central and southern basin.

Numerous roads, sheep-tracks, and mule paths led out from Aeclanum, following the natural routes, to which were eventually added the Appian Way from west to east, and the Via Herdonia, which headed to Herdonia (modern Ordona) in Apulia. One of the most important cities in Hirpinian Samnium, Aeclanum was occupied by Sulla in 89 B.C., during the Social War. According to Appian, he destroyed its wooden defensive walls by setting fire to them:

*Sulla moved the army toward another population, the Hirpinians, and attacked Aeclanum. The inhabitants, who had been waiting that very day for the Lucanians to come to their aid, asked Sulla for time to make up their minds. Sensing a trick, he granted them one hour, and in the meantime placed faggots of vine-twigs outside the city walls, which were made of wood. When the hour was up, he set fire to them. Terrorized, the people of Aeclanum surrendered the city, which Sulla then put to the sack for having given up not spontaneously, of its own will, but because it had been forced.*[16]

When it came under the dominion of Rome, Aeclanum was definitively given the status of *municipium*. Only in the second century A.D., under the emperor Hadrian, did it reach the height of its prosperity as a colony under the name of Aelelia Augusta Aeclanum. The most notable archaeological sites—the baths, the *macellum*, the forum—date in fact from this period.[17]

Excavations have made it possible to individuate the defensive wall, which follows the irregular unfolding of the upland plain in its own irregular fashion. One can easily make out the semicircular and square towers, and the three access gates.

what must have been the *macellum*, the covered market for foodstuffs.

As the social fulcrum of the ancient population center, the site—with its round central piazza paved in marble and the gushing fountain at the center—expresses the pride of what was certainly a minor city of Hirpinian Campania, but one that did not lack dignity and beauty. One can make out several different architectural phases in the excavated area, including the more external zone, in which one glimpses a few tokens of the later development of the center, such as the layout of an early Christian basilica, with a cross-bearing baptismal font beside it.

In the baths, one can recognize without difficulty the *calidarium* with *suspensurae*, the *laconicum*, the *tepidarium*, the *natatio*, and even the *palaestra*.

Next to these, a few private dwellings give way, in the peristyle area, to a *domus* of late antiquity that still has its domestic workshop.[18] Above, one can make out, contained within its round structure,

This is one stretch of the Campanian countryside whose bucolic charm remains intact, thanks to a felicitous blend of nature and history. The fine white *opus reticulatum* framing the red brickwork creates a chromatic effect that complements the green of the fields. The Hadrian-era architecture harmonizes with the natural setting of sheep and corn, creating a decidedly late-Romantic picture.

**From Aeclanum to Melfi**

We continue along the State Route SS 303, which roughly retraces the route of the ancient road. A small detour along an ancient sheep-track leads to a solitary landscape and all the way to the Ansanto valley. An acrid, sulfurous odor seems to lead to what could rightly be called a volcano in the

process of extinction.[19] The site, famous since antiquity, could only be attributed to the cult of Dis.[20] It was believed that the gates to the Underworld were here, and that the dead gathered here to begin their journey to the next world.

It is a landscape whose strong stench and boiling aperture in the earth crystallized in the mythic memory into the attributes of the Mouth of Hell. Virgil wrote:

*In midst of Italy, well known to fame,*
*There lies a lake (Amsanctus is the name)*
*Below the lofty mounts: on either side*
*Thick forests the forbidden entrance hide.*
*Full in the center of the sacred wood*
*An arm arises of the Stygian flood,*
*Which, breaking from beneath with bellowing*
  *sound,*
*Whirls the black waves and rattling stones around.*
*Here Pluto pants for breath from out his cell,*
*And opens wide the grinning jaws of hell.*[21]

A slimy, smoky pond makes this place particularly unsettling. It is assigned by tradition to the goddess Mefitis, object of an archaic cult linked to a sanctuary on this site from the sixth century B.C. onward.[22] The recent discovery of a wooden statue gives an idea of her anthropomorphized aspect.[23]

Back on the SS 303,[24] we continue along a mountain route that, from the ridge over which the modern road passes, affords a vista over vast horizons of farmland dotted by an almost uninterrupted sequence of wind turbines. It is a limitless landscape, bare, and airy, that passes through Guardia dei Lombardi and La Toppa (which probably corresponds with the Roman way station of Sub Romula) on its way to Lacedonia, probably the site of the ancient Aquilonia.[25]

Boundless panoramas of wheat fields accompany this stretch of road, which after a few kilometers breaks away from the ancient route and heads down to the Ofanto River,[26] crossing it by means of the Pons Aufidi, the modern S. Venere bridge. The ancient bridge actually stood a bit downstream from the current one, being linked to another *statio*. The present-day bridge spans the Ofanto with six fine arches over great buttressed piles, blending in with the dense vegetation and a newer bridge towering over it crosswise. The road

*Facing page: Detail of the bell tower of Melfi Cathedral, twelfth century. To the sides of the higher mullioned window are two lava-stone griffins, symbol of the Norman dynasty of Sicily.*

*Above: The famous sarcophagus of Rapolla, kept in the clock tower of Melfi Castle (Museo Archeologico Nazionale del Melfese).*

*Below: View of the city of Melfi, from the stone bridge of its imposing castle.*

*On pages 162–63: Melfi Castle. Its most ancient nucleus dates to the Norman-Swabian domination. It was here that Frederick II made public his legal code, the so-called Constitutions of Melfi or* Liber Augustalis.

continued to the north of Melfi as far as Madonna di Macera, where a celebrated sarcophagus was found.

Hoisted like a ship's prow atop a volcanic hill at the northern foot of Monte Vulture, Melfi is a town with a predominantly Norman face. Despite its important Neolithic vestiges, in the Roman era it was of little importance for the nearby colony of Venusium, a way station along the Via Appia. Closed in behind its walls, Melfi almost jealously guards an interesting medieval urban fabric dotted by craggy churches. It assumed its current Norman flavor in 1041, when the little town underwent a burst of urban development that in barely a century brought the historic center to its current size.

The castle that dominates the heights with its quadrangular profile remains the most valuable reminder of this period of growth. Its powerful towers, its masonry bridge (originally a drawbridge), and its deep moat declare its military purpose in forceful terms.

Actually the fortress, within the compact, imposing shell of its architecture, displays a complex structure stratified into different nuclei that recall the city's own vicissitudes over different historical eras. There is the most ancient nucleus, the Norman-Swabian (twelfth–thirteenth centuries), then the Angevin, then the renovations of John II Caracciolo (1456–60) and Marcantonio del Carretto (1549–70).[27]

Hidden away like a precious jewel box inside the Torre dell'Orologio, the Sarcophagus of Rapolla, with its extraordinary reliefs and the great refinement of its modeling, exemplifies the lofty artistic refinement attained by the workshops in Asia Minor in creating these extraordinary funerary objects. Its name derives from the place where it was found in 1856: the village of Rapolla, not far from Melfi. Its bright white marble stands out sharply between the rough walls of the tower. It is very well preserved, and its superb craftsmanship dates from the second century A.D. Rarely have sarcophagi of such value been preserved with their lids intact. For this reason alone, a visit to the castle of Melfi is indispensable to any travel itinerary along the Appian Way.

On the cover of the sarcophagus, a young woman with fine features and a hairstyle typical of the Antonine era lies on her deathbed with a

mournful, sober look. At her feet are the vestiges of what is recognizably a dog to keep her company in her eternal rest; at her head, a cupid holds a garland of flowers in one hand, and in the other a torch, turned downward, in a clear allusion to death.[28]

On the sarcophagus itself, in the upper part, a fine frieze of tritons and sea monsters creates a counterpoint to the scene above. Beneath this, between a rich architectural composition of aediculae supported by fluted columns, a chorus of deities displays exquisite modeling, being sculpted almost entirely in the round. Persephone, in her aspect as queen of the Underworld, oversees this theophanic manifestation of gods and heroes, watching over the young woman's sleep with peerless sovereignty.

### From Melfi to Venosa

Just past Madonna di Macera, the Appian Way continued eastward[29] to Venusium (modern Venosa). Resting on the floor of a Pleistocene basin, the city of Venosa is one of the most important stops along this ancient route.

Dominated from above by the jagged profile of Monte Vulture, Venosa is the hometown of the celebrated Latin poet Horace, Quintus Horatius Flaccus, born here in 65 B.C. Situated at the frontier between Apulia and Lucania, it was an important Roman center and reached the height of its splendor between the fourth and fifth centuries as the *splendida civitas Venusinorum*. The town, with the square mass of its sixteenth-century Aragonese castle looming above it, unfolds in a fabric of small but architecturally interesting buildings that bear witness, with ancient elements scattered here and there in the walls, to an extraordinary historic continuum. "At each step," wrote François Lenormant in 1883, "one comes across an inscription or an architectural fragment: architrave, column-shaft, capital. Even the uninscribed stones indisputably bear the mark of the Roman chisel. . . ; a Latin epigraphy of astonishing richness."[30]

The strategic position of the Appian Way, and the town's felicitous topographical location, made it one of the most important hubs of exchange in southern Italy, a point of traffic confluence between Campania and Apulia.

*Facing page: General view of the archaeological complex adjacent to the abbey of Santissima Trinità at Venosa. In the foreground, the mosaic flooring of the* frigidarium *of the first–second century A.D. bath complex; in the background, the bell tower of the "new" or "unfinished" church.*

*Above: Detail of one of the floor mosaics from the bath complex.*

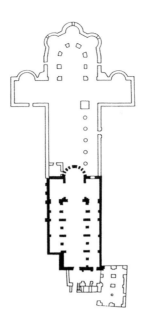

*Above: The plan of Santissima Trinità Abbey.*

*Right: The "new" church of Santissima Trinità Abbey. Left unfinished, the building was constructed over the course of the twelfth century, as an extension of the old church, built in the early Christian era. Construction ceased after the outer walls, apse, transept, and the row of clustered columns on the right side had been built.*

The Appian Way passed directly in front of the famous Abbey of the Santissima Trinità and the archaeological complex beside it, which, aside from being an important ancient legacy, presents a scene of incomparable beauty and charm with its array of architectural ruins beside the unfinished church. Rarely do Romanesque and Roman forms stand side by side in a united whole and in such happy synthesis, showing how the site came to be consolidated over time.

The area is articulated into different spaces and structures. One can easily recognize the baths, the early Christian baptistery, and the houses. In the abbey complex, one can make out various elements: the old church, the guest house, the monastery, and the new, unfinished church.

One first comes across the archaeological vestiges of the bath complex, which dates from the first–second centuries A.D. It is a vast, open area, with a jumble of different spaces whose decoration and structure often reveal their ancient functions: the *frigidarium* with a fine mosaic floor, the *calidarium* with its hypocausts (underground heating systems).[31]

That a *statio* along the Appian Way would have a place of recreation and rest such as a bathhouse should come as no surprise. We know that all the ancient centers of any importance had bathing complexes. But here there were also homes and residences. Along the paved street that runs past the baths are private dwellings, two *domus* of some importance. The first, adjacent to the bath building, was built around the end of the second century B.C., from brickwork of the Republican era, then restructured at the start of the first century A.D.

The typology is the usual one we encounter in luxury dwellings, with the atrium flooring decorated with plant motifs, the *impluvium* at the center, the bedrooms and the *tablinum* all around, and, on the opposite side, the service rooms. Facing the baths is the second *domus*, which is bigger but not as well preserved.

Between the *domus* and the unfinished church are the remains of a trilobate building with an outer corridor. The presence of two baptismal fonts, one hexagonal and the other cruciform, indicates that this was an early Christian baptistery. Just beyond this lies the medieval complex, a series

of architectural works articulating different spaces including the old church, the chapter house, the guest house, and the unfinished church. It is a nucleus of great charm and fascination, with its combination of structures and its felicitous situation in the landscape.

The old church, as is often the case, is founded on an ancient Roman temple, in this case one dedicated to Hymen. By an historical concatenation of events, this temple was overwhelmed first by the early Christian building, then the Benedictine one, and finally by the Norman church.

Prefacing the entrance on the simple, modest facade, two column-bearing lions remind us to heed the warning in the inscription above them: "One passes through a narrow door to the broad atrium of the Temple, so that one may see how difficult is the path to virtue. Thus anyone who offend religion must flee the life of the cloister, and commit outrage and violence against the heavens."

The inner layout shows a typical early-Christian structure, with a nave divided into four bays by as

many transverse arches. On the walls, fragments of frescoes make way for the Norman tombs, including the elegantly sober tomb of Alberada, wife of Robert II Guiscard.[32] On the opposite wall, the other sepulcher contains the mortal remains of the Altavilla (Hauteville),[33] a noble Norman house that dominated southern Italy between 1030 and 1189. Inside lie the remains of, among others, Robert Guiscard himself. "This Robert was tyrannical in character," wrote Anna Comnena, Princess of Byzantium (1083–1148), "highly astute in purpose and brave in action. . . . So great in stature as to tower over the tallest, and his eyes did nothing but throw fiery sparks. With all these gifts of fortune, he was naturally indomitable and subordinate to no man on earth."

The underground crypt, reached by two flights of stairs on the sides, is noteworthy; on the walls are fragments of frescoes in the Greco-Byzantine style.

Going back outside, we encounter the unfinished church. Its roofless structure seems purposely

truncated to create an extraordinary scene open to the heavens. The rows of clustered pillars and the cadenced sequence of columns seem to hold up the sky itself with their capitals, intoning, in the warm amber color of the stone, a hymn to the constructive wisdom of the Benedictines, who left here one of the most exciting examples of unfinished architecture in existence. "It was worked on repeatedly over the first two centuries after the year 1000, but was left unfinished," wrote Piovene. "It looks, however, without being so, a ruin lost in solitude, with its high walls rising up in the middle of the fields, and the stone lions in front in of the portal. As one walks around it, every step releases a scent of aromatic herbs."

When, in the first half of the twelfth century, the old church was deemed insufficient to the needs of their religious practice, the Benedictines planned a grandiose extension behind the apse, with the intention of turning it all into one vast basilica. The plan was never brought to completion.

### From Venosa to Taranto by Way of Gravina and Altamura

From Venosa the road continues on toward Gravina, roughly retracing an ancient sheep-track

"No trace of trees except for two or three kilometers around the towns," wrote Tommaso Fiore in a letter to Piero Gobetti in 1925, "under the ocean of clear, even light, under the great accumulations of clouds, even the naked highland plain is a succession of gray, steely, lightly moving waves stretching to infinity, broken only by the darker, cultivated terrains and dull dark greens of the meadows."[34]

Here, on the heights of the Botromagno, the archaic Peucetian settlement was renewed in the Roman way station of Silvium.[35] This was destroyed during the barbarian invasions, during which the natives, to protect themselves, fled into the caves carved into the tufaceous walls of the gorge, which still exist.

Present-day Gravina[36] is located, however, on the other side of the ravine. From here one must descend into the depths (to the Fondovico district) to find, in the sheer rock-face of the gorge, the church of S. Michele dei Grotti. In this craggy landscape of incomparable beauty and charm, the church, carved directly into the tufa, presents the usual layout of the early Christian basilicas, with nave and four aisles on quadrangular pillars. In the center, a chorus of four small altars rises to overlook the sacred space of the presbytery.[37] Here and there one finds traces of frescoes, attesting to the existence of pictorial decorations long since lost.

Driven by hardship, the Latin and Greek monks created a singular fusion of art and life in this harsh setting of grottoes and passages in rock. They animated these ancient caverns and refuges with furnishings and frescoes and gave light to a Christianity still gravid with primordial spiritualism.

As we proceed, the air is suffused with thyme and wild mint across a horizon serrated with endless hillocks and jags, evidence of a solitary, neglected civilization. We resume our way along the ancient route, which for the stretch of the Tarantine sheeptrack retains the name of Via Appia Antica as far as Altamura.

Perched on a height in Le Murge, the ancient Peucetian[38] center of Altamura returned to life, in all likelihood, in the Roman settlement of Blera. "In Apulia," wrote Piovene, "you have a complex of Romanesque cathedrals comparable to the complex of Gothic cathedrals in Northern France. They are scattered everywhere, and even when one arrives from Basilicata, the first sign of Apulia is Altamura

that, after crossing two ravines, passes between Palazzo S. Gervasio and the railroad line. From there it heads past Costa Boldini and the Spinalva bridge, until it reaches Gravina di Puglia.

The landscape is marked by karst topography, with its barren, desolate outer horizon and the craggy vistas boiling up at its center. It is a harsh, pure land, a realm of erosion caused by a rich underground watercourse that has carved out grottoes, sinkholes, and karst basins, and has produced vast uncultivated grazing lands that teem with life on the surface and with arcane spiritualism below it.

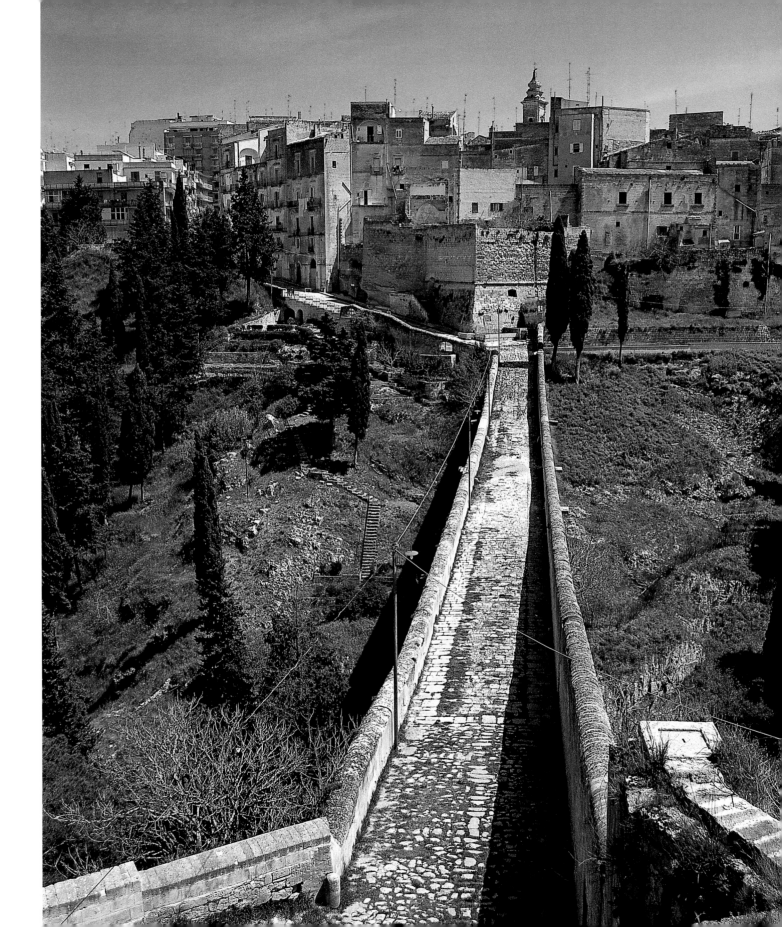

*Above left: Altamura Cathedral, founded by Frederick II and rebuilt during the reign of Robert d'Anjou.*

*Above right: The splendid portal of Altamura Cathedral, fourteenth–fifteenth century. Inside a protruding gable resting on two ferocious lions, refashioned in 1533, is a triumphant cycle of decorative and illustrative sculpture, masterpieces of Apulian Gothic art.*

*Facing page: The fourteenth-century rose window of Altamura Cathedral.*

and its palatine basilica with sculpted portal and rose window."

A superb, surviving monument of medieval art, the cathedral was built at the behest of the emperor Fredrick II of Swabia between 1232 and 1242.[39] A remarkable fusion of Romanesque and the so-called "Federician" style, it looms in the distance, its powerful facade of brown stone united by the two sixteenth-century bell towers and marked by the fine plasticism of the portal and the magnificent rose window. The interior is a good nineteenth-century restoration accompanied by nineteenth-century paintings and a fine Renaissance marble pulpit.

After Altamura, we continue along our route (SS 97), which preserves both the name and the route of the ancient road, heading down an open straightaway[40] toward a flat, wheat-planted coun-

tryside that still retains traces of the ancient Roman land division known as centuriation.

The scene opens onto a horizon of vast, well-groomed plots, broken up here and there by the compact, reassuring geometries of old farm-estates called *masserie*. After Masseria Cangiulli, there is Masseria Taverna, whose very name preserves the memory of the shelter that was probably the Roman *statio* of Sub Lupatia.

At Castellaneta, the Tarantine sheep-track (SS 97) vanishes only to reemerge in the current Appian Way (SS 7). Further on, near Palagiano, interwoven into the tight rows of vines and olive trees, are the remains of a great defensive wall done in *opus reticulatum*. They are the ruins of Parete-Pinto, possibly identifiable with the ancient center of Ad Canales, the last way station on the Appian Way before Taranto (Tarentum).

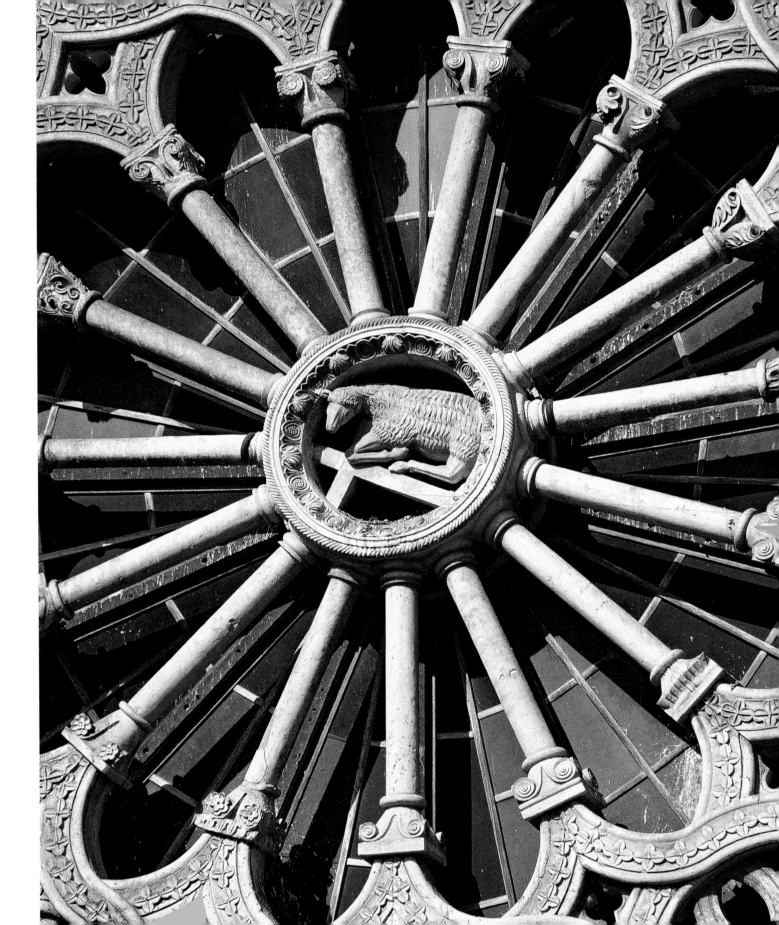

**Taranto**

It is not hard to imagine how impressive the sight
of the city must have once been for someone
approaching it from inland. Indeed it still
impresses. After a flat, monotonous stretch of landscape dominated by olive trees and repetitive wheat
plantations that follow the ancient centuriations,
the vision of Tarentum in the distance must have
been breathtaking. Wrote Gregorovius:

*The view of the Gulf of Taranto at last opens up
from San Giorgio. The broad circuit of slopes almost
form a vast amphitheater around a rather limited
base, where emerges a basin of water shooting forth
flashes at once purple and blue. It is the Mar Piccolo
of Taranto! . . . Now the city itself appears with its*

*walls and towers, like an island amidst the bewitching sparkle of the two seas.*[41]

It must not have been any different in antiquity,
when despite the defeats suffered by the Romans,
Tarentum remained the splendid capital of Magna
Graecia, cradle of a mixed civilization in which
Orient and Occident blended together in wondrous
synthesis.[42] Strabo described it in his *Geography*:

*Although the Gulf of Tarentum is for the most part
devoid of natural harbors, Tarentum nevertheless
possesses a rather large and excellent port, with a
perimeter of 100 stadii and enclosed by a great
bridge. The innermost part of the port forms an
isthmus with the sea outside, so that the city is situ-*

ated on a peninsula and sailing vessels are easily transported over land from one side to the other, since the neck of the isthmus is not very elevated. . . .

Tarentum also possesses a magnificent gymnasium and a vast, beautiful square in which stands the colossal bronze statue of Zeus, the biggest known to exist, with the exception of the Colossus of Rhodes.[43]

The Appian Way made its entrance into the city via a majestic, elevated bridge[44] under which ships could pass. It was a stately, movable bridge worthy of one of the most important capitals in the Mediterranean, with its two natural harbors—called Mar (or Mare) Piccolo and Mar Grande—giving onto the east.

It reached the height of its splendor at the time of Archytas, who created a Pythagorean city that stood out in all of Magna Graecia for its cultural and political primacy. Strabo wrote:

They had also embraced Pythagorean philosophy, in which Archytas, who was long the leader of the city, especially distinguished himself. Afterward, however, because of their prosperity, a loosening of morals so great prevailed that there were more public celebrations held during the year than there were days in the calendar.[45]

Even under imperial rule[46] the city remained Greek in appearance and customs, proud of the favorable location that had brought it such glory and wealth. In the Roman era, however, this primacy gradually shifted to Brundisium (modern Brindisi).

Of that early greatness, unfortunately, very little remains today. Much of it has been ruined by a careless and perverse building craze, unstoppable since it first began in the last century. It has destroyed the ancient city, creating an atmosphere of deterioration and real decay.

The rare vestiges that still survive are in the Museo Nazionale and the ruins of a great Doric temple,[47] which in its gloomy solitude sings the hymn of a now lost grandeur. Cesare Brandi writes:

Of Tarentum, the Greek city, once splendid and opulent, and then gradually as though wiped off the face of the earth, reduced to that islet that at once

closes and opens the Mar Piccolo: how many golden crowns of tremulous rose and myrtle have issued from this pillaged ground and now bring back to life for the astonished visitor, through the showcases of the museum, the splendor, the richness of that time when it was capital of Magna Graecia and perhaps not even Syracuse was greater. But the temples have fallen, the marble has been used to make lime, and what is best preserved is what seems most fragile: the terra-cottas, the graceful figurines, always a bit dusty, but graceful, almost endless in number, and the beautiful vases—and yet how many have been stolen!—and a stupendous, almost archaic bronze, and an evanescent marble head. A bit outside of Taranto, the Palatine Tables at Metaponto, at the entrance to old Taranto, the vestiges of a temple.[48]

The rest is medieval history. Until 1080, Taranto remained Byzantine. Then came the Norman conquest. The Duomo, dedicated to the city's patron saint, Cataldo, is from the tenth to eleventh centuries. As with most Italian buildings, it is a palimpsest in which one can retrace the various additions. Its lateral facings still show the original Romanesque foundation in the elegant sequence of blind arches supporting the fine round tiburio with Byzantine-style cupola. The facade, on the other hand, is Baroque, made in 1713 by Manieri. Gregorovius wrote:

Very ancient basilica, begun under the Archbishop Drogo in 1070, [was] then rebuilt in 1588 under Pope Sixtus V. It has a nave and two aisles: round arches rest on twenty-four ancient columns with Corinthian capitals, magnificent vestiges of some pagan temple. The floor is white-and-black marble, the ceiling gilded wood. The main altar has a fine red-marble tabernacle.[49]

The interior, still in the process of being restored, is nobly austere in the play of fine ancient columns, which in the luminous dynamism of their capitals seem to echo the sculptural vibrations of the fine, coffered ceiling. Especially noteworthy is the Cappellone di S. Cataldo, whose decorative exuberance places it firmly within the richest vein of southern Italian late-Baroque style. It is embroidered with

On page 178: Columns of the Doric temple in Piazza Castello, Taranto.

On page 179: Side view of S. Cataldo Cathedral in Taranto.

a luxuriant multicolor facing of marble inlay, which the fine bronze gate seems to herald proudly.

## From Taranto to Brindisi

"The inland route from Brentesium to Tarentum can be traveled by courier in a single day and forms the isthmus of the abovementioned peninsula," Strabo wrote in his *Geography* (6.3.5). The forty-four mile (65 km) route between these two cities could be traveled in a single day following a recti-linear course that passed through the centers of Mesochorum, Urbius, and Scamnum.

The Appian Way left Tarentum as a broad car-riageway[50] that headed in the direction of S. Giorgio Ionico toward the Masseria Misicuro—whose name still preserves the ancient place-name of Mesochorum. The meaning of the term—"halfway down the road"—apparently alludes to the specific position of the way station, which must have stood somewhere near the present *masseria*. The road passed through vineyards and olive groves along a flat route as far as Uria (modern-day Oria). According to Gregorovius:

*The landscape presents itself always the same, monotonously flat, with luxuriant, unending thick-ets of olive trees that alternate with fields of grain. Only toward the north does a chain of heights begin ever so slowly to rise, atop which one can see a great city with white walls, dominated by a great castle in the middle. This is the very ancient Oria or Uria. . . . With longing we gazed from afar at the monumen-tal city, whose age is beyond measure and whose walls, towering over the pale blue mount and radi-ant with sunlight, had something at once splendid and majestic about them, while a strange breath, wholly of mythic, pre-Hellenic times, seemed to come forth and cascade down from the castle above.*[51]

As one of the major centers of ancient Messapia,[52] the city dominates the surrounding plain with its massive Federician castle. The old nucleus of the town, with its unusual elliptical configuration, its narrow, tortuous streets, its whitewashed and ocher houses, huddles under the vigorous protection of the fortress, almost forming a city in the shape of a castle.

As symbol and master of the city, this architec-tural complex may rightly be considered one of the

*The Aragonese castle of Taranto, at the far corner of the peninsula of the old city. The structure's original nucleus was built by the Byzantines atop the ruins of the ancient city, destroyed in a Saracen raid. They called it La Rocca, or "the fortress."*

*Pages 182–83: Frederick II's castle in Oria.*

most original of Swabian monuments, built and shaped to the will of Frederick II, atop the ruins of the ancient Messapic acropolis between 1227 and 1233.[53] Sovereign of the heights, with its triangular shape it looks—as Paul Bourget wrote in his *Sensation d'Italie*—like "a ship afloat in the air," "a gigantic jewel of stone."

The Appian way station Urbius was located at a still-unspecified spot not far from the town center. The road continued on toward Latiano, to the station of Scamnum,[54] where the *masseria* of Muro Tenente now stands. From here the road headed on toward Messania (modern Mesagne), another ancient Messapic center. The name derives perhaps from the Latin *mediania*, meaning "city in the middle," underscoring its geographic and cultural centrality. It was a *vicus* (district) of Brundisium, and the penultimate population center before the terminus of the route. The Appian Way then continues on to Brindisi along one last straightaway where the ancient and modern roads coincide.

## Notes

1. A cart drawn by two or four horses that made it possible to transport baggage and in some cases also provided cover from the elements.
2. Horace *Satires* 1.5.77–85 (trans. Jacob Fuchs).
3. Ibid., 1.5.71–76.
4. The Second Samnite War was marked by the humiliating episode of the Caudine Forks (321 A.D.) that the Samnites inflicted on the Romans. Thereafter the Appian Way, whose first route linked Rome and Capua, was extended to the Caudine valley, reaching Caudium and, just after that, an early suburb that would soon be made into the Roman colony of Beneventum.
5. George Berkeley, "Journal of Travels in Italy (May 17, 1717)," in *The Works of George Berkeley, Bishop of Cloyne*, eds. A. A. Luce and T. E. Jessup (London: Nelson, 1955), vol. 7, pp. 269–70.
6. It was originally called the Ponte Marmoreo ("marble bridge"). The name of Leproso was probably conferred in the Middle Ages to indicate a district in which there was a leper colony. First built by the Samnites, it was renovated by Appius Claudius Caecus, and again by Septimius Severus and Marcus Aurelius Antoninus.
7. Entering over the Leproso bridge, the Via Appia formed a *decumanus* along the axis of the current *vie* of SS. Filippo, Rummo, and Annunziata, parallel to the *decumanus maximus*, corresponding to the modern Viale S. Lorenzo and Corso Garibaldi.
8. *Letters*, Naples, August 28, 1753. A recent edition of this travelogue is Luigi Vanvitelli, *Le lettere di Luigi Vanvitelli della biblioteca palatina di Caserta*, ed. Franco Strazzullo (Galatina: Congedo, 1976–77).
9. It was also known for having made famous the sort of script called "Beneventan."
10. It was founded, together with the adjacent monastery, by Arechis II, in 762, when he became duke of Benevento. Over time it has suffered various violations (especially in the twelfth century), not least of them being the damages wrought by the earthquake of 1688. In 1952–57 it was restored to its original form. Today it has been cleaned and newly restored.
11. Guido Piovene, *Viaggio in Italia* (Milan: A. Mondadori, 1957; rpt. 1966).
12. SS 7 (a state road), upon leaving Benevento, passes through S. Giorgio del Sannio and Castello del Lago over a route of about 20 km, about one and a half times as long as the original route. In all likelihood the original did not go to S. Giorgio, but went directly from Benevento to the Ponte Rotto.
13. On the archway overhead one can still see remains of the amphorae used to lighten the vault.
14. Its origins are probably more ancient, but it was completely remade in Hadrian's time, to bring it up-to-date with the increase in commercial traffic.
15. F. M. Pratilli, *Della via Appia riconosciuta e descritta da Roma a Brindisi* (Naples, 1745; rpt. Sala Bolognese: A. Forni, 1978).
16. Appian *Bella Civilia* 1.51.
17. A large part of the city still lies buried, yet to be excavated.
18. This house possesses a circular kiln and some basins revetted in *opus signinum* (a mosaic-like fine concrete consisting of river gravel, small pieces of stone, or terra-cotta fragments cemented in lime or clay).
19. It is a small lake that percolates up a sludgy water, releasing carbon dioxide and sulphuric acid. Inhalation of its fumes is harmful to small animals and the surrounding vegetation and is not without danger for humans as well, when they are exposed to it over a long period of time.
20. Pliny writes about it in *Naturalis historia* 3. It is also mentioned by Claudian in *De raptu Prosperpinae* and by Cicero in *De divinatione*.
21. Virgil *Aeneid* 7.776–86, trans. John Dryden (London: Grant Richards, 1903).
22. Archaeological finds show the sanctuary of the goddess Mefitis to have been on this site. Inscriptions and ex-votos in bronze and clay confirm this hypothesis beyond any shadow of a doubt.
23. The statue measures 1.40 m (a little over 4.5 ft.), and can rightly be considered the largest wooden statue thus far recovered.
24. Along this stretch, State Route SS 303 roughly retraces the route of the Appian Way.
25. The Hirpinian city where the Romans dealt the Samnites a mortifying defeat in 293 B.C.
26. A sheep-track that descends in a straight line toward Candela, coinciding with the route of the Appian Way.
27. The castle now houses the Museo Nazionale del Melfese and its archaeological finds from the eighth to the sixth centuries B.C., which document the presence of the populations that settled in those territories during that period: the Dauni, Samnites, and Lucanians. The finds from the Roman period were put in the nearby Museo Archeologico Nazionale di Venosa.
28. The lowered *face* (torch) is a consistent reference to death in Roman funerary iconography.
29. Along a route no longer known to us, it crossed the Arcidiaconata gorge before continuing on its way to Venosa.
30. François Lenormant, *À travers l'Apulie et la Lucanie: notes de voyage* (Paris: A. Levy, 1883) is one of this author's many learned travelogues.
31. This is the typical Roman system of heating, using small brick pillars to support the flooring from below and brick conduits beneath, through which the hot air circulated on its way to piping along the walls.

32  She was both Guiscard's wife and the mother of Bohemond, the hero of the First Crusade who is buried at Canosa.

33  It holds the remains of Prince "Bras de Fer" William, Humphrey, Drogo, Robert Guiscard, and William "of the Princedom."

34  A volume of correspondence between these two has been published: Tommaso Fiore, *Un popolo de formiche: lettere pugliesi a Piero Gobetti* (Bari: Laterza, 1952).

35  This was an important Peucetian city, perhaps Sidion (or Sides). Significant Peucetian artifacts, especially tombs, have also been found in the contemporary population center of Gravina.

36  The name obviously derives from the deep gully (*gravina* means "gorge") over which the charming town is located. By the fifth century the new center had begun to be built, and it was given the name of Civitas Gravinae, later shortened simply to Gravina.

37  The altars are more recent, having been remade in 1690. The human bones in one corner of the church are most likely those from the bloody massacre of the Saracens in 983.

38  Settlements in the area are documented dating as far back as the Aeneolithic era (before 4000 B.C.). Modern-day Altamura stands on an ancient Peucetian center whose name remains unknown, but whose period of greatest development was around the sixth–fifth centuries B.C. The visible remains of a double ring of defensive walls date from this period.

39  Dedicated by Frederick himself to the Virgin of the Assumption, the cathedral, at the emperor's command, was to be free and independent of any episcopal jurisdiction. Rather it would be directly dependent on the emperor, who would appoint its archpriest. Following an earthquake that probably occurred in 1316, part of the church collapsed. On the orders of Robert d'Anjou, the facade was disassembled piece by piece and reconstructed where it currently stands.

40  Its only curves are in places where the ancient route was altered.

41  Ferdinand Gregorovius, *Nelle Puglia (Wanderings through Apulia)*, trans. Raffaele Mariano (Florence: G. Barbera, 1882).

42  Taras (Tarentum in Latin), named after a hero considered to be the son of Poseidon and Satyra, daughter of Minos, appears, according to tradition, to have been founded by Spartan colonists in 706 B.C. We do know, however, that the site was already an important destination by that time.

43  Strabo *Geographia* 6.3.1.

44  Its location does not, however, correspond to the current one, the swing bridge built in 1886 to replace the ancient Angevin bridge. It was rebuilt in 1958.

45  Strabo *Geographia* 6.3.4.

46  After the campaigns of Pyrrhus (280–275 B.C.), Tarentum was defeated by the Romans in 272 B.C. In 123 B.C., the colony of Neptunia was established there. In 89 B.C. it was granted the status of *municipium*.

47  The remains date from the sixth century B.C. and seem to have belonged to a large Doric temple, probably devoted to Poseidon.

48  Cesare Brandi, *Terre d'Italia* (Rome: Riuniti, 1991).

49  Gregorovius, *Nelle Puglia*.

50  At Cimino near Taranto, the remains of the original pavement were discovered. The road's width at this point appears to have been no less than 7 m, attesting to the importance of the suburban traffic. One could indeed avoid passing through the city by way of an alternate route that ran along the shore of the Mar Piccolo to the north and passed through Masseria S. Pietro, where a Byzantine church now stands to bear witness to St. Peter's passage here.

51  Gregorovius, *Nelle Puglia*.

52  Strabo tells us that the royal palace of the Messapic kings and the Temple of Saturn were still visible in his day. Various archaeological finds from this period (sixth to third centuries B.C.) have been excavated in the area.

53  The castle underwent various modifications in different periods. It was enlarged and completed in the fourteenth century, then later transformed and restored by its owner, Count Giuseppe Martini Carissimo.

54  Nothing is left of the area of the ancient *statio*. One can, however, see vestiges of the vast, fortified Messapic defense wall scattered about the countryside (the area is actually called Paretone).

# The Via Appia Traiana

IVANA DELLA PORTELLA

**The Arch of Trajan and the Via Appia Traiana**
With the unveiling of the great triumphal arch of
Beneventum, Trajan (53–117 A.D.) symbolically
announced one of the most important of the works
for which he would go down in history: the Via
Appia Traiana. It was an extraordinary project most
worthy of remembrance, as confirmed by the many
epigraphs and carved scrolls posted on milestones
still preserved today.[1]

More than sixty milestones from this road have
Trajan's name on them. In its customary cylindri-
cal column form, each one bears an inscription on
the scroll carved into its face. The text changes only
in its indication of the mileage in the first line. It
says: *Imp[erator] Caesar/Divi Nervale f[ilius]/Nerva
Traianus/Aug[ustus] Germ[anicus] Dacic[us]/Pont[ifex]
Max[imus], tr[ibunicia] pot[estate]/XIII, im[perator]
VI, co[n]s[ul] V/p[ater] p[atriae] viam Benevento/
Brundisium Pecun[ia]/sua fecit* ("The Emperor
Caesar, son of the god Nerva, Nerva Traianus,
Augustus, victor over the Germans and Dacians,
Supreme Pontiff, in the thirteenth year of his tri-
bunician power, six-time triumphator, six-time con-
sul, father of his country, constructed the road from
Beneventum to Brundisium at his own expense.")

An early French chronicler, Jean-Claude
Richard de Saint-Non, wrote:

*We reached Benevento around midday and, though
weary from the chaos of a horrendous road, upon
arrival we wanted to go see the famous Arch of
Trajan, one of the best-preserved monuments to be
found in Italy, and perhaps the most intact, since it is
missing only a few pieces from the cornice. As a whole
and in its details, this monument, made entirely of
marble, is so similar to the Arch of Titus in Rome,
that there can be no doubt it is an imitation thereof.
The architecture did not seem particularly noteworthy
to us, either in nobility or proportion, despite the
praises lavished on it in certain Italian texts, and even
though it is not unlikely its author was the famous
Apollodorus of Damascus, the celebrated architect who
lived under Trajan and erected many monuments
under this Emperor's rule.*

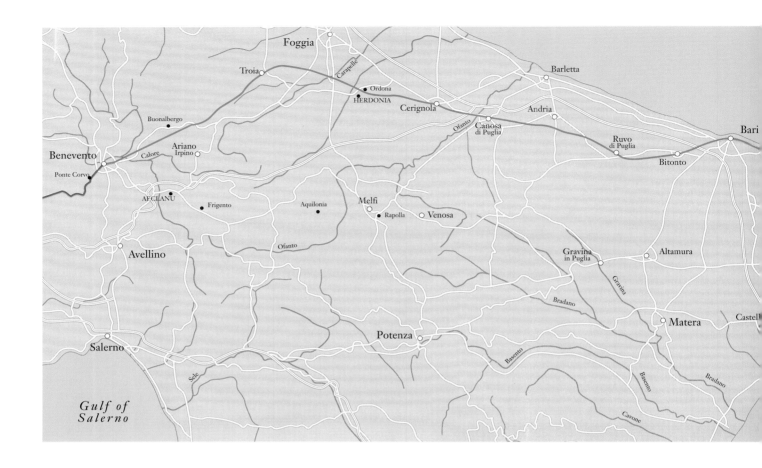

*Above: Map of the route of the Via Appia Traiana, from Benevento to Brindisi.*

*To us, in truth, it seemed, in style and in the characteristics of its sculptures, quite inferior to the Arch of Titus. The bas-reliefs are generally a bit heavy, the figures are short, and only their heads reflect the character and harsh pride of the ancients. It is clear that the bas-reliefs of this Arch are related to the various achievements of the Emperor Trajan, but it is difficult to establish precisely which.[2]*

A masterpiece of Trajanian rhetoric, it was built where the *decumanus maximus* and the *cardo* of the city intersect. It is a creation of the productive stonecutter who has, after careful study, come to be called simply the Master of the Arch of Benevento. Some traditionally identify him as the same Apollodorus of Damascus much celebrated for the remarkable achievements of the Arch of Trajan in Rome.[3]

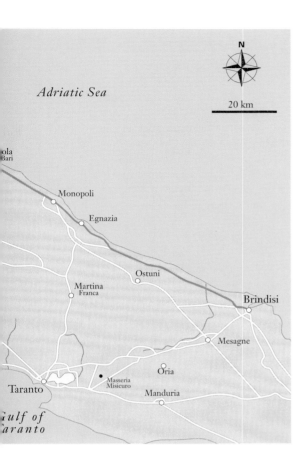

Adriatic Sea

20 km

Monopoli

Egnazia

Ostuni

Martina
Franca

Brindisi

Mesagne

Òria

Masseria
Misicuro

Manduria

Taranto

Gulf of
Taranto

Bari

since it was transformed, in the Middle Ages, from *caput viae* [the roads' beginning] and triumphal arch into a defensive gate of the walled city. At last it has shaken off the filthy burden of a handful of hovels and the even more odious burden of a few pretentious, dressed-up bourgeois homes. Today it has completed what, for better or worse, was begun by an Italian pope, Pius IX, and now it is finally free and, alone in its triumphant beauty of marbles and sculptures, it looks out onto the long expanse of the Via Appia Traiana, the new road the Emperor had wanted to shorten the route to the Adriatic, Epirus, and the East. And the road descends straight and steep in a single leap, so that the Arch looms high, rising up, seeming to indicate, from up there, a finishing line for a race or a target for a lance.

Even before the Arch has finished donning its warrior paints, I can again see the reliefs of the great barrel vault, with the incomparable scene of the emperor in the act of issuing the tabulae alimentariae, *the food relief for the children of the people: boys rushing boldly up to him with the frank nonchalance of the children of this region; one is holding out the hem of his tunic to collect what he has coming to him; two smaller children are sitting astride their father and mother respectively, and we can be sure they didn't just sit there in silent amazement, but were accompanying the chorus of acclamation with cries and shouts. If Dante had seen this relief, what other brilliant terzinas might he have given us to sing the "glory of the Roman prince" in the city where Paul the Deacon, guest of the court of Arichis and Adalperga, must have raised his eyes to look at the Admirable arch.*[4]

In a classicizing style, he created the reliefs and sculptures recounting the victorious undertakings and good government of the *Optimus Princeps*, constructing, in a work of rare beauty, a panegyric to Trajan's policies and his prudent management of economic, social, and military affairs. It is a true monument of celebration and consensus. This *proemio felix* of the Appian Way was inaugurated by the emperor in 114 A.D., when he created a faster, more comfortable alternate route for reaching Brundisium.

Amedeo Maiuri wrote:
*The Arch of Trajan stands in the middle of a sea of pebbles, as if it had been inundated by a river overflowing its banks: this is from the demolition of the buildings still besieging it. It has been freed from the walls and little houses clinging to its sides ever*

On the northern side of the arch, on the lower left, it is not difficult to make out *The Pacification of Germania*, which occurred just after Trajan had been elected emperor in 98 A.D. On the right, we see Trajan together with Hercules, god of the legions, concluding *The Pacification of the Danube Regions* (symbolized by pear trees), which took place before his return to Rome in 99 A.D.

On the southern side, at the bottom, a single scene covers both panels: *Trajan's Re-entry into Rome*, in 99 A.D., which seems to be a translation in stone of Pliny the Younger's *Panegyric*. On the left, we see Trajan in front of the Temple of Vespasian, being received by the Genii of the Roman people:

a toga-clad old man (Senate); a man wearing a crown (the Equestrian Order), and a young man (the People); on the right, the *Praefectus Urbis* without any ceremony invites him to enter.

On the northern side, on the second level to the left, we see *The Reorganization of the Army in the Provinces*, with *Honos* (Honor) presenting Trajan with a recruit and the *delectator* in front of the goddess Roma wearing a crown with towers; on the right, Trajan extends to all of Italy the *Institutio alimentaria* promoted by Nerva: The emperor, seen with the Virtues *Indulgentia* and *Felicitas*, is watching an infant and a young girl rise from the tilled soil. To the side are the goddess Roma with a plough and Mars clad in armor.

On the southern side, at the second level on the left, one finds *The Foundation of the Five Ulpian Colonies* favoring the veterans of the Rhine and Danube regions. A crowned matron is bearing the standard with five eagles, commending to the emperor's service two legions on leave. On the right, *Trajan's Provisions for Commerce*: three *mercatores* thanking the sovereign, in the presence of Portus (the early port of Rome) with an anchor symbolizing the safe haven of the port, Hercules with club and lion's skin, and Apollo with naked torso.

On the northern side, on the left-hand attic, are representations of the Four Deities that protect Dacia: Liber Pater, Ceres, Diana, and Sylvanus welcome Trajan among the lictors. On the right is *The Subjugation of Dacia*. A crowned woman is kneeling before a Trajan wearing a tunic and *paludamentum* (general's cloak). To the sides, the rivers of the region: the Tisia to the west, the Alutus to the east. Above the bridge over the Tisia appears Hadrian, who in 106 A.D. returned to Rome to assume the office of praetor, while Trajan remained behind to pacify the region with Lucius Licinius Sura as his advisor.

On the southern side, on the attic, both panels form the single scene of *The Second Dacian Triumph*, celebrated in 107 A.D. To the left, in front of the Temple of Jupiter Optimus Maximus on the Capitol, is the Capitoline Triad welcoming Trajan: Jupiter is giving him the lightning; he is accompanied by Juno with veiled head and Minerva representing Wisdom. On the right: Trajan, in the Campus Martius, at the back of the temple, in

front of the Triumphal Door, receives the consuls bearing the Senate decree to celebrate the triumph. The goddess Roma is bearing witness, along with the *penates* (household gods) of the Roman people. Hadrian is also present, getting ready to leave to quell a revolt in Pannonia.

Under the barrel vault, on the eastern side, is the panel of *The Institutio Alimentaria Being Granted to Beneventum*, in 101 A.D.; on the western side we see *Trajan Celebrating the Sacrifice at Beneventum*, in inauguration of the Via Appia Traiana in 109 B.C. The coffering inside the vault, with its impressive chromatic effects, has on its center panel a scene of *Trajan Being Crowned by Victory*.

The sculptural program is rounded out by the allegories in the pendentives. On the northern side is the Source of the Tisia and the Danube, the Genius of Autumn and the Genius of Winter; on the southern side, two Winged Victories, the Genius of Spring, and the Genius of Summer.

The creation of a new route, faster and more flexible than the old course of the Appian Way, corresponded to an obvious social consensus, but also displayed the Empire's technical and strategic skills.[5] The end product was a direct link between Rome and Brundisium that, by crossing the Apennine watershed at Beneventum, saved the traveler a good day's journey (200 miles, or about 296 km).

The Via Appia Traiana headed into the eastern horizon with a bold series of bridges and viaducts, perfect straightaways, and direct cuts into the rock of the mountains. The pride of the Empire thus grew with this direct challenge to the future, and with an awareness that it was defying nature by creating works that corresponded to the Vitruvian principles of "solidity, usefulness, and beauty." Strabo the geographer observed, "The Romans had the best foresight in those matters which the Greeks made but little account of, such as the construction of roads and aqueducts, and of sewers that could wash the filth of the city into the Tiber" (*Geography* 5.3.8).[6]

After the fall of the Western Empire (476 A.D.), the invading peoples, who had put the peninsula to fire and sword, continued to use the consular roads. Invaluable testimony in this regard is given us by Procopius of Caesarea, who in his ponderous work *History of the Wars*, discusses in great detail the merits, usefulness, and qualities of the Appian Way, as noted above (see "Origins and Historic Events"). In addition to his general description of the construction and quality of the road, he noted that "Belisarius led the army from Naples along the Via Latina, leaving the Via Appia to his left, a road built 900 years earlier by the consul Appius, from whom it took its name. To travel the Appian Way from Rome to Capua it takes an unencumbered traveler five days."[7]

On this basis, the road came to define the Dark Ages, continuing its purpose of conveying people toward the East, even as it became somewhat run-down.

The wayfarers who traveled the Via Appia Traiana in the Middle Ages were above all pilgrims, merchants, thieves, and crusaders—so much so that the road can rightly be considered the Via Francigena (Road to France) of the South, as Renato Stopani called it.[8] Columns of devout travelers would head out on the Trajanian paving stones in the direction of Jerusalem, with only their spiritual strength and their crooked walking-sticks to hang onto. They were often people who came from beyond the Alps along a lengthy and exhausting route that began at Santiago de Compostela in Spain, passed through Rome, and ended in Jerusalem. But it was a purifying experience, one that led people from a variety of cultures to test their mettle on an uncomfortable, uncertain journey full of dangers and temptations.

Hotels, guest houses, inns, and homes grew beyond measure along its route. Often they were run by the Hospitaler orders, which gave "chivalric" lodging under the aegis of the Knights Templar, the Knights of St. John of Jerusalem, or the Teutonic Knights. Next to these sites, places of worship sprang up, churches as well as cathedrals. The pilgrimage to the Holy Lands thus became enriched with spiritual stopping places on the way to new and important holy places: way stations like the *stationes* of antiquity, but replete with the thaumaturgical necessities for salvation. And thus began one of the most outstanding episodes in medieval European architecture: Apulian Romanesque.

Cesare Brandi writes:

*But as many races had come together in the Apulians, many styles merged in an original, felicitous way: with its extraordinary monuments, Apulian Romanesque, which is in fact an offshoot of Emilian Romanesque, represents a beautiful meeting of North and South, which yielded architectural, and not only painterly, results. Churches such as S. Nicola and Bari Cathedral create airy spaces and grow into stupendous plastic aggregates in which an Islamic aura of the most ancient era also manages to penetrate. Out of these two churches comes a proliferation of examples of development, which, in remaining faithful to certain canons, brings the fantastical element of a vigorous plasticism into the equation. As a result, some of the finest sculptures we know are Apulian, like St. Elia's episcopal chair [cathedra].[9]*

Travel writer H. V. Morton wrote at some length about this architectural phenomenon:

*Nowhere in Europe are so many Norman cathedrals to be found so close together, and should the pedant rebuke for calling them Norman and not Apulian-Romanesque, I can only say that the dark and solemn naves, with their rounded arches, the carved, massive doorways, the delicate arcading and a hundred other details, are essentially Norman. It is difficult to say which is the most beautiful or the most interesting of these Norman cathedrals, but their accessibility within walking distance one from the other makes it a simple matter to re-visit and compare them. Ten miles from Bari is the cathedral of Giovinazzo, built in 1283; two miles farther on is lovely Molfetta, where a white cathedral with three domes and two bell-towers is reflected in rock pools; eight miles on is Bisceglie with its twelfth century cathedral; then another five miles and one comes to the cathedral of Trani (1096) with its superb bronze doors and, also, like Molfetta, upon the edge of the sea. Another ten miles brings one to the coast town of Barletta, with a cathedral that dates from 1139. And one is still only thirty-five miles from Bari.*

*To leave the coast at Barletta and to return to Bari by inland roads is to arrive, after eight miles, at the site of the battle of Cannae; another eight and one sees the cathedral of Canosa and the tomb of the crusader Bohemund, who captured Antioch in 1098; another twelve miles and one is in Andria, in whose cathedral was buried the English wife of Fredrick II; then to Ruvo with its Norman cathedral, and twelve miles farther on to the exquisite cathedral of Bitonto, which was built in 1200; and so back to Bari.*

*I cannot think of any other small area that holds so much of interest for the historian and particularly for the architect. These Apulian cathedrals and minor churches are a relatively unknown chapter in the history of Norman architecture and scarcely anything has been written about them. They remain in delightful obscurity, the timeless activities of small harbours going on all round them and weekly markets being held in their shadows. They are the most beautiful surviving memory of the Norman conquest of Southern Italy.*[10]

### From Benevento to Troia

After emerging from the Arch of Trajan, the road descends in a straight line down to the Ponticello ravine, which today is crossed by a bridge that rests in turn on a more ancient one.[11] The road then gradually narrows until it becomes a country cart-track headed in the direction of Masseria Morante.

At the Paduli station, the Via Appia Traiana spanned the river over the powerful arches of the San Valentino Bridge.[12] The bridge—a proud, audacious project (76 m long and 6.5 m wide)—still rests on its pylons over the Calore River, spreading out in three, lightly pointed arches. Its strong curvature betrays its transformation in the Middle Ages, although one can still glimpse, behind the brick facing, the Roman-era part in large blocks of limestone.[13]

From here the road, which has not been preserved, went on to the first *statio*, Forum Novum.[14] This stopping place survives only in the name of the present-day Forno Nuovo, perpetuating its memory albeit in corrupt form. The road then clambered uphill toward Aequum Tuticum, overcoming the steep slopes and harsh terrain, not to mention the rivers, by means of a series of bridges whose substantial and grandiose vestiges bear witness to the high quality of their construction techniques.

Four of the bridges have survived, and it is not hard to find them amidst the rows of olive trees and tobacco plants. Proceeding toward northeast, we find the so-called "Bridge of Thieves" (Ponte dei Ladroni),[15] spanning the Vallone della Ferrara; its name, probably medieval in origin,

*Above: The San Valentino Bridge, over which the Via Appia Traiana crossed the Calore River.*

*Facing page: Detail of the apse of Troia Cathedral.*

recalls the problems of travel in those days and the ambushes that were a constant threat to pilgrims, merchants, and anyone who might use the bridges and roads.

Then in rapid succession one encounters, after some effort negotiating the steep vale of Le Cesine, the Ponte San Marco and the Ponte delle Chianche, which originally spanned the Buonalbergo torrent with six broad arches. Further along, over the Ginestra torrent, we find the isolated remains of a pylon belonging to the so-called Ponte di Santo Spirito.

The Appia then proceeded toward the *statio* of Aequum Tuticum, identifiable today as the Masseria Sant'Eleuterio. It has a spectacular view of the hills sloping down to the Apulian plain, stretching as far as the most elevated point of the Via Appia Traiana, near the Masseria S. Vito,[16] where the *statio* called *mutatio* Aquilonis was located. The fine sixteenth-century farming complex has an *osteria* (inn and tavern). It thus maintains the character of the ancient shelter (*mutatio*), which took its name from the Celone river, formerly known as the Aquilone. Wrote Horace:

*From here on, Apulia starts to display some mountains*
*familiar to me, those with the sirocco parches, . . .*
*Then we're whisked twenty-four miles by carriage*
*to stay in a village whose name won't fit into meter,*
*so I offer an obvious hint: the most common of things*
*must be brought here—water. But its bread is*
    *the best,*
*and wise travelers usually bring some along for*
    *future use.*
*For in Canusium it's gritty, and they don't have*
    *any water*
*there either, in that town brave Diomedes founded*
    *long ago.*

(*Satires* 1.5.77–92, trans. Jacob Fuchs)

The road thus arrives in "*siticulosae Apulia*" (Apulia's familiar heights), near the Tavoliere plain, a terrain once used for transhumancy and now filled with waves of grain and rows of vines.

It is not clear exactly which locality Horace was referring to in his text, but it obviously was in this general area. A land of princes and brigands, desolate and golden with sunburnt crops, it is still today the source of very good bread.

An arid, monotonous, treeless landscape surrounds the road. Piovene wrote:

*With the destruction of the trees. . . , caused by the hatred of the shepherd who would not tolerate a shadow where his flock might graze, . . . [t]he poverty can be explained. But it is a poverty converted into moralism. Not only is the tree judged detrimental because it occupies an area of earth; it is abhorred as a plunderer, a "land-thief." It is a feeling of envy for the unproductive being (or the being thought to be so), that does not work, does not toil, and yet presumes to live: an act of primitive justice against the idle, the parasite, whose right to life is called into question. It is a moralistic condemnation, the capital punishment of an alleged criminal.*[17]

This landscape accompanies the traveler as far as the *statio* of Aecae (modern Troia).[18] Clustered around its cathedral in a natural amphitheater looking out onto the Tavoliere, the town of Troia stretches along the route of the Traiana.[19] F. Hamilton Jackson described this city and its history in 1906:

*The town of Troja crests a hill seven miles from the railway station of Giardinetto and about twelve miles from Foggia by road. From the railway quantities of giant asphodel may be seen growing on the slope of the hills, higher than the backs of the horses which feed among it. . . .*

*The present cathedral (which is dedicated to S. Maria Assunta) was commenced in 1093 under Bishop Gerard, but one must have existed already or John XIX would not have sent relics to the bishop, and the Amalfitan chronicler says that Robert Guiscard brought to Troja from Palermo, as signs of victory, iron doors and many marble pillars with capitals, in 1073. The greater part of the building was done by Bishop William II, Bigoctus, after a fire which took place in 1097, and it was nearly finished in 1105, when he brought thither many relics of saints. The celebrated bronze doors are of his time, and are dated 1119 and 1127.*[20]

The pearl of its main street, the cathedral proudly flaunts the charm of its Romanesque with Pisan influences. One must step back a bit from the square to take in all of its rare beauty, the facade

with its marvelous rose window and the exquisite bronze door. The upper section, with pitched roof vigorously supported by two lions, rises up like a sailing ship over the delicate rose window. Executed between 1160 and 1180, the window combines Moorish and Angevin styles in perfect synthesis; between columns and pointed arches, the twenty-two fields enclose stone openwork patterns of great elegance, reminiscent of the Islamic windows in an Eastern *gynaeceum* (the part of a *domus* set aside for women). It is proof, if any were needed, of the cultural ferment to which the Via Appia Traiana contributed when between the tenth and eleventh

*Right: Ruins of the ancient Herdoniae, one of the most important way-stations on the Appia Traiana.*

*Facing page: The arch of Canosa.*

centuries, it became the southern route of the Via Francigena, traveled by people of different nations and cultures.

The lower part of the facade features the great bronze doors, a testimony to the city's prosperity and some of the finest in Italy.[21] They are the work of Oderisius of Beneventum, completed in 1119, and, like the rose window, they commingle Byzantine traditions with Arab and local influences, in an extraordinary and original combination.[22]

### From Troia to Ruvo di Puglia

The Via Appia Traina continued on in the general direction of Foggia along a route that the modern provincial Foggia road retraces. Thereafter it broke off and headed toward Masseria Pozzorsogno, where the *mutatio* Ad Pirum appears to have been located.

From there the road turned southward, crossing the Cervaro torrent by way of the Ponte Rotto ("Broken Bridge").[23] After this, it headed toward Ordona (ancient Herdoniae), meeting up with another important public work, also called Ponte Rotto,[24] and, like the other one, a viaduct of splendid proportions rather than a bridge. Around this leg of the route, as if by miracle, a seemingly vanished rural culture still survives; for mile after mile, there are only the wide-open spaces of well-tilled fields, dotted here and there by peasant houses and farm structures. The terrain slopes gently down from the Apennines to the sea, covered with crops, haystacks, and olive groves. Cesare Brandi writes:

*The extreme variety of the terrain, with its highly distinct and diversified urban centers, is basically agricultural, as we see with the vast, endless olive plantations, which, together with the vineyards, give the Apulian landscape the quality of representing a pre-Indo-European countryside, since "oil" and "wine" do not have Indo-European roots but rather reflect an etymon of an unknown language related perhaps to the Pelasgians. And in no other region— not Greece, nor Sicily—are olive groves and vineyards so universally widespread. One might think they were born here. Besides, the legend of Athena's having caused the olive tree to sprout from her spear stuck*

*Right: Episcopal throne in the Canosa Cathedal, eleventh century. Supported by two elephants who seem to be advancing forward, it is the work of a sculptor named Romualdo, as attested by the inscription on the outside of the left arm.*

*Far right and facing page: The marble pulpit of Canosa Cathedral.*

*into the ground might, at least for the Greeks, imply that this most Mediterranean of plants was imported from elsewhere. What the olive tree, with its often spare and fragile foliage, really represents can be easily seen in Tuscany, where, because of the very cold winter of 1985, almost all of the plants are dry and have to be cut down to the trunk. Now, alas, it looks like another region altogether. For Apulia, the colossal olive trees are features of the land itself and the great vineyards are practically their only grasslands: a sunny land, it seems to drive away darkness and gloom, along a clean, azure sea, under a rather tender, celestial, almost African sky.[25]*

Apulia is a land flooded with light, where the Romanesque cathedrals rise up into the air like chants. Time here seems to have stopped, in an almost suspended, solidified atmosphere. Thus it is not unusual that, upon entering an old *masseria*, one might find, side by side, animal pens and ancient ruins.

Herdonia, the ancient Daunian center and one of the most important way stations of the Appia, thrived in this proud, solitary peasant reality.[26] A crossroads of the transhumance routes and the traffic of southern Italy, it was destroyed by Pyrrhus before it was reborn again 279 B.C. It played a much more than secondary role in the second war against Hannibal. Hannibal punished the city by transferring its inhabitants to Thuris and Metapontos.

Substantial ruins of the ancient city remain. Scattered across the fields, the walls surround the citadel with a ring of *opus reticulatum*, leaving its remote heart immersed in an idyllic pastoral atmosphere. The Via Appia Traiana passed through its main gate in triumphal style, cutting a swath through its center and leaving its urbanistic mark upon it. Like the major *municipia* of the era, it had a basilica, two temples, a forum, and a *macellum* with its typically circular layout.[27] The sense of oblivion emanating from these ruins is quite unusual, as if man's neglect had allowed nature to pursue its inexorable

reconquest of the space, leaving the tale of these vestiges to be sung only by the birds.

Beyond Ordona, the road is identifiable in the path of a sheep-track that passes through the Masseria Durando on its way to Cerignola, where the Mansio Furfane, cited in the *Tabula Peutingeriana*, is supposed to have been located. The road then went on to Canusium (modern Canosa di Puglia) and crossed the Ofanto River via a majestic bridge. Today this bridge can be seen in its medieval guise, bending hog-backed over five imposing spans.

Here, as a kind of preface to the city, two important tombs, both from the second century A.D., stood by the road. Today they are called Tomba Bagnoli[28] and Torre Casieri.[29] Another mausoleum of the Augustan age[30] anticipated the entrance to the city, which is announced in triumphal fashion by the great, single-spanned Arch of Trajan, also known as the Porta Varrone.[31]

The city is laid out like a balcony over the Ofanto Valley and the Tavoliere, dozing lazily behind its former grandeur. Situated at the border between Peucetia and Daunia, Canusium, according to myth, was founded by Diomedes and then grew dynamically under the aegis of the Greeks and later the Romans:

*It was a Greek colony with the name of Κανυσιον, as shown by coins found on the site. Livy notes it as the refuge of the few Romans who escaped from Cannae, and it appears to have been one of the most magnificent and cultured cities in Italy, if one may judge from the cameos, objects of gold and silver, and Greek and Roman coins which have been frequently dug up—as well as fragments of columns, architectural carvings, and mosaic pavements. It was much larger than the modern Canosa, which stands on part of its site.*[32]

The Canusians in fact remained bilingual until the age of Augustus and made their cultural and geographical primacy a point of honor.[33]

During the Empire, Canusium retained its importance thanks to its fortunate location along the Appian Way and its economic strength, which was due mainly to commerce in wheat and wool. As a crossroads in the Adriatic segment of the Via Appia Traiana, it played an important role in the Middle Ages as well, acting as an essential way station for the Christian religion. As the most ancient diocese in Apulia, it still has two extraordinary monuments from the Dark Ages: the cathedral and the Tomb of Bohemond.

It is inside that the cathedral preserves its ancient heart, in the splendid, peaceful rhythm of its five domes, and in the beauty of the episcopal chair and pulpit—the cathedra of St. Elia. Here the influence of Byzantium is decisive, since several masters who signed their work here are believed to have been educated in Constantinople.

Next to the cathedral, in a small, sunken courtyard, as if squeezed in there by force, is the Tomb of Bohemond,[34] a work freely inspired by the Temple of the Holy Sepulcher. This votive chapel, effectively the casket of the Norman prince's mortal remains, fits tightly into its central structure, nodding to its models in Byzantium and Jerusalem while bearing a local imprint as well. The outside is faced in marble, with a curtain of blind arches and pilaster strips, while the inside dissolves in an intense, naked sobriety interrupted only by the floor inscription, which reads like an invocation: *Boamundus*.

After Canusium, the Via Appia Traiana headed toward Andria, diverging slightly from the present-day drove way bearing the name of Appia Traiana. Then it passed to the north of Corato. The *mutatio* of Quintumdecimum must have been nearby and can perhaps be placed at the site of the Masseria Quadrone, near Monte Faraone. The next *mutatio* was Rubos, which obviously corresponds to modern-day Ruvo.

*Here Varius leaves us, which makes all his friends upset.*
*From there we move on to [Rubos], tired when we arrive,*
*having gone rather far on a road that was all mud.*
   (Horace *Satires* 1.5.93–95; trans. Jacob Fuchs)

One of the most important population centers of the Peucetians, Rubos later became a Roman *municipium*, holding a position of particular importance because of its Greek heritage and its advantageous location. Jackson wrote:

*[Ruvo] must have been a very large city in antiquity, since wherever foundations are dug on the hill which*

seem to raise the rose window[36] to a position of visual and aesthetic preeminence, with the impassive statue called the *Sitter* above it.[37]

Facing west, in the finest symbolic tradition of the great cathedrals, it breaks the monotony of its dark stone with the round-arched openings of the three portals, counterbalancing its lofty grace with a Romanesque calm. The very fine center portal splays outward in a sequence of reliefs and medieval *drôleries* with apocalyptic overtones and references. Carved with mastery and careful refinement, they seem unconcerned with the scowling lions and griffins held aloft by the tireless suffering of the inevitable telamons.[38]

Gregovarius wrote of it:

*The architectural style of Ruvo Cathedral shows that it belongs to the twelfth or thirteenth century: a modest basilica with nave and two aisles, and corresponding apses. In between the lateral doors is the central portal, richly adorned with sculptures. The upper part of the facade has a round window. Yet another time-blackened bell-tower stands next to the church. This severe, gloomy mass, seen there surrounded by narrow little streets, creates a strange impression: it is as though the three-dimensional figure of a now obscure past were suddenly riding up before our eyes!*[39]

Not to be missed is a visit to the Museo Jatta, which houses a rich and splendid nineteenth-century collection of ancient vases, the pride of a local ceramic art long since lost.[40]

**From Ruvo to Bari**

After Ruvo the road continued on with an eastern deviation toward the *mutatio* of Bitunti (modern Bitonto). Based on what the poet Martial says, the Roman Bitunti appears to have been a rather marginal center, the butt of mockery and disdain:

*So these names so rustic make you laugh? Then laugh, laugh:*
*Better rustic than to hail from Bitunti.*
(Martial *Epigrams* 4.55)

In reality the low regard in which the Latin poet held the town dates from a time prior to the opening of the Via Appia Traiana, which actually gave

*it occupies, vases, coins, and ornaments are found. It is believed to have been twenty times as large as the present town. The Greek coins found here have the name "PYBA" with an owl and the head of Pallas, which shows that it was an Athenian colony.*[35]

The cathedral is the city's most outstanding monument. With its great, flat, elongated facade, it seems to bring a touch of the Gothic to Apulian lands. But upon close examination, its steeply pitched gables recall nothing from beyond the Alps; rather, they

*The Cathedral of Bitonto, dedicated to St. Valentine and built in the second half of the thirteenth century, using the basilica of S. Nicola in Bari as model.*

*Facing page: Detail of the right-hand, lateral facade of Bitonto Cathedral.*

a considerable boost to this population center of Le Murge.[41]

Imbedded in a plain of olive groves, vineyards, and almond orchards, Bitonto stands out proudly with its ever-fascinating cathedral.[42] The local brown limestone dresses this abode of St. Valentine in French garb, a kind of counterpoint to the Mediterranean severity of the local taste. A fine example of mature Romanesque architecture, it launches a historical high note into the sky over Bari province. It does so by quoting that city's basilica of S. Nicola with its spires, steeply pitched eaves, and blind arches. It culminates with a flourish in the precious carving of the portal and the rose window, the latter almost protected by a fine archivolt supported by animals atop hanging columns. According to Jackson:

*Round the door runs a double band of arabesques; in the inner monsters intertwine with the stems in a masterly fashion, the outer has rosettes as the center of each convolution. Above is a projecting hood-mould richly carved with acanthus and volutes which are made to form a band outside the foliage. The lower portion of the composition is the usual crouching lion on a bracket-kind of pedestal, with a beautifully proportioned column and cap which support rather more foolish-looking griffins than usual.[43]*

The right side, cadenced by the chiaroscuro sequence of the six deep arch-spans, supports a delicate upper gallery of six-arched openings balanced on colonnettes which, with their different shapes, highlight this outpouring of feverish sculptural fantasy. The Latin-cross interior comes alive

*Lunette with New Testament scenes over the central portal of Bitonto Cathedral.*

*Facing page: Detail of the arcade on the right-hand side of Bitonto Cathedral.*

*On pages 208–209: The famous marble pulpit in Bitonto Cathedral, signed by the sculptor Nicolaus in 1229. The work's interest, beyond the elegance of the carving and openwork, lies above all in the triangular slab laid into the parapet of the stairway, with its bas-reliefs of four figures traditionally identified as members of the Swabian ruling family.*

in a rarefied, filtered light that runs over the shading of the capitals, galleries, and arches, condensing on the sculptural shapes of the figures, animals, and various mythical creatures: "The carving of the caps shows great variety and fancy. Many of them have monsters seated back to back, griffins with men's heads, apes with the heads of cats, &c., and others fill the long side with interlacing stems and foliage."[44]

One feels almost like crying out, as did St. Bernard of Clairvaux in his famous *Letter to Guillaume de Saint-Thierry* (1150), "That wondrous deformed beauty, that beautiful deformity!"[45]—except that one is repeatedly distracted by the refined workmanship of the ambo with its jumble of symbols and figures, signed by the same Nicolaus who established himself at Trani.

Descending into the crypt, an extraordinary forest of arches and capitals, one cannot help but reflect on the motivations and influences that led to this prodigious architectural phenomenon in Apulian territory, on how the Normans, who gave expression to the culminating moment of the Romanesque, insinuated themselves, with their Northern imprint, into a syncretistic fabric enriched by preexisting Byzantine, Lombard, and Islamic sensibilities. From this cauldron of experiences and cultures one emerges bedazzled, especially thinking back on the fantastical creations and diverse monsters. It reminds one of the gloomy note struck by Bernard de Clairvaux in the letter mentioned above:

*What on earth are they doing there, those grotesque monsters, those strangely deformed beauties and comely deformities, in your many cloisters where the friars devote themselves to sacred readings? What do they signify, these filthy apes, ferocious lions, bizarre centaurs that are only half-men? And those tigers with striped fur, those knights in battle, those hunters blowing their horns? Here you see at times several bodies under a single head, at times several heads on a single body. Here a quadruped has a serpent's tail, there a fish has a quadruped's head. And further on, behold an animal that looks like a horse in front and a billy goat behind. And vice versa, a horned beast that ends up as a horse.*

*In short, the variety of these shapes seems so great and so wondrous that one is more drawn to reading*

*sculptures than manuscripts. And the day, which should be used to meditate upon the law of God, is spent contemplating these frivolities.*

*My lord, if we do not blush at these absurdities, let us at least regret what they have cost.*

From Bitonto, the route bifurcated. One branch, from the Porta di Egnazia, followed an inland route, retracing what had once been the Via Minucia.[46] The other ran along the coast, following the route of the Via Gellia, heading toward Bari.

As a road hub and strategic center, Bari progressively gained in importance over time, growing from a simple Peucetian town and port into a Roman *municipium*, eventually assuming the role of the region's capital for the Byzantines and then the Normans. From Bari the knights and soldiers would set out on their Crusades, and the pilgrims on their journey to the Holy Lands.

In 1087, three Barese caravels with sixty-two sailors aboard made off from Myra in Lycia (coastal Asia Minor) with the mortal remains of St. Nicholas, forever marking the city's destiny. To honor the prestige of those relics, one of the finest Romanesque basilicas in Christendom was built there. The whole city wanted it to be erected in the middle of the court of the Byzantine catapan (governor), as if to symbolically mark its limit.[47]

Regarding the cult of St. Nicholas, Piovene wrote:

*Apulia is the region [of Italy] where one most strongly feels the East. . . . St. Nicholas, worshiped in Bari, is a Russian saint as well. . . . In the old section of Bari, the stupendous Apulian Romanesque unfolds, tinged with Eastern influences. Massive S. Nicola, with its broad, full facade pierced by towers, is one of the great churches of Italy. It was built, after various vicissitudes, to house the body of St. Nicholas, which had been stolen from Myra. It is said that his bones exude the purest of water, distilled as if in a laboratory. The basilica, which served as the prototype of Romanesque architecture for the entire region, was restored between the two wars and now appears in all its original starkness. Only in the crypt is work still ongoing. The other great church of Bari, the Cathedral, which possesses almost the same beauty, is*

*also being restored with similar intentions. In both, Apulian Romanesque sculpture takes wing, meticulously refined, dense, and Orientalizing in its arabesques of animals and flowers.*[48]

Far from being an exclusively sacred and spiritual heritage, the Romanesque cathedrals of Bari province are the synthesis of a civic culture linked to that flow of vital energies that manifested itself around the eleventh and twelfth centuries and was nurtured with great vigor by the Apulian cities. The cities indeed became the focal point of a great variety of interests and concerns that were, of course, connected with the Holy Lands and the traffic in relics, but also with the intense agricultural and commercial activity spurred by the presence of numerous ports and communication routes such as the Via Appia Traiana.

The facade of S. Nicola, with its upward thrust to a sky often swept clean by the west wind, is as though contracted and buttressed by the massive bell towers on either side. Morton described his first encounter with this cathedral:

*In a few minutes I entered a different world. It happened to be a singularly noisy night in New Bari, with loud speakers casting the voices of nasal giants into the darkness as some civic occasion was being celebrated in the open air. . . . The moonlight, spilling itself over white archways and ancient doorways, led into courtyards where outside steps rose to houses which had been lived in for centuries.*

*I was soon hopelessly lost and found that I had left in the hotel the small pocket compass which I usually carry for such occasions. Unwilling to betray my foreignness by speaking to any of the figures who brushed past me in the narrow lanes, I wandered on, turning now left, now right, attracted by a moonlit courtyard or by the sound of high-pitched voices singing songs with the Arab semi-tones which you hear all over the south, or by some ancient building, massive as a fortress, which looked as though it must have numbered crusaders among its lodgers. I began to wonder if chance would lead me out of this maze or at what point I should be obliged to ask for help.*

*Emerging from an alley way, I found myself in a wide and empty piazza where, like a stately ship,*

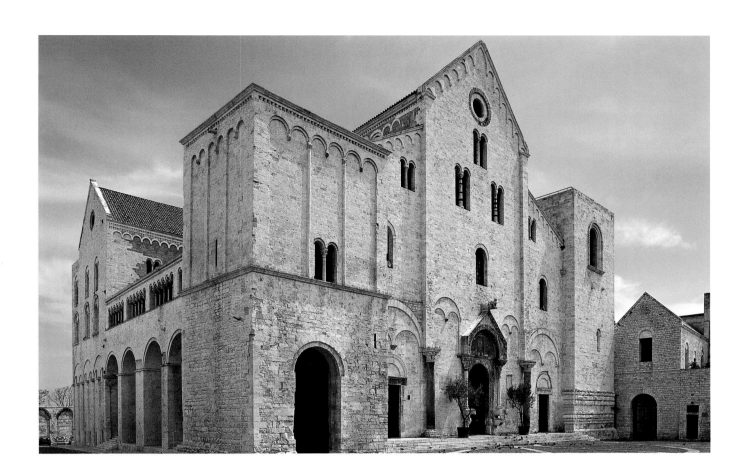

a splendid Norman church rose in the moonlight.
*Floodlights picked out a tower which I recognized as
the campanile that the porter had told me was the
bell-tower of the cathedral. This beautiful building,
with a rose window above the west front, reminded
me of some of the Norman churches in England, but
with a difference. Where, for example, in England
would one find the side columns of a window resting
on the backs of two elephants? Still, I thought, the
men who had built this basilica had spoken the same
language as those who had built Durham and Ely,
and it occurred to me that possibly one reason why one
feels at home in Apulia is that every town contains
Norman buildings which correspond to the Norman
buildings of English towns and villages.*[49]

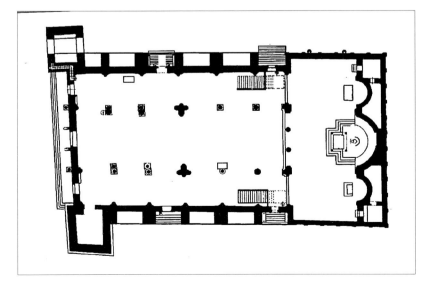

*Facing page, left: Main portal of the basilica of S. Nicola.*

*Facing page, right: One of the two bulls flanking the main portal of S. Nicola.*

*On pages 214–15: The cathedra of Bishop Elia, a masterpiece of Romanesque art, in the basilica of S. Nicola. On page 214, a detail of the rear of the throne.*

*On page 216, top: The so-called amphitheater of ancient Gnathia. It is called an "amphitheater" purely by convention. In fact it was simply an enclosure that formed a piazza next to the forum.*

*On page 216, bottom: The trapezoidal area identified as the forum of ancient Gnathia.*

*On page 217: A stretch of the Via Appia Traiana, which used to pass through Gnathia.*

*On pages 218–19: The port of Egnazia.*

The vast, welcoming interior was a place of primitive, apotropaic worship, a crossroads of people and nations of different origins and cultures who would press into the crypt to capture crumbs of heady sainthood in their rags and handkerchiefs. It is noteworthy for its exceptional *ciborium* (altar canopy),[50] and especially for the artistic mastery of the cathedra of St. Elia, previously mentioned. Brandi discusses it at length:

*This beautiful sculpture is supposed to date back to Bishop Elia of Bari in the year 1098, a very distant date that has raised fierce doubt. In any event the cathedra is an isolated monument, since one can attribute to the same sculptor, and with some doubt, only one capital of the iconostasis of S. Nicola. . . .*

*[T]he sculptor of the cathedra emphasizes openings, separating the limbs of the Telamons and perforating them without creating a background. In this sense, the Byzantine-style openwork of the transennae (the screens under the chair's arms) are fully harmonized with the whole play of transparencies created by the arms and legs. . . . The Telamons in Bari are animated and do not seek unity in a single verticle body; they resemble neither a column nor a spiral column. This freedom is so astonishing that it leaves one far more perplexed as to the very early dating of 1098 than do its vague and entirely external resemblances to Wiligelmo [act. Modena, 1099–1120] and Aquitanian sculpture. However, it is not possible to establish any line of development, since the monument stands alone, even were it to be placed a century later in time. This should be recognized and underscored: not even by arbitrarily changing the date of the cathedra of Bari is its situation in the overall history of art made any easier or more verifiable.*

*What remains is this extraordinary monument, whose beauty is so great, its accents so new, its proportions so lithe as to make it unique in every sense. And just as it has no precedents in time for its understanding of plasticity in space, it likewise has no descendents either. For this reason, in my opinion, one might as well keep to the traditional dating.*[51]

**From Bari to Ostuni**

After Bari, the coastal branch of the Via Appia Traiana continued along a route roughly retraced by the present-day state road, SS 16, following the jagged basalt configuration of the so-called "crenellated coast"[52] to Egnazia (ancient Gnatia or Gnathia).

The inland branch headed instead toward Ceglie (ancient Caeliae),[53] through a sweet, luxuriant landscape carpeted with fruit and almond orchards and the customarily large, contorted olive trees. It then continued along a sheep-track that led to the *statio* of Ad Veneris (corresponding to the modern town of Monopoli), before hooking back up with the coastal route as far as Egnazia.

*The weather improves next day, but the footing is worse right up to fishy Barium's walls. Then Gnatia, built while water spirits sulked, gives us good reason to laugh: they try to tell us incense melts upon their temple's steps without fire. Apella the Jew may believe this if he likes, not I; I've learned about the tranquil life the gods enjoy and know, whatever miracle nature makes, the gods won't give up their peace to send it down from heaven.*

(Horace *Satires* 1.5.96–103; trans. Jacob Fuchs)

According to Horace, Gnathia[54] was "*lymphis iratis extructa*"—built over irate waters, in spite of the nymphs' desires. This would remain as a kind of curse, or rather, an inescapable fate for the city, which has been left half swallowed up by slow earth subsidence.[55] At the border between Peucetia and Messapia, Gnathia stands proudly with its acropolis atop a promontory that soars high over the sea.[56] Its position would ensure its good fortune as a complementary seaport to Brindisi. Strabo wrote, "As one sails from Brentesium along the Adriatic seaboard, one comes to the city of Egnatia, which is the common stopping-place for people who are traveling either by sea of land to Barium" (*Geography* 6.3.8).[57]

Egnazia is now cut in two by the modern road, leaving the acropolis outside the archaeological area that lies below. We head straight down to the forum with its trapezoidal piazza surrounded by porticoes, which conserves part of the original Doric decoration (first century A.D.). At the center is an ancient speaker's rostrum and various honorary pedestals. Further on, one can see the remains of a great basilica dating perhaps as far back as the fourth century B.C.

At last we come to the Via Appia Traiana, which cuts across the city with its white paving stones, worn and grooved by the friction of cart-wheels. After all this straying from the road, one feels almost emotional at rediscovering it in an ancient site, so well paved and preserved. The shops lining its path still remain, testaments to the intense commercial activity of the nearby port and forum. For a moment this patch of antiquity seems to come alive with swarms of diverse people: sailors, prostitutes, merchants, and marauders coming and going without any visible end. But suddenly the spell is broken, and the amphitheater, which also once teemed with people, now appears mute before us.[58]

Leaving Gnathia behind, the Via Appia Traiana continued its coastal route along the foothills of Le Murge, heading toward Brundisium. After Terme di Torre Canne, near Torre S. Leonardo, it came to the *mutatio* of Decimum, then headed further inland in the direction of Ostuni. Jackson wrote:

*The towns which lie between Brindisi and Bari have an Eastern appearance to a considerable extent. They are uniformly white, and, if the wind happen to be blowing, raising a haze of dust, look luminous. There are no dark spots, even in open windows and doors, and the effect is fairy-like and unreal. The roofs are most of them flat, and the trees are generally olive, carob, and orange, with an occasional palm, so that the traveler feels that he is near the magic East.[59]*

Messapian in origin, Ostuni may perhaps be identified with the city of Stulnium mentioned by Pliny and Ptolemy. Thereafter, it leaves no mark on

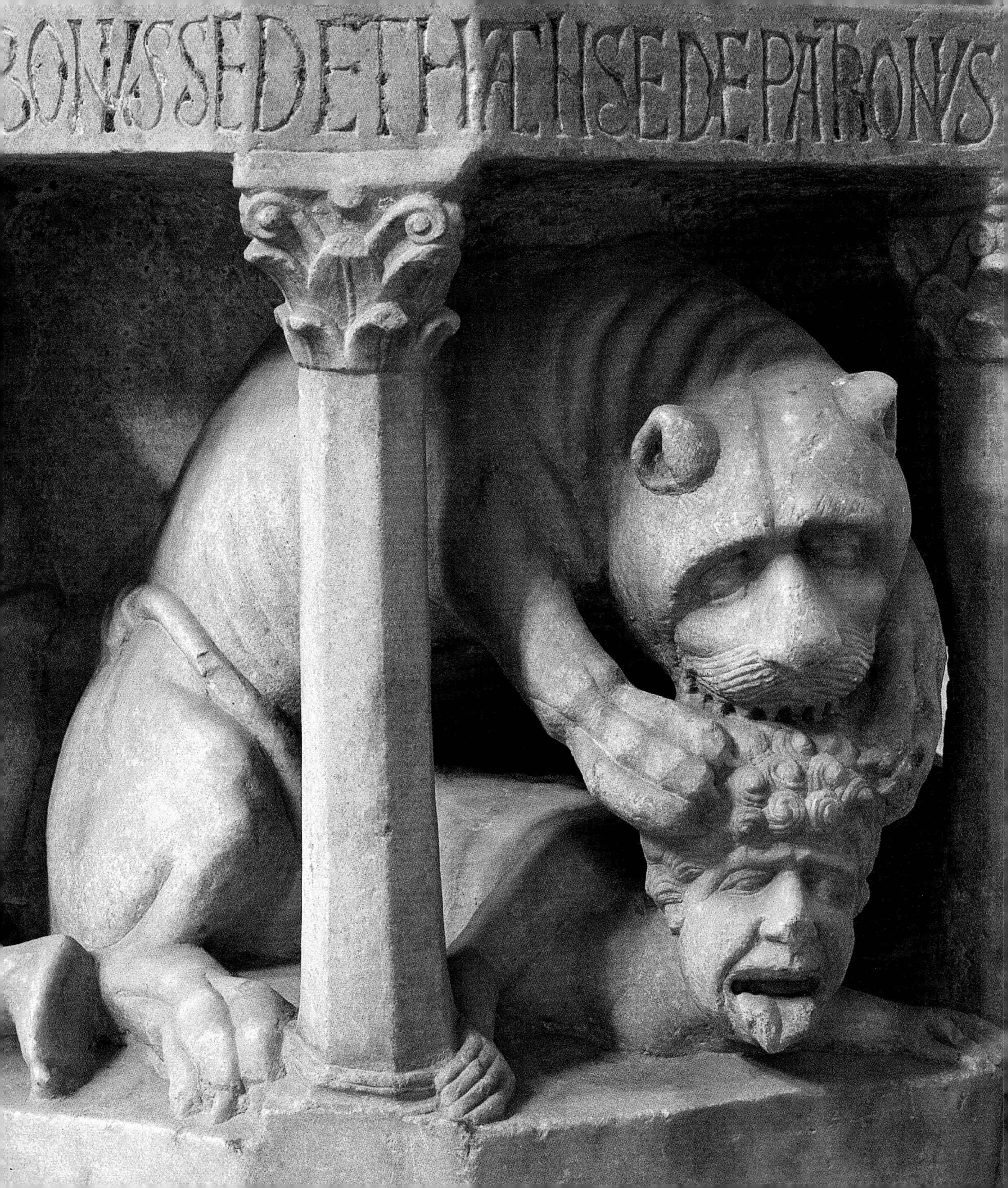

best face, its whitewashed facades. In a very ancient tradition, a spring rite of renewal is repeated every year by repainting the gray stone of Le Murge white. "Ostuni is beautiful in and of itself," wrote Piovene, "with a cathedral whose late-Gothic facade stands in counterpoint to the predominant Baroque."

Only the architecturally important buildings are spared the obligatory whitewashing of narrow streets, staircases, archways, and courtyards. The splendid cathedral[60] dominates the city from above with its whimsical profile and pensile arches. It speaks a new language, different from the other nearby cathedrals, which are all Romanesque: It is a late-Gothic dialect with Dalmatian and Venetian inflections, revised and corrected with local cadences.[61] The result: a magnificent *coup de théatre* for anyone clambering up to the citadel and passing under the great arch.

## Brindisi

After Ostuni, the road ran along the seaboard, following the route of the modern coastal road, SS 379. Just ahead, near the coastal tower of S. Sabina, in the town of Mezzaluna, some concrete ruins, a series of cave dwellings, and some tombs identify the site as the former *statio* of Ad Speluncas. From here, the Via Appia Traiana proceeded another sixteen miles to Brundisium.[62] A nineteenth-century traveler wrote:

*Brindisi! The name inspires deep veneration! . . . In Roman times it was the capital of the Salentini: such is how Florus defined it. The magnificent harbor that nature gave it determined its prosperity. After having built the Appian Way from Rome to Capua, the Romans, wanting to spread their conquests to Greece and Asia, extended it all the way to Brindisi, and thus it earned its name as Queen of Roads. And so the Republican armies began taking ship at Brindisi.*[63]

Gateway to the East, Brindisi thrusts its promontory between two inlets (the Eastern Inlet and the Western Inlet) enclosed within a single bay. It is an extraordinary natural setting, and its harbor, with its stag's-head shape, was a source of ancient pride:

*Brentesion [Brindisi], moreover, is situated in a most favorable position also as concerns harbors. Indeed it*

history until the ninth century A.D., when it was taken by Basilius the Macedonian and became a Byzantine diocese. Captured by the Normans in 1071, it belonged variously to the count of Lecce, the prince of Taranto, and the duke of Bari in accordance with the respective histories of these cities.

Perched on a hill with its small white houses reflecting the intense sunlight, the light of the Orient, it seems concerned only with showing its

*Above left: Ostuni Cathedral.*

*Above right: Late-Gothic portal of Ostuni Cathedral. The lunette contains a bas-relief of the Virgin and Child.*

*possesses several ports untroubled by waves, enclosed within a single bay, which comprises several inlets, so that its shape resembles that of a stag's horns, and the city's name derives from this. Indeed the site as well as the city very closely resemble the head of a stag, and in the Messapic tongue a stag's head is, in fact, called "brentesium." (Strabo Geography 6.3.6)*

First a Messapic port, then a Roman one. Brindisi's role grew increasingly important after it was occupied by Rome in 266 B.C. As a naval base facing east, it quickly became one of the most prominent commercial and military hubs of the Mediterranean, also by virtue of being the terminus of the Via Appia Antica.

A composite city frequented by people from different countries, it had a forum, temples, baths, and theaters. Nothing remains of these ancient

expressions except for the two columns that constitute the terminus of the Appian Way at the port. Morton describes it as follows:

*I was standing upon the most celebrated spot in the city: the summit of the beautiful flight of steps from which rises the tall Roman column that marks the termination of the Via Appia. The column commands the port today as it did centuries ago. The harbour is one of Nature's supreme achievements. The sea flows in through a narrow entrance and forms two wide protected arms or bays, to the left and right of the town where ships may anchor in safety even should a gale be blowing.[64]*

The road indeed completed its itinerary through the south of the Italic peninsula triumphantly, with a dramatic, symbolic prospect of monumental pro-

portions. When he set about restoring the Appian Way, Septimius Severus had wanted to emphasize its start and finish with notes of solemn grandeur, with the Septizodium as an overture, opening the route at Rome, and the two commemorative columns as the finale and epilogue.[65]

Like columns of Hercules reaching out to an unknown world, those monoliths of African cipollino marked the termination of an extraordinary itinerary that had defied nature by overcoming its challenges. It was a bridge to the East, in which the building skill of the Romans measured itself against a limitless horizon. *Queen of Roads*: a justly deserved title, and an unequaled, eternal supremacy.

In the dark centuries, pilgrims, merchants, and crusaders took ship at Brindisi and set sail for the Holy Land, on a journey full of hope and expecta-tion. The Templars built a support house there, of which the fine portico in the Piazza del Duomo is an elegant reminder. Here ended the Via Francigena of the South.

It was around midday in the spring of 37 B.C. when Horace arrived at Brundisium. The city was flooded with a noontide sunlight that obliterated all contrast and shade. Under that sky of a blue one sees only in Apulia, he caught a glimpse of the port like a mirage.

*At Brundesium the long trip is over; now this long
page is too.*
(Horace *Satires* 1.5.104; trans. Jacob Fuchs)

*Above and facing page: The so-called Portico of the Templars in Brindisi, today incorporated into the Museo Provinciale. The loggia, which served as a support station for crusaders, dates from the thirteenth–fourteenth centuries.*

## Notes

1 More than sixty milestones survive with the name of Trajan on them (there were originally about 200).

2 Jean-Claude Richard de Saint-Non, *Voyage pittoresque, ou Descriptions des Royaumes de Naples et de Sicile*, 1781. Published in 5 vols. (Paris: Imprimerie de Clousier, 1781–86).

3 But he was probably only one of Apollodorus's better collaborators on the Roman work.

4 Amedeo Maiuri, *Passeggiate campane*, 1938. Originally published by Hoepli, a newer edition of this work appeared in 1990 (Milan: Rusconi).

5 We know that already in the Republican era, another road, a Via Minucia, was used from Beneventum as a much longer alternative to the Appian Way.

6 Trans. Horace Leonard Jones (Cambridge, MA: Harvard University Press, 1969).

7 Procopius *De bello Gothico* 5.14.5–6.

8 See Renato Stopani, *La via Francigena del Sud* (Florence: Le Lettere, 1992).

9 Cesare Brandi, *Terre d'Italia* (Rome: Riuniti, 1991).

10 H. V. Morton, *A Traveller in Southern Italy* (New York: Dodd, Mead & Co., 1969), pp. 117–18.

11 The little bridge has a stone semicircular arch that was enlarged in the Roman era and again in the modern age.

12 The bridge takes its name from a church that is no longer standing.

13 The climbing brick arches and the parapets done in *opus quadratum* are Roman.

14 The *statio*, as was often the case with these stopping places, was located about ten miles from Beneventum.

15 All that's left of the bridge are fragments of the pylons on which two or perhaps three great arches rested.

16 Located about 1 km from Monte S. Vito.

17 Guido Piovene, *Viaggio in Italia* (Milan: A. Mondadori, 1957; rpt. Milan: Baldini & Castoldi, 1993).

18 We know that ancient Aecae stood about 2 km west of present-day Troia. It was an Augustan colony and is mentioned by Polybius and Livy. After the battle of Cannae (216 B.C.), the city probably went over to Hannibal's camp, but it was retaken by Fabius Maximus in 214 B.C.

19 It was founded as a Byzantine fortress in 1019 by the catapan Basil Boioannes on the ruins of the ancient city; in 1022 it repeatedly resisted the attacks of Henry II.

20 F. Hamilton Jackson, *The Shores of the Adriatic: The Italian Side* (London: John Murray, 1906), pp. 146–48.

21 On the right side is another extraordinary bronze door (1127) by the same artist.

22 Particularly noteworthy for their splendid workmanship are the outside of the apse, with its double rows of colonnettes, and inside, the magnificent pulpit (1169), featuring a fine bas-relief of a struggle between wild beasts.

23 The ruins of this bridge can be seen near the Masseria Ponte Rotto. It was a considerable work both for its exceptional length and for its monumental structure, composed of about 30 pylons with central arches a good 15 m wide.

*The commemorative columns in the port of Brindisi, which marked the terminus of the Appian Way at the shoreline. Only a stump remains of one, the rest of which was transported to Lecce in the seventeenth century; there it was placed in the central square to serve as a base for a statue of the town's patron saint. The other column, which one may still admire in the port, is currently being restored.*

24 This spanned the Carapelle torrent on an embankment several hundred meters high, which made the road more comfortable and overcame the unevenness of the surrounding terrain.
25 Brandi, *Terre d'Italia*.
26 It was prominent above all in the fourth and third centuries B.C., during which time it even minted its own coins.
27 A thirty-year excavation campaign (by a Belgian university) has brought this center to light. Despite substantial surviving vestiges, it is still in a state of complete abandon.
28 A two-story funerary monument with an elegant polychrome brick facing with moldings. The bottom story had a barrel vault, while the upper, almost entirely destroyed, had two great arches giving onto the road.
29 A square-plan sepulcher in stone blocks at the base and brick in the upper part. The inner chamber still has the niches for the cinerary urns of the deceased.

30 All that is left of this is its great square base with some remnants of the large stone revetment blocks.
31 It is not clear whether this is a triumphal arch or a city gate deriving its name from the Roman consul defeated at Cannae (Varro). In all likelihood it was originally faced with marble.
32 Jackson, *The Shores of the Adriatic*, pp. 131–32.
33 Canusium was actually occupied by the Romans in 318 B.C., but long remained autonomous as a federated city.
34 Son of Robert Guiscard, hero of the First Crusade, who died in 1111.
35 Jackson, *The Shores of the Adriatic*, p. 83.
36 Some date it back to 1237, although others date it 1297. It has 12 small columns (12 apostles, 12 hours) with rounded trefoil arches with acanthus leaves.
37 Some consider this statue a portrait of Frederick II.
38 The interior, which features a Gothicizing verticality, has a basilican plan with three

semicircular apses which the facing cuts obliquely. Several times remodeled, it also features a fine gallery, supported on corbels with human, animal, and other phytomorphic figures, and connecting the bays.

39  Gregorovius, *Nelle Puglia.*

40  The collection features more than two thousand vases and ceramics of the region, passionately catalogued and saved from an otherwise irreversible spoliation by Giovanni Jatta, Sr., and the archaeologist Giovanni Jatta, Jr.

41  At first a Peucetian center, it became a Roman *municipium,* then grew as a way station of the Via Appia Traiana.

42  Built in the second half of the thirteenth century, it was supposed to have had a porch in front—as one can see from the vestiges of the springers over the facade's pilasters—but this project was never realized.

43  Jackson, *The Shores of the Adriatic,* pp. 70–71.

44  Ibid., p. 72.

45  See the passage from a letter by St. Bernard of Clairvaux quoted in the next paragraph of the text.

46  The *Tabula Peutingeriana* indicated the following *stationes:* Butontos VIIII (Bitonto)—Celia (Ceglie)—VIII Ezetium (Rutigliano)—XX Norve (Conversano)—VIII Ad Veneris (Monopoli)—VIII Gnatie (Egnatia).

47  The basilica is surrounded to this day by four courtyards, which were originally bordered by walls and towers marking the abbey's jurisdiction.

48  Piovene, *Viaggio in Italia,* 1957.

49  Morton, *A Traveller in Southern Italy,* pp. 92–93.

50  This dates from the twelfth century and is the work of *maestri comacini* (master craftsmen from Como in northern Italy). It rises up on four breccia columns, with very fine carved capitals, supporting an architrave adorned with a bronze inscription and a double-octagonal pyramidal baldacchino.

51  Brandi, *Terre d'Italia.* The full text of his argument is as follows:
   "This beautiful sculpture is supposed to date back to Bishop Elia of Bari in the year 1098, a very distant date that has raised fierce doubt. In any event the cathedra is an isolated monument, since one can attribute to the same sculptor, and with some doubt, only one capital of the iconostasis of S. Nicola. Thus rivers of ink have flowed about this year 1098, and the final hypothesis is that it is a conscious falsification having to do with a quarrel over proprietary rights between the diocese of Bari and the contiguous dioceses at a time when the presence of so ancient an episcopal cathedra would ensure precedence for the bishop's seat. The true reason for all this disputation, however, is to be found in the fact that it looks like too advanced a sculpture for that period, being even ahead of Wiligelmo of Modena Cathedral, whose dates, themselves often

*Above: The columns marking the terminus of the Appian Way in Brindisi, in a nineteenth-century engraving by Cucinello and Bianchi.*

*Left: Detail of a capital, with pagan gods, from one of the commemorative columns in Brindisi.*

disputed, fall somewhere between 1106 and 1110. The reason for this latter dispute is based on similarities with French Aquitanian sculpture—that is, from Toulouse and Moissac—which should come before it, even if only by very few years, and which displays certain patterns in common with Wiligelmo, especially in the characteristic folds in the garments, which are resolved as seams.

"Now the connections between Wiligelmo and the Cathedra of Elia are not superficial: in Wiligelmo's reliefs at Modena, we find the Telamon—i.e., a male caryatid—at the center of the Sacrifice of Cain and Abel, and it is highly reminiscent of the three Telamons of the cathedra in Bari. But this, with its folds, is the only similarity, because the cathedra is Apulian in style and recalls the one in the Cathedral of Canosa, sculpted by Romualdo in 1078-1079, a date no one has invalidated. But the elephants supporting the bishop's throne at Canosa are an imitation of Fatimite bronzes and have nothing to do with the Telamons of the cathedra of Elia. In the latter, one also finds decorative motifs in the Muslim style and openwork in the Byzantine style, cultural components that are absent in Wiligelmo and Aquitanian sculpture. In a word, the 'Apulianness' of the cathedra of Elia cannot be called into doubt, and the arguments marshaled to undermine the date are, if not gratuitous, at least entirely without any documented historical foundation.

"We must, moreover, bear in mind that Wiligelmo did not necessarily begin with Modena Cathedral, and that, apart from the lone element of the folds, there is no other stylistic relationship between Wiligelmo of Modena and the cathedra of Elia. Especially different is the manner of understanding plasticity and space. In the Modena reliefs, the references to the background are explicit: the figure is not conceived within a closed perimeter; gestures are rare, the arms, for the most part, are attached to the body, creating a discrete volumetric unit; the tree of good and evil, with the snake, looks like a spiral column; the tree's branches barely protrude from its surface. A similar sort of plastic condensation is also used to give hands and feet a pronounced bulkiness, and proves so highly distinct in the whole of the composition that it could not be attributed to other works where one does not find the same degree of plastic condensation.

"Let us now see if we encounter anything of this sort in the cathedra of Elia. We should say at once that the plasticity of the latter is almost the opposite of Wiligelmo's. Where Wiligelmo unites masses and volumes, the sculptor of the cathedra emphasizes openings, separating the limbs of the Telamons and perforating them without creating a background. In this sense, the Byzantine-style openwork of the transennae (the screens under the chair's arms) are

fully harmonized with the whole play of transparencies created by the arms and legs. Now, observations such as these decidedly establish a difference from Wiligelmo: this is not to say that the sculptor of the cathedra is greater or lesser than Wiligelmo, but that he certainly was different, and specific stylistic elements such as the folds are not of the sort as would make it possible to establish, let alone a sameness of hand, but even so much as a common provenance, aside from that found earlier in Aquitanian sculpture. Moreover, in his way of presenting the Telamons, the cathedra sculptor is keen not to block all the masses and bodies together, whereas Wiligelmo's bas-relief caryatids, on the contrary, form a block, practically fused together in a single piece. The Telamons in Bari are animated and do not seek unity in a single verticle body; they resemble neither a column nor a spiral column. This freedom is so astonishing that it leaves one far more perplexed as to the very early dating of 1098 than do its vague and entirely external resemblances to Wiligelmo and Aquitanian sculpture. On the other hand it is not possible to establish any line of development, since the monument stands alone, even were it to be placed a century later in time. This should be recognized and underscored: not even by arbitarily changing the date of the cathedra of Bari is its situation in the overall history of art made any easier or more verifiable.

"What remains is this extraordinary monument, whose beauty is so great, its accents so new, its proportions so lithe as to make it unique in every sense. And just as it has no precedents in time for its understanding of plasticity in space, it likewise has no descendents either. For this reason, in my opinion, one might as well keep to the traditional dating."

52  The *stationes* recorded in the *Itineraria* are, in order: *mutatio* Turris Julianae (near Masseria Vito Luigi); *mutatio* Turres Aurelianae (Torre Ripagnola); and Vertum or Diriam (Torre d'Orta).

53  It then continued on toward Norba, corresponding to present-day Conversano.

54  It was already constituted a Roman *municipium* after the First Social War (90–89 B.C.). Vespasian, however, turned it into a colony.

55  This type of seismic activity, called bradyseism, is characteristic of the region.

56  The only monumental vestiges here are the foundations of a fourth-century B.C. temple and the remnants of an early medieval fortification with square defensive walls and bastions.

57  Trans. Horace Leonard Jones.

58  The recently built Antiquarium features the most interesting of the archaeological finds recovered here. Particularly noteworthy are a fine floor mosaic with a representation of the Three Graces, and some characteristic local ceramics (glossy black

with white, yellow, and red painted on top). This sort of ceramic is called Gnathia.

59  Jackson, *The Shores of the Adriatic*, p. 44.

60  Begun in 1435 and completed in 1495.

61  The tripartite facade has a fine coping that plays entirely on the movement of the outlines. In the middle section this forms a tympanum created by two inverted arches, and it is continued on the wings with two half-moons. The interior was remade in predominantly eighteenth-century forms.

62  After the Ad Speluncas station, the road in fact veered away from the present-day coastal road and followed a more direct path to Masseria Apani. A little bit past the Masseria there is still a large well-preserved viaduct of the Via Appia Traiana done in *opus reticulatum* with brick layerings and buttresses.

63  Guiseppe Ceva Grimaldi, *Itinerario da Napoli a Lecce, e nella provincia di Terra d'Otranto nell'anno 1818* (Naples: Tip. di Porcelli, 1821).

64  Morton, *A Traveller in Southern Italy*, p. 161.

65  It was a truly monumental complex that culminated in the harbor, embracing all who came in from the sea. Of the two great cipollino columns, each 19 m high, one survives intact. All that remains of the other, which collapsed in 1528, is a stump. They might have held aloft a kind of beacon or searchlight. On their beautiful capitals, in the composite style, is a fine relief of a chorus of gods (Jupiter, Neptune, Mars, Pallas, and eight tritons).

# Horace's Journey

*SATIRES* 1.5

TRANSLATED BY JACOB FUCHS

*lines 1–3. First Day: Rome—Ariccia (16 miles = ca. 24 km)*
*lines 3–9. Second Day: Ariccia—Forappio (27 miles = ca. 40 km)*
*lines 9–23. Night of the Second Day: On the canal, from Forappio to the source of Feronia*
*(16 miles = ca. 24 km)*

Rome's grandeur left behind, I was met in Aricia
with moderate hospitality. Heliodorus the rhetorician,
most learned of Greeks, came with me. Then, off to Forum Appii,
full of boatmen and crooked innkeepers. We were lazy
5    and spent two days getting there. Those with quicker legs
do it in one. The Appian Way is easier if you go slower.
Here, since the water was unspeakably bad, I declared war
upon my stomach, waiting in sour spirits for the others
in the party to finish eating. Now Night brought darkness
10   forth upon the earth and prepared to flood heaven with stars.
Now shout followed shout, slaves to boatmen and boatmen
to slaves: "Land here!" "Don't overload us, dammit!" "Enough,
we're packed!" Settling the money and hitting up the mule
waste at least an hour. The horrible gnats and swamps frogs
15   forbid all sleep. Drunk on cheap wine, the boatman sings
about his girl back home. A passenger joins in to make
a contest. Eventually he gets tired and goes to sleep,
so the lazy boatman lets the mule feed itself its dinner,
tying its rope around a stone, and then flops down and snores.
20   Come daybreak and we see that our boat isn't moving at all;
but finally someone with a temper pounces on the mule
and on the boatman, whacking away at skulls and butts
with a willow rod. By midmorning we've barely made port.

Egressum magna me accepit Aricia Roma
Hospitio modico: rhetor comes Heliodorus,
Graecorum longe doctissimus: inde Forum Appi,
Differtum nautis, cauponibus atque malignis.
Hoc iter ignavi divisimus, altius ac nos
Praecinctis unum: minus est gravis Appia tardis.
Hic ego propter aquam, quod erat deterrima, ventri
Indico bellum, cenantes haud animo aequo
Exspectans comites. Iam nox inducere terris
Umbras et caelo diffundere signa parabat:
Tum pueri nautis, pueris convicia nautae
Ingerere: 'huc appelle'; 'trecentos inseris'; 'ohe!
Iam satis est.' Dum aes exigitur, dum mula ligatur,
Tota abit hora. Mali culices ranaeque palustres
Avertunt somnos, absentem ut cantat amicam
Multa prolutus vappa nauta atque viator
Certatim. Tandem fessus dormire viator
Incipit ac missae pastum retinacula mulae
Nauta piger saxo religat stertitque supinus.
Iamque dies aderat, nil cum procedere lintrem
Sentimus; donec cerebrosus prosilit unus
Ac mulae nautaeque caput lumbosque saligno
Fuste dolat. Quarta vix demum exponimur hora.

*lines 24–33. Third Day: Temple of Feronia – Terracina (3 miles= ca. 4.5 km; after a night on the canal, a day of rest)*

| | |
|---|---|
| We wash our hands and faces, Feronia, in your waters. | Ora manusque tua lavimus, Feronia, lympha: |
| 25   After breakfast, we creep along three miles, climbing | Milia tum pransi tria repimus atque subimus |
| white rocks—visible, gleaning, far away—to high Anxur. | Impositum saxis late candentibus Anxur. |
| Here we're to meet Maecenas and the distinguished | Huc venturus erat Maecenas optimus atque |
| Cocceius, both authorized to speak in great affairs | Cocceius, missi magnis de rebus uterque |
| of state, both skilled at solving problems between friends. | Legati, aversos soliti componere amicos. |
| 30   And here I get an inflammation and have to smear my eyes | Hic oculis ego nigra meis collyria lippus |
| with black salve. Soon Maecenas arrives, and also | Illinere. Interea Maecenas advenit atque |
| Cocceius. Fonteius Capito comes then too, a man | Cocceius Capitoque simul Fonteius, ad unguem |
| with no flaw in him anywhere, and Antony's best friend. | Factus homo, Antoni, non ut magis alter, amicus. |

*lines 34–38. Fourth Day: Terracina – Fondi – Formia (26 miles = ca. 38.5 km)*

| | |
|---|---|
| Fundi, in the magistracy of Aufidius Luscus, we leave | Fundos Aufidio Lusco praetore libenter |
| 35   with joy, laughing at the crazed ex-clerk and his prizes, | Linquimus, insani ridentes praemia scribae, |
| the purple-bordered robe, striped tunic, pan of coals. | Praetextam et latum clavum prunaeque vatillum. |
| In the Mamurrae's hometown, exhausted, we rest a while, | In Mamurrarum lassi deinde urbe manemus, |
| Murena supplying us a place to live, Capito a kitchen. | Murena praebente domum, Capitone culinam. |

*lines 39–46. Fifth Day: Formia – Sinuessa – Ponte Campano (27 miles = ca. 40 km)*

| | |
|---|---|
| The next morning's sun rises most happily for me, since | Postera lux oritur multo gratissima: namque |
| 40   Plotius and Varius meet us at Sinuessa, and Vergil | Plotius et Varius Sinuessae Vergiliusque |
| is there with them. Nobler souls than these never dwelled | Occurrunt, animae, quales neque candidiores |
| on earth, and no one has closer ties to them than I. | Terra tulit neque quis me sit devinctior alter. |
| O what embraces we shared, and what great rejoicing! | O qui complexus et gaudia quanta fuerunt! |
| Nothing compares, I think, when thinking right, to a good friend. | Nil ego contulerim iucundo sanus amico. |
| 45   Near the Campanian bridge a government hostel shelters us, | Proxima Campano ponti quae villula, tectum |
| and the officers in charge give us supplies. | Praebuit, et parochi, quae debent, ligna salemque. |

*lines 47–70. Sixth Day: Ponte Campano – Capua – Caudio (38 miles = ca. 56 km)*

| | |
|---|---|
| Then, at Capua, the mules put their saddles down early. | Hinc muli Capuae clitellas tempore ponunt. |
| Maecenas goes to play games, Vergil and I go to sleep; | Lusum it Maecenas, dormitum ego Vergiliusque: |
| ball throwing doesn't amuse the red-eyed and sour-stomached. | Namque pila lippis inimicum et ludere crudis. |
| 50   We stay at Cocceius's well-stocked farm, north of Caudium | Hinc nos Coccei recipit plenissima villa, |
| and its inns. At this point that little sharp-talking leech | Quae super est Caudi cauponas. Nunc mihi paucis |
| Sarmentus had a fight with Messius Cockadoodle, of which, | Sarmenti scurrae pugnam Messique Cicirri, |
| Muse, I would hear, beginning with the parentage of those | Musa, velim memores, et quo patre natus uterque |
| who met in war. Messius is of noble Oscan blood; | Contulerit lites. Messi clarum genus Osci; |
| 55   Sarmentus's line goes back to his owner. Thus their lineage. | Sarmenti domina exstat: ab his maioribus orti |
| And now the battle: First Sarmentus. "A wild horse, that's you, | Ad pugnam venere. Prior Sarmentus 'equi te |
| a real snorting stallion." We laugh. Messius doesn't mind. | Esse feri similem dico.' Ridemus, et ipse |
| "Damn right," he says, and jerks his head. "And if your brow | Messius 'accipio', caput et movet. 'O, tua cornu |
| still had its horn uncut," Sarmentus adds, "you'd be a terror; | Ni foret exsecto frons', inquit, 'quid faceres, cum |

| | |
|---|---|
| 60 even with it cut, you're quite a fright." For an ugly scar | Sic mutilus minitaris?' At illi foeda cicatrix |
| disfigured his forehead on the left, beneath its bristles. | Saetosam laevi frontem turpaverat oris. |
| Campanian rot, jokes Sarmentus, and goes on about his face. | Campanum in morbum, in faciem permultam iocatus, |
| Then he asks him to perform Cyclops' shepherd dance: | Pastorem saltaret uti Cyclopa rogabat: |
| with those looks he'd need no tragic mask or heavy boots. | Nil illi larva aut tragicis opus esse cothurnis. |
| 65 Now Cockadoodle has a lot to say. Would Sarmentus give | Multa Cicirrus ad haec: donasset iamne catenam |
| his slave chain to the lares? And though now a clerk, | Ex voto Laribus, quaerebat; scriba quod esset, |
| didn't his old mistress own him just the same? He ends | Nihilo deterius dominae ius esse: rogabat |
| by asking why he ever fled: for he could fill himself | Denique, cur umquam fugisset, cui satis una |
| upon a pound of corn a day, he was then skinny and small. | Farris libra foret, gracili sic tamque pusillo. |
| 70 That's the kind of dinner we like, and we take our time. | Prorsus iucunde cenam producimus illam. |

*lines 71–85. Seventh Day: Caudio – Benevento – Trivico (36 miles = ca. 53 km)*

| | |
|---|---|
| Then we go straight to Beneventum, where a diligent host | Tendimus hinc recta Beneventum ubi sedulus hospes |
| nearly burns his place down while cooking bony thrushes. | Paene macros arsit dum turdos versat in igni: |
| For through his old kitchen a vagrant flame veered, | Nam vaga per veterem dilapso flamma culinam |
| from a fallen volcano of logs, mounting high to lick the roof. | Volcano summum properabat lambere tectum. |
| 75 Hungry guests, terrified slaves, snatch the food to safety, | Convivas avidos cenam servosque timentes |
| everyone tries to put the fire out—quite a scene. | Tum rapere atque omnes restinguere velle videres. |
| From here on, Apulia starts to display some mountains | Incipit ex illo montes Apulia notos |
| familiar to me, those with the sirocco parches, and which | Ostentare mihi, quos torret Atabulus et quos |
| we would never have crawled over if near Trevicum | Numquam erepsemus, nisi nos vicina Trivici |
| 80 a farm hadn't given us a reception, including teary smoke | Villa recepisset lacrimoso non sine fumo, |
| from wet branches and leaves smoldering in the fire. | Udos cum foliis ramos urente camino. |
| Here, utter moron that I am, I lie awake til midnight | Hic ego mendacem stultissimus usque puellam |
| waiting for a liar of a girl who never came. Sleep takes me | Ad mediam noctem exspecto: somnus tamen aufert |
| in the middle of a fantasy and my dreams are so real | Intentum Veneri; tum immundo somnia visu |
| 85 that I make a mess on my clothes and on my belly. | Nocturnam vestem maculant ventremque supinum. |

*lines 86–90. Eighth Day: Trivico – "Oppidulum quod versu dicere non est"*
*(24 miles = ca. 35.5 km)*

| | |
|---|---|
| Then we're whisked twenty-four miles by carriage | Quattuor hinc rapimur viginti et milia raedis, |
| to stay in a village whose name won't fit into meter, | Mansuri oppidulo, quod versu dicere non est, |
| so I offer an obvious hint: the most common of things | Signis perfacile est. Venit vilissima rerum |
| must be brought here—water. But its bread is the best, | Hic aqua, sed panis longe pulcherrimus, ultra |
| 90 and wise travelers usually bring some along for future use. | Callidus ut soleat umeris portare viator: |

*lines 91–93. Ninth Day: "Oppidulum . . ." – Canosa (35 miles = ca. 52 km)*

| | |
|---|---|
| For in Canusium it's gritty, and they don't have any water | Nam Canusi lapidosus, aquae non ditior urna |
| there either, in that town brave Diomedes founded long ago. | Qui locus a forti Diomede est conditus olim. |
| Here Varius leaves us, which makes all his friends upset. | Flentibus hinc Varius discedit maestus amicis. |

From there we move on to Rubi, tired when we arrive,
95  having gone rather far on a road that was all mud.

Inde Rubos fessi pervenimus, utpote longum
Carpentes iter et factum corruptius imbri.

The weather improves next day, but the footing is worse
right up to fishy Barium's walls. Then Gnatia, built
while water spirits sulked, gives us good reason to laugh:
they try to tell us incense melts upon their temple's steps
100  without fire. Apella the Jew may believe this if he likes,
not I; I've learned about the tranquil life the gods enjoy
and know, whatever miracle nature makes, the gods
won't give up their peace to send it down from heaven.

Postera tempestas melior, via peior ad usque
Bari moenia piscosi; dein Gnatia lymphis
Iratis exstructa dedit risusque iocosque,
Dum flamma sine tura liquescere limine sacro
Persuadere cupit. Credat Iudaeus Apella,
Non ego: namque deos didici securum agere aevum,
Nec, siquid miri faciat natura, deos id
Tristes ex alto caeli demittere tecto.

At Brundisium the long trip is over; now this long page is too.

Brundisium longae finis chartaeque viaeque est.

# Bibliography

**List of Abbreviations**

| | |
|---|---|
| *L* | Corpus Inscriptionum Latinarum |
| *ILLRP* | A. Degrassi (ed.), *Inscriptiones Latinae Liberae Rei Publicae* |
| *ILS* | H. Dessau (ed.), *Inscriptiones Latinae Selectae*, 1892–1916 |
| *Inscr.Ital.* | A. Degrassi (ed.), *Inscriptiones Italae Academiae Italicae Consociatae ediderunt* |
| *LTUR* | Lexicon Topographicum Urbis Romae |
| *MEFRA* | Mélanges de l'École française de Rome, Antiquité |
| *QuadAEI* | Quaderni del Centro di Studio per L'Archeologia Etrusco-Italica |


**Bibliography**

Ashby, Thomas, *The Roman Campagna in Classical Times* (New York: Macmillan, 1927).

———, and R. Gardner, "The Via Traiana," *Papers of the British School at Rome* 8 (1916).

Battista, A., and V. Giacobini, "Il paesaggio vegetale del comprensorio dell'Appia Antica," *Piano per il parco dell'Appia Antica*, Italia Nostra, Sezione di Roma; V. Calzolari, coord.; M. Olivieri, ed. (Rome: The Association, 1984), pp. 47–54.

Bellini, G. R., ed., *Minturnae, l'area archeologica*, exh. cat. (Marina di Minturno, 1994).

Bellino, S., *Dizionario Epigrafico di antichità romane*, vol. 2, Ettore Ruggiero, ed., s.v. "*cursus publicus*" (Rome: Pasqualucci, 1895–), 2.1404–25.

Berkeley, George, "Journal of Travels in Italy [May 17, 1717]," *The Works of George Berkeley, Bishop of Cloyne* 7, A. A. Luce and T. E. Jessup, eds. (London: Nelson, 1955), pp. 269–71.

Bertinetti, M., "La cura viarum," *Viae Publicae Romanae*, Rosanna Cappelli, ed., exh. cat., Castel Sant'Angelo, (Rome: Leonardo-De Luca, 1991).

Bevilacqua, G., *LTUR Suburbium* 1 (Rome, 2001), s.v. "*Appia, via*," pp. 98–99.

Bianchini, F., *Camera ed iscrizioni sepulcrali de' liberti, servi ed ufficiali della casa di Augusto scoperte nella via Appia* (Rome, 1727).

Bisconti, F., "La via delle catacombe," *Via Appia: Sulle ruine della magnificenza antica*, I. Insolera and D. Morandi, eds., exh. cat. (Rome: Fondazione Memmo, 1997), pp. 74–77.

Brandi, Cesare, *Terre d'Italia* (Rome: Riuniti, 1991).

Bruni, S., "La via Appia Antica: gli scavi tra Settecento ed Ottocento," *Via Appia: Sulle ruine della magnificenza antica*, I. Insolera and D. Morandi, eds., exh. cat. (Rome: Fondazione Memmo, 1997), pp. 23–24.

———, *LTUR Suburbium* 1 (Rome, 2001), s.v. "*Appia, via*," pp. 84–95.

Camardo, Carmelina, et al., *La villa di Massenzio sulla via Appia*, vol. 2: *Il circo* (Rome: Editrice Colombo, 1999).

Cambedda, Anna, and Alberta Ceccherelli, "Le mura di Aureliano dalla Porta Appia al bastione Ardeatino," *Itinerari d'arte e di cultura: Via Appia* (Rome: Fratelli Palombi, 1990).

Canina, L., "Esposizione topografica della prima parte dell'antica via Appia dalla Porta Capena alla stazione di Ariccia," *Annali dell'Instituto* (1851), pp. 303–24; (1852), pp. 254–300; (1853), pp. 132–87.

_____, _La prima parte della via Appia, dalla porta Capena a Boville, descritta e dimostrata con i monumenti superstiti_ (Rome, 1853).

Cappelli, Giovanna, and Susanna Pasquali, eds., _Tusculum: Luigi Canina e la riscoperta di un'antica città_, exh. cat. (Rome: Scuderie Aldobrandini di Frascati, 2002).

Cappelli, Rosanna, ed., _Viae Publicae Romanae_, exh. cat. (Rome: Castel Sant'Angelo, 1991).

Carbonara, Andrea, and Gaetano Messineo, _Via Appia_, vol. 3: _Da Cisterna a Minturno_ (Rome: Libreria dello Stato, 1998).

Cassanelli, L., "Schede di storia territoriale," _Piano per il parco dell'Appia Antica_, Italia Nostra, Sezione di Roma; V. Calzolari, coord.; M. Olivieri, ed. (Rome: The Association, 1984), pp. 81–108.

Castagnoli, Ferdinando, "Il tracciato della via Appia," _Capitolium_ 44, nos. 10–12 (1969), pp. 77–100.

_____, Antonio Maria Colini, and Giovanni Macchia, eds., _La via Appia_ (Rome: Banco di Roma, 1972).

Cecchini, M. G., M. N. Gagliardi, and L. Petrassi, "Cavalcavia tra via Cilicia e via Marco Polo (Circ. I–IX)," _Bullettino della Commissione Archeologica Comunale_ 91, no. 2 (1986) pp. 595–601.

Ceva Grimaldi, Guiseppe, _Itinerario da Napoli a Lecce, e nella provincia di Terra d'Otranto nell'anno 1818_ (Naples: Tip. di Porcelli, 1821).

Chiarini, Paolo. "Goethe, Roma e il viaggio in Italia," _Goethe a Roma, 1786–1788: Disegni e acquerelli da Weimar_, P. Chiarini, ed., exh. cat. (Rome: Museo Napoleonico, 1988), pp. 15–25.

Chioffi, L., "Epigrafia e insediamenti: il caso del suburbio di Roma," _La forma della città e del territorio. Esperienze metodologiche e risultati a confronto_, Stefania Quilici Gigli, ed. (Rome: L'Erma di Bretschneider, 1999), pp. 56–60.

Coarelli, Filippo, _Dintorni di Roma_ (Bari: G. Lazerta, 1981).

_____, _Lazio_ (Rome and Bari: Guide Archeologiche Laterza, 1982).

_____, "Colonizzazione romana e viabilità," _Dialoghi di Archeologia_, ser. 3a, 6, 2 (1988), pp. 35–48.

_____, _LTUR_ I (Rome, 1993), s.v. "_arcus stillans_," p. 107.

_____, "La costruzione del Porto di Terracina in un rilievo storico tardo-repubblicano," _Revixit ars_ (Rome, 1996), pp. 434–54.

Coppola, Maria Rosaria, _Terracina: Il foro emiliano_, exh. cat. (Rome: Comune di Terracina, 1986; 2nd ed., 1993).

Coste, J., "La Via Appia nel Medioevo e l'incastellamento," _Via Appia_, QuadAEI 10.1 (Rome, 1990), pp. 127–37.

D'Andria, F., "La via Appia in Puglia," _Via Appia: Sulle ruine della magnificenza antica_, I. Insolera and D. Morandi, eds., exh. cat. (Rome: Fondazione Memmo, 1997), pp. 95–104.

D'Onofrio, Cesare, and Carlo Pietrangeli, _Le Abbazie del Lazio_ (Rome: Staderini, 1971).

D'Urso, Maria Teresa, _Il tempio della Dea Marica alla foce del Garigliano_, vol. 1 (Scauri: Archeoclub d'Italia, Sede di Minturnae, 1985).

De Caro, Stefano, and Angela Greco, _Campania_ (Rome and Bari: Guide Archeologiche Laterza, 1981).

De Rossi, Giovanni Maria, _Lazio meridionale_ (Rome: Newton Compton, 1980).

De Seta, Cesare, "Luoghi e miti del 'viaggio'," _Goethe a Roma, 1786–1788. Disegni e acquerelli da Weimar_, P. Chiarini, ed., exh. cat. (Rome: Museo Napoleonico, 1988).

Eck, W., "Der administration der italischen Strassen: das Beispiel der Via Appia," _Via Appia_, QuadAEI 10.1, p. 31 ff.

_Enea nel Lazio: archeologia e mito, bimillenario virgiliano_, exh. cat. (Rome: Palazzo dei Conservatori, 1981).

Fagiolo dell'Arco, M., "Esotico e pittoresco alle porte di casa," _La Campagna Romana da Hackert a Balla_, Pier Andrea De Rosa and Paolo Emilio Trastulli, eds., exh. cat. (Rome: Museo del Corso, 2001), p. 13 ff.

Fancelli, P., and P. Tamaro, "Antonio Canova tra archeologia e restauro: il monumento di M. Servilio Quarto sulla via Appia," _Studi in onore di Renato Cavese_ (Vicenza: Centro internazionale di studi architettura Andrea Palladio, 2000), p. 230.

Ferrua, A., and C. Carletti, _Damaso e i martiri di Roma_ (Vatican City: Pontificia commissione di archeologia sacra, 1985).

Filetici, M. G., "Otto mausolei fra il terzo e quarto miglio della via Appia, dal restauro di Canina del 1851 a quello del Giubileo del 2000," _Tusculum: Luigi Canina e la riscoperta di un'antica città_, Giovanna Cappelli and Susanna Pasquali, eds., exh. cat. (Rome: Scuderie Aldobrandini di Frascati, 2002), pp. 225–29.

Fiorani, L., "L'Appia Antica nel Medioevo," _Capitolium_ 44, nos. 10–12 (1969), pp. 121–26.

Friggeri, R., "I miliari," _Viae Publicae Romanae_, Rosanna Cappelli, ed., exh. cat. (Rome: Castel Sant'Angelo, 1991), pp. 39–40.

Goethe, J. W., _Selected Works of J. W. von Goethe_ (New York: Knopf/Everyman, 2000).

Gori, E., _Monumentum sive columbarium libertorum et servorum Liviae Augustae et Caesarum_ (Florence, 1727).

Gregorovius, Ferdinand, _Nelle Puglia (Wanderings through Apulia)_, Raffaele Mariano, trans. (Florence: G. Barbera, 1882).

_Horace's Satires and Epistles_, Jacob Fuchs, trans. (New York: W. W. Norton, 1977).

Insolera, Italo, and Domatilla Morandi, eds., *Via Appia: Sulle ruine della magnificenza antica*, exh. cat., Fondazione Memmo, Rome (Milan: Leonardo Arte, 1997).

Jackson, F. Hamilton, *The Shores of the Adriatic: The Italian Side* (London: John Murray, 1906).

Kammerer Grothaus, H., "Camere sepolcrali de' liberti e liberte di Livia Augusta ed altri Cesari," *MEFRA* 91 (1979), pp. 315–29.

Lenormant, François, *À travers l'Apulie et la Lucanie: notes de voyage* (Paris: A. Levy, 1883).

Le Pera, S., and R. Turchetti, "Thomas Ashby e la via Appia," *Sulla via Appia da Roma a Brindisi. Le fotografie di Thomas Ashby 1891–1925*, exh. cat. (Rome: British School in Rome, 2003), pp. 15–18.

Liverani, Paolo, "L'antro del Ciclope a Castel Gandolfo. Ninfeo Bergantino," *Ulisse, il mito e la memoria*, exh. cat. (Rome: Palazzo delle Esposizioni, 1996), pp. 332–41.

Lugli, Giuseppe, "Il sistema stradale di Roma antica," *Études Etrusco-Italiques* (Lovanio, 1963), pp. 112–18; republished in G. Lugli, *Studi minori di topografia antica* (Rome: De Luca, 1965), pp. 223–28.

Maiuri, Amedeo, *Passeggiate campane* (1938; Milan: Rusconi, 1990).

Marazzi, F., "Il patrimonium Appiae: beni fondiari della Chiesa Romana nel territorio suburbano della via Appia fra il IV e il IX secolo," *Via Appia*, QuadAEI 10.1 (Rome, 1990), pp. 117–26.

Mari, Z., *LTUR* 3 (Rome, 1996), s.v. "*miliarium aureum*," pp. 250–51.

Marigliani, C. and S., eds., *Vedute della campagna romana nei secoli XVII–XIX*, exh. cat. (Rome: Complesso del Vittoriano, 2003).

Martinori, Edoardo, *Lazio Turrito: Repertorio storico ed iconografico*, vol. 2 (Rome, 1934), pp. 99–102; vol. 3 (Rome, 1934), pp. 114–15.

Massafra, M. G., "Via Appia illustrata ab Urbe ad Capuam. Un itinerario attraverso i disegni di Carlo Labruzzi e le memorie archeologiche di Thomas Ashby," *Sulla via Appia da Roma a Brindisi: Le fotografie di Thomas Ashby 1891–1925*, exh. cat. (Rome: British School in Rome, 2003), pp. 33–38.

Mazzarino, S., "Aspetti di storia dell'Appia antica," *Helikon 8* (1968), pp. 195–96.

———, "L'Appia come prima via censoria," *Capitolium* 44, nos. 10–12 (1969), pp. 101–20.

Meomartini, Almerico, *Del cammino della via Appia verso Brindisi nel Territorio di Benevento* (Benevento: De Martini, 1907).

Mineo, S., *LTUR Suburbium* 1 (Rome, 2001), s.v. "Via Appia, IV miglio," pp. 113, 118, 122, 128, 132.

Mingazzini, P., "Il santuario della Dea Marica alla foce del Garigliano," *Monumenti Antichi dei Lincei* 37 (1938), coll. 684–983.

Monti, Pier Giorgio, *Via Latina*, Antiche Strade, Lazio (Rome: Libreria dello Stato, 1995).

Morton, H. V. Canova, *A Traveller in Southern Italy* (New York: Dodd, Mead & Co., 1969).

Mosca, A., "Restauri tardo-antichi sulla via Appia," *Via Appia*, QuadAEI 10.1 (Rome, 1990), pp. 182–85.

Nicosia, Angelo, *Il Lazio meridionale tra antichità e medioevo* (Marina di Minturno: Caramanica, 1995).

Palma, Antonio, *Le 'curae' pubbliche. Studi sulle strutture amministrative romane* (Naples: E. Jovene, 1980).

Palombi, D., *LTUR* 1 (Rome, 1993), s.vv. "*arcus Traiani*" and "*arcus divi Veri*," p. 112.

Paris, R., "Il mausoleo di Cecilia Metella e il Castrum Caetani sulla via Appia," *Via Appia: Sulle ruine della magnificenza antica*, I. Insolera and D. Morandi, eds., exh. cat. (Rome: Fondazione Memmo, 1997), p. 54.

———, "L'Appia Antica oggi," ibid., pp. 21–22.

———, *Via Appia: Il mausoleo di Cecilia Metella e il castrum Caetani* (Milan: Electa, 2000).

———, "Luigi Canina e il museo all'aperto della via Appia," *Tusculum: Luigi Canina e la riscoperta di un'antica città*, Giovanna Cappelli and Susanna Pasquali, eds., exh. cat. (Rome: Scuderie Aldobrandini di Frascati, 2002), pp. 221–24.

Pflaum, H.-G., "Essai sur le cursus publicus sous le haut-empire romain," *Mémoires de l'Académie des Inscriptions et Belles Lettres* 14 (1940).

*Piano per il parco dell'Appia Antica*, Italia Nostra, Sezione di Roma; V. Calzolari, coord.; M. Olivieri, ed. (Rome: The Association, 1984).

Piovene, Guido, *Viaggio in Italia* (Milan: A. Mondadori, 1957; rpt. Milan: Baldini & Castoldi, 1993).

Pisani Sartorio, Guiseppina, "Mezzi di trasporto e traffico," *Vita e costumi dei Romani antichi 6* (Rome, 1988).

———, *LTUR* 3 (Rome, 1996), s.v. "Muri Aureliani. Portae, Porta Appia," pp. 299–300; *LTUR* 4 (Rome, 1999), s.v. "Septizodium, Septisolium," pp. 269–72; *LTUR Suburbium* 1 (Rome, 2001), s.v. "Almo," pp. 45–47.

———, and R. Calza, *La villa di Massenzio sulla via Appia*, vol. 1: *Il palazzo, le opere d'arte* (Rome: Istituto di studi romani, 1976), pp. 131–41 (with bibliography).

Pratilli, Francesco Maria, *Della via Appia riconosciuta e descritta da Roma a Brindisi* (Naples, 1745; Sala Bolognese: A. Forni, 1978).

Quilici, Lorenzo, *La via Appia da Roma a Boville* (Rome: Bulzoni, 1977).

_____, "La via Appia Antica," *Piano per il parco dell'Appia Antica*. Italia Nostra, Sezione di Roma; V. Calzolari, coord.; M. Olivieri, ed. (Rome: The Association, 1984), pp. 61–80.

_____, *La Via Appia dalla Pianura Pontina a Brindisi* (Rome: Fratelli Palombi, 1989).

_____, *Via Appia*, vol. 1: *Da Porta Capena ai Colli Albani*; vol. 2: *Dalla Pianura Pontina a Brindisi* (Rome: Fratelli Palombi, 1989).

———, "Il rettifilo della via Appia tra Roma e Terracina," *Via Appia, QuadAEI* 10.1 (Rome, 1990), pp. 41–60.

———, "Le strade. Viabilità tra Roma e il Lazio," *Vita e costumi dei Romani antichi* 12 (Rome, 1991).

_____, *La via Appia: Regina Viarum* (Rome: Viviani, 1997).

_____, "La Via Appia attraverso la Gola di Itri," *Le vie romane nel Lazio e nel mediterraneo*, Atti della Giornata di Studio (Rome, 2001); *Lazio ieri e oggi* 38, no. 1 (2002).

Quilici Gigli, Stefania. "Gli sterri per la costruzione dei forti militari," *L'archeologia in Roma Capitale tra sterro e scavo*, Giuseppina Pisani Sartorio and Lorenzo Quilici, eds. (Venice: Marsilio Editori, 1983), pp. 91–96.

_____, ed., *Via Appia, decimo incontro di studio del Comitato per l'archeologia laziale, QuadAEI* 10.1 (Rome: Consiglio nazionale delle richerche, 1990).

Radke, Gerhard, *Viae Publicae Romanae*, Italian trans. (Bologna, 1981).

Rossetti, C., "Materiali per la storia della tutela dell'Appia. Scavi privati post-unitari nei documenti della Direzione Generale di Antichità e Belle Arti," *Bullettino della Commissione Archeologica Comunale di Roma* 102, 2001 (2002).

Rossini, Luigi, *Viaggio pittoresco da Roma a Napoli* (Rome, 1839).

Saint-Non, Jean-Claude Richard de, *Voyage pittoresque, ou Descriptions des Royaumes de Naples et de Sicile*, 5 vols. (Paris: Imprimerie de Clousier, 1781–86).

Scamuzzi, U., "Aedes Tempestarum," *Rivista di Studi Classici* 11 (1963), p. 98 ff.

Severini, Francesca, *La Via Appia*, vol. 2: *Da Bovillae a Cisterna di Latina* (Rome: Libreria dello Stato, 2001).

Silvestrelli, G., *Città, castelli e terre della regione romana*, vol. 1, 2nd ed. (Rome, 1940).

Spera, L., "Il paesaggio suburbano di Roma dall'antichità al Medioevo: il comprensorio tra le vie Latina e Ardeatina dalle Mura di Aureliano al III miglio," *Bibliotheca Archeologica* 27 (Rome, 1999).

———, *LTUR Suburbium* 1 (Rome, 2001), s.v. "Appiae patrimonium."

Staccioli, R. A., "La via Appia: Storia e monumenti della 'regina viarum,'" *Roma tascabile* 84 (Rome, 1998).

Sterpos, D., *Roma-Capua* (Novara, 1966).

Stopani, Renato, *La via Francigena del Sud* (Florence: Le Lettere, 1992).

*Sulla via Appia da Roma a Brindisi. Le fotografie di Thomas Ashby 1891–1925*, exh. cat. (Rome: British School in Rome, 2003).

Tomassetti, G., *La Campagna Romana antica, medievale e moderna*, L. Chiumenti and F. Bilancia, eds., vol. 2 (Rome: Banco di Roma, 1975).

Touring Club Italiano, *Itinerari turistici illustrati da Bari e dale coste Pugliesi* (Milan, 1989).

Uggeri, G., *La viabilità romana nel Salento* (Mesagne: Grafischena Fasano, 1983).

———, "La via Appia nella politica espansionistica di Roma," *Via Appia, QuadAEI* 10.1 (Rome, 1990), pp. 21–28.

Zevi, F., *LTUR* 4 (Rome, 1999), s.v. "*sepulcrum (Corneliorum) Scipionum*," pp. 281–85.

Ziolkowski, A., *LTUR* 5 (Rome, 1999), s.v. "*Tempestates, aedes*," pp. 26–27.

# Index